The Eucharistic Spirit

WORD AND SPIRIT:
PENTECOSTAL INVESTIGATIONS IN THEOLOGY AND HISTORY

The *Word and Spirit* series will make space for the pneumatological emphasis typical of Pentecostal/charismatic approaches to theology without eclipsing the discernment that comes with the Word of God (that is the Word both christological and scriptural). This series will not be narrowly *Pentecostal* but will include other approaches deemed charismatic as well. Furthermore, the series will also have an ecumenical horizon. Contributors will be encouraged to write in a way that would make these books relevant to other denominational traditions. These books are *Investigations* in that they are scholarly treatments of topics that will seek to remain accessible to pastors as well as seminary and upper division college readers. *Theology* in the series name signals that these are constructive works engaging biblical, systematic, and historical theological discourse, with an eye towards offering contributions of contemporary relevance to the church.

The series will contract academic monographs that offer a solid Pentecostal and ecumenical discussion of key loci, but also of key trajectories in Pentecostal thought and experience.

EDITORS:

FRANK D. MACCHIA: Professor of Systematic Theology at Vanguard University of Southern California.

DALE M. COULTER: Professor of Historical Theology at the Pentecostal Theological Seminary.

ASSOCIATE EDITORS:

DAVID D. DANIELS III: Henry Winters Luce Professor of World Christianity at McCormick Theological Seminary

LISA P. STEPHENSON: Associate Professor of Systematic Theology at Lee University

NÉSTOR MEDINA: Director of Master of Theological Studies and Associate Professor of Religious Ethics and Culture at Emmanuel College of Victoria University in the University of Toronto.

The Eucharistic Spirit

A Renewal Theology of the Lord's Supper

WORD AND SPIRIT: PENTECOSTAL
INVESTIGATIONS IN THEOLOGY AND HISTORY

FLORIAN M. P. SIMATUPANG

Foreword by CHRIS E. W. GREEN

CASCADE *Books* · Eugene, Oregon

THE EUCHARISTIC SPIRIT
A Renewal Theology of the Lord's Supper

Word and Spirit: Pentecostal Investigations in Theology and History

Copyright © 2025 Florian M. P. Simatupang. All rights reserved. Except for brief quotations in critical publications or reviews, no part of this book may be reproduced in any manner without prior written permission from the publisher. Write: Permissions, Wipf and Stock Publishers, 199 W. 8th Ave., Suite 3, Eugene, OR 97401.

Cascade Books
An Imprint of Wipf and Stock Publishers
199 W. 8th Ave., Suite 3
Eugene, OR 97401

www.wipfandstock.com

PAPERBACK ISBN: 978-1-6667-8793-1
HARDCOVER ISBN: 978-1-6667-8794-8
EBOOK ISBN: 978-1-6667-8795-5

Cataloguing-in-Publication data:

Names: Simatupang, Florian M. P. [author] | Green, Chris E. W. [foreword].

Title: The eucharistic Spirit : a renewal theology of the Lord's Supper / Florian M. P. Simatupang.

Description: Eugene, OR: Cascade Books, 2025 | Series: Word and Spirit: Pentecostal Investigations in Theology and History | Includes bibliographical references and index.

Identifiers: ISBN 978-1-6667-8793-1 (paperback) | ISBN 978-1-6667-8794-8 (hardcover) | ISBN 978-1-6667-8795-5 (ebook)

Subjects: LCSH: Lord's Supper—History of doctrines. | Holy Spirit. | Pentecostal churches—Doctrines. | Pentecostalism.

Classification: BV825.3 S56 2025 (print) | BV825.3 (ebook)

Unless otherwise noted, Scripture quotations marked NRSV are from the New Revised Standard Version, copyright 1989, Division of Christian Education of the National Council of the Churches of Christ in the United States in the United States of America. Used by permission. All rights reserved.

Scripture quotations marked AT are the author's translation.

Scripture quotations marked KJV are from the King James or Authorized Version.

For Arlene

major autem horum est caritas

The indwelling of God, of the redeeming Trinity which inwardly re-creates us in Christ and makes us *filii in Filio*, children of the same Father, is the overwhelming effect of a fruitful sacrament, and it is faith that gives us a conscious and living awareness of this.

—Edward Schillebeeckx, OP

Table of Contents

Abbreviations ix
Foreword by Chris E. W. Green xi
Preface xv
Acknowledgments xvii

1. Introduction 1
2. Analysis of Pentecostal Eucharistic Theology 25
3. Analysis of Ecumenical Eucharistic Theology 62
4. Rereading the Biblical Text 96
5. A Renewal Theology of the Eucharist 139
6. Conclusions and Implications for Ecclesial Practices 182

Bibliography 195
Name Index 205
Subject Index 209

Abbreviations

AARAS	American Academy of Religion Academy Series
AG	Assemblies of God
AThR	*Anglican Theological Review*
BDAG	Danker, Frederick W., Walter Bauer, William F. Arndt, and F. Wilbur Gingrich. *Greek-English Lexicon of the New Testament and Other Early Christian Literature*. 3rd ed. Chicago: University of Chicago Press, 2000 (Danker-Bauer-Arndt-Gingrich)
GOTR	*Greek Orthodox Theological Review*
Ign. Eph.	Ignatius, To the Ephesians
NICNT	New International Commentary on the New Testament
SET	search-encounter-transformation
SP	Sacra Pagina
TS	*Theological Studies*
VCSup	Vigiliae Christianae Supplements

Foreword

I'M DELIGHTED TO INTRODUCE Simatupang's *The Eucharistic Spirit: A Renewal Theology of the Lord's Supper*. Florian's work is traditional in the best sense—scholarly without being merely academic, tactful without being evasive, innovative without being novel, orthodox without being conventional. Both the tone and content reflect his deep love for the Pentecostal movement and his commitment to the fullness of the Spirit, the fullness that manifests itself in the unity and catholicity of the church.

Building on my work and that of others, Florian presents the Eucharist as a many-splendored reality—a meal of solidarity, a celebration of justice, a witness to hunger, a sign of healing, a call to mission, and a preview of the redemption of all things. For him, as for the mothers and fathers of the faith, the Eucharist is far more than a ritual, more than a symbolic act; it is nothing less than the giving and receiving of Christ himself through the Spirit, to the Father's delight and for the joy of the world. While the destiny of a book is impossible to predict, I hope Florian's work will be recognized in the future as having made a significant contribution not only to Pentecostal sacramental theology but also to a broad and deep renewal of the sacramental life within and beyond Pentecostal communities.

Florian's work resonates deeply with the sacramentality I found in the early Pentecostal periodicals I read during my PhD research. And reading him reminds me that we need to continue rediscovering our tradition's sacramental theology, fragmented and inchoate as it may be. But rediscovery is not enough. We must also critically engage with traditional sacramental theologies and the metaphysics that underpin them. In order to receive Florian's work for all its worth, we need to understand that there is no competition between the Creator and the creaturely, because God is not just another being in existence or one cause among the many; God is the very source, guide, and goal of all things. Because that is true, the sacraments do not come between God and us but are the very material of our communion. They are not tokens of an absent Christ but the here-and-now presentation of the bodily risen Jesus by the Father through the Spirit. At the table, we do not merely remember Christ. The Father, through the Spirit, makes him present, uniting us with him, with the Father, and with each other. A. B. Simpson had this exactly right: the Lord's Supper is "a direct personal touch of God."

As a Pentecostal, I'm particularly struck by Florian's suggestion that reordering our worship around the call to the Lord's table could remedy the spiritual fatigue plaguing so many of our communities. He argues that this exhaustion stems from the relentless pressure to replicate dramatic altar experiences. So, by centering our worship on the Eucharist, we would position ourselves to receive a more peaceful encounter with Christ—one less about spectacle and more about the quiet, sustaining presence of the Spirit who is our peace.

Karl Rahner famously said that the Christian of the future will be a mystic or will not be a Christian at all. I agree. But this mysticism must be sacramentally grounded; otherwise, it will devolve into mere pietism and superstition. So, as we move into that future, we must guard against the temptation to see the sacraments as tools to deliver a desired experience of God. Pentecostals often speak of the sacramental when they really mean the mediational. But Florian pushes us deeper. Holy communion is not just a means of grace; it is grace himself.

God's presence is never under our control, of course. Even as we develop a recognizably Pentecostal sacramentality we must resist clericalism, ritualism, and any theology that limits the freedom of God. The first Pentecost spilled out from the upper room into the streets, and that is always the way of the Spirit of the Eucharist: overflowing our limits and transgressing our expectations. Nevertheless, we can be sure that Christ will be where he said he would be, doing what he said he would do—renewing the face of the earth. "Behold, I make all things new!"

Chris E. W. Green
 Professor of Public Theology, Southeastern University
 Bishop of the Diocese of St Anthony
 Director of The St Anthony Institute of Theology, Philosophy, and Liturgics

Preface

WHAT SORT OF EXPERIENCE of grace does the Holy Spirit give a Pentecostal believer when one celebrates the Eucharist? In this book, I aim to answer that question by looking theologically into the Eucharist through a Pentecostal spirituality framework and process known as search-encounter-transformation (SET). Looking at the Eucharist using the SET paradigm will inform the theology and spirituality of Pentecostalism in a way that will broaden the Pentecostal understanding of the journey of salvation (*via salutis*). I will demonstrate that the broadening is achieved by emphasizing the place and importance of the *anamnēsis* in the Eucharist. As the Holy Spirit is called upon in the *epiclēsis*, he allows the church to attain a pneumatological imagination, enabling the church to remember the work of Christ well. By employing a pneumatological imagination afforded by the SET paradigm, this book will present a rereading of the biblical text and comparative retrieval of other Christian traditions. The outcome is the construction of a renewal theology of the Eucharist that will provide several explicit meanings in the Eucharist. There are at least seven meanings that can be deduced in this construction, namely, the Eucharist as (1) solidarity, (2) justice, (3) hunger management, (4) healing, (5) missional meal, (6) eschatology, and (7) preview of the restoration of all things (*apokatastasis*) in the wedding supper of the Lamb.

By constructing this renewal theology of the Eucharist, my hope is this book will encourage the Pentecostal church to move to a weekly celebration of the Eucharist instead of the typical practice of only once every month. By doing so, I am convinced that the Pentecostal church will become truly *Pentecostal*!

Acknowledgments

I THANK THE SERIES editors, Frank D. Macchia and Dale M. Coulter, for including my book in the Word and Spirit series. I am honored and could not think of a better place to publish my doctoral studies research. I especially want to thank Frank for his great encouragement through our email communications and conversations when we both were at an event hosted by the Asia Pacific Theological Seminary in Baguio, Philippines. Frank also gave invaluable input and suggestions, but unfortunately, due to the deadline, I was not able to incorporate most of them into the final version of the book. It shows that the work of theology is always incomplete, never finished, and always requires further investigations.

I am grateful to our church, Christ the King, where I serve as the lead pastor. I am glad we can experiment with my research in our community and witness how we may experience a transformative encounter every time we celebrate the Eucharist. As a church that seeks to develop a culture of belonging for all through our commitment to living and sharing the deep truth of God's love to all and for all, during the process of finishing this book, we went through quite a difficult time. In hindsight, I am glad that the difficulties we experienced strengthened our understanding of what it means to be a community of disciples who desire to be Spirit filled and are on a journey living the story of Jesus in every area of life.

I am profoundly thankful to my parents, Patuan and Lamida Simatupang. I would not have imagined writing a book when I was much younger. After ten years of playing around, I dropped out of college. In the early 2000s, when the university I dropped out from offered e-learning, my mother urged me to finish my bachelor's degree so that "the future is open for you," she said. I followed her advice. The rest, as they say, is history. This book is a testament to that opened future (and the benefit of listening to your parents' advice!).

As this book originated from my doctoral dissertation, I also want to express my gratitude to Mark J. Cartledge, who took me as his supervisee and not only served as a kind and gracious teacher, advisor, and mentor who pushed me to think things through in my arguments but, with his wife Joan, also offered friendship and hospitality, especially during the doctoral residency trips. Years ago, when Mark was still teaching at Birmingham, I emailed him expressing my interest in studying under him. That email that was sent during Mark's sabbatical was lost. Little did I know that I would have him as my doctoral advisor a few years later. It has been my honor to have studied under such a respected theologian in Pentecostal/charismatic studies.

I am deeply grateful to Chris E. W. Green for his generous foreword, which greatly honors this work. Chris, whose expertise in the theology of the Lord's Supper I deeply respect, was also a member of my dissertation committee. His insights have greatly enriched both my thinking and this project. I also want to thank Rebecca Abbott, my copy editor, whose sharp editorial eye and careful attention to detail helped refine the final version of the manuscript.

Finally, I reserve the greatest gratitude for my wife, Arlene, who is my constant source of support and encouragement. You are a true sacrament of grace and love in my life. It is a great blessing to be married to your best friend and ministry partner. I dedicate this book to you! Also, to our two beautiful young ladies, Tedra and Katriel, you have always been my biggest fans (as I am yours). At the same time, you both also taught me discipline. The last stretch of completing my dissertation took place during COVID-19. Your diligence in doing online school then was what made this book possible. As a family, I pray that we continue to experience the world as a sacrament, allowing us to taste and see the Lord's goodness (Ps 19:1, 34:8).

> Now to him who is able to keep you from falling, and to make you stand without blemish in the presence of his glory with rejoicing, to the only God our Savior, through Jesus Christ our Lord, be glory, majesty, power, and authority, before all time and now and forever. Amen. (Jude 24–25)

1

Introduction

WHY THIS BOOK

IN THIS BOOK, I set to investigate whether and in what ways the Eucharist can be understood within the Pentecostal spirituality process of search-encounter-transformation (SET).[1] Historically, Pentecostals have paid little attention to the theology—and, therefore, the spirituality—of the Eucharist. In the past, except until relatively recently, most of the attention given to the Lord's Supper would fall into an approach considered biblicist apologetics. Pentecostals often define their beliefs by stating what they *do not* believe about the Eucharist.[2]

A transformative encounter is essential to Pentecostalism; hence, understanding the Eucharist as a "journey of discovery" mediating the experience with the Divine, bringing total transformation in how a person sees God and the world—which is the aim of this study—is necessary.[3] In this book, I will argue that looking at the Eucharist using an SET paradigm will inform the theology and spirituality of Pentecostalism in a way that mediates the *via salutis*.[4] What I mean is that as Pentecostals "taste

---

1. Cartledge, *Encountering the Spirit*, 25–27.
2. Menzies, *Bible Doctrines*, 111; Bricknell, "Ordinances," 217.
3. Cartledge, *Encountering the Spirit*, 27.
4. Cartledge, *Mediation of the Spirit*, 65.

and see [in the Eucharist] that the Lord is good" (Ps 34:8), the Pentecostal understanding of the journey of salvation is broadened. In making this argument, I aim to bring into the focus of Pentecostal theology the place and importance of the Eucharist from the perspective of pneumatological remembrance or *anamnēsis* so that a concrete understanding of the meaning of the Eucharist can be made. The goal is to construct several explicit descriptions of the meaning contained in the Eucharist by employing a pneumatological imagination afforded by the SET paradigm. This will make more cohesiveness between the Pentecostal's *lex orandi* and its *lex credendi* and *lex vivendi*; that is, the way Pentecostals worship will reflect what they believe and determine how they will live. In saying this, I do not—at least for this discussion—necessarily seek to develop a specifically "Pentecostal" eucharistic prayer; instead, what I am trying to suggest is for Pentecostals to see the Eucharist as an intentional formative practice that may—and should—lead to the shaping of our doctrine.[5] In accomplishing this goal, this book also seeks to contribute constructively to the larger theological conversation already taking place that attempts to advance and push the boundaries of Pentecostal theology, specifically in the area of ecclesiology. Although in this book there will be places where there is some continuity with classic Pentecostal theology, there will also be a noticeable discontinuity, as what I seek to do is to present a constructive and distinct contribution, which will include new knowledge, at least for Pentecostalism, related to the Eucharist.

To accomplish the goal I have set above, this book will provide an analysis of the current Pentecostal interpretation of the Eucharist through a careful reading of systematic theologies that are representative of Pentecostal denominations, i.e., Assemblies of God, Church of God (Cleveland, Tennessee), and Foursquare, and also to look into some of the most recent literature on the Eucharist published by Pentecostals. Following this, an analysis of selected Roman Catholic, Eastern Orthodox, and Protestant interpretations of the Eucharist will be conducted to understand their theological contexts and contributions. The eucharistic theology of these three traditions will be read to see whether and how the theology of these traditions, at least implicitly, appreciates the Eucharist as an SET process. Subsequently, using the Pentecostal "text-community-Spirit"

5. See what Green calls *particular shaping* ("Saving Liturgy," 108); Archer argues that religious experience shapes our beliefs, and our beliefs shape our activities ("Nourishment for Our Journey," 81). See also Stephenson's *regula spiritualitis, regula doctrinae* proposal (*Types of Pentecostal Theology*, 115).

hermeneutic, this book will attempt to provide a rereading of eucharistic texts of Scripture (1 Cor 10:14–22, 11:23–34; Matt 26:26–30; Mark 14:12–26, Luke 22:14–20, 24:13–33; John 6:25). This is achieved through an ecumenical dialogue that comes from reading interpretations of other Christian traditions and maintain their compatibility with the inherent Pentecostal interpretation of the Eucharist. The outcome of that will be the ability to construct, expand, and precisely locate the understanding of the Eucharist of the latter within an SET paradigm. As I will demonstrate in chapter 4, reading the biblical text eucharistically, that is, noticing that the formation and redaction of the text were done to serve a eucharistic purpose, will exhibit an SET framework within the text. What Amos Yong calls "pneumatological imagination"[6] found in "text-community-Spirit" (the specific terminology he uses is "Spirit-word-community") is especially helpful to achieve the goal. The goal is for Pentecostals to gain an ecumenical awareness—which is essentially an enlarged understanding of the Spirit-led "community" of readers, thus are enabled to embrace how other traditions interpret the "text" (I will give an example of how this works in more detail in when I present my methodology). The expected result will be a productive, distinct contribution to Pentecostal theology and spirituality that, in the end, will constructively enhance the Pentecostal *lex orandi, lex credendi, lex vivendi*.[7]

ENTERING THE CONVERSATION

When someone goes into a room in which a conversation on a particular topic is already taking place and joins in, as the newcomer, that person has to be aware of what has been talked about in the conversation so that what that person says later has some connection to the topic being talked about and does not come out of nowhere. I imagine joining in a theological conversation to be the same, and the literature presentation below is the first step I take in entering that conversation. I aim to see how Pentecostal/charismatic theologians have understood the Eucharist and investigate how other Christian traditions, namely Protestant, Roman Catholic, and Eastern Orthodox, see the celebration as a divine SET

---

6. Yong, *Spirit, Word, Community*, 119.

7. See Warrington, *Pentecostal Theology*, 219–21. This distinct contribution would combat what he points out, that the concept of worship is myopically understood as singing, and go back to the Pentecostal claim that the way they worship is as the New Testament church.

event. If Pentecostal/charismatic theology is about the transformative divine encounter, the aim is to see whether this notion has been presented in their understanding of the Eucharist and if the three older traditions have something to contribute to Pentecostal eucharistic theology. Concerning Pentecostal literature, I attempt to listen as much as possible to what has been covered in the scholarly body of knowledge. However, with the other three traditions, presenting a view that is truly representative of the theology of each of them is difficult, if not impossible; therefore, this presentation seeks to give only a sample of their respective traditions. Some of the presented literature will be further analyzed as dialogue partners in either chapter 2 (Pentecostal) or chapter 3 (ecumenical).

Pentecostal/Charismatic Literature

Pentecostal/charismatic literature will form the bulk of this presentation as I attempt to cover as much of the published scholarly work on the Eucharist as possible. The literature presented is arranged in two ways. First, I will present systematic theology volumes from three Pentecostal denominations: the Assemblies of God, Church of God (Cleveland, Tennessee), and Foursquare. These volumes of systematic theology are by no means official positions, but they will at least give us an idea of how Pentecostal denominations state their understanding of the Eucharist. Second, in chronological order from earlier works to the more recent, discussions on the Eucharist by Pentecostal/charismatic theologians will be reviewed to capture the key ideas presented. These works will then be engaged more thoroughly in the second chapter on the Pentecostal theology of the Eucharist.

Assemblies of God

Myer Pearlman's volume *Knowing the Doctrines of the Bible*, first published in 1937, is one of the earliest works of Assemblies of God systematic theology. In a chapter entitled "The Church," Pearlman devotes a section to discussing "The Ordinances of The Church." Predictably for a classic Pentecostal, he begins by stating that "New Testament Christianity is not a ritualistic religion [because] at the heart of it is man's direct contact with God through the Spirit."[8] As a classic Pentecostal, Pearlman

---

8. Pearlman, *Knowing the Doctrines*, 352.

prefers the word "ordinances" to refer to water baptism and the Lord's Supper as a way to indicate that they are "ceremonies ordained by the Lord Himself," yet his explanation of the word "sacraments"—which to him means "sacred things" and "oaths consecrated by a sacred rite" does not suggest he opposes the word entirely.[9] While beginning with stating that Christianity is "not a ritualistic religion," Pearlman puts baptism as a "rite of entrance into the Christian church"—which is closer to Paul (1 Cor 12:13) than the typical "outward expression of inward faith" explanation—and the Lord's Supper as a "rite of communion."[10] For Pearlman, the Lord's Supper contains five "keynotes," namely commemoration of Jesus's atoning sacrifice, instruction or object lesson regarding the incarnation and the atonement, inspiration for the faithful to become partakers in the life of Christ, assurance of the new covenant that Christ instituted, and responsibility of the believers to lead their life as disciples.[11]

The following Assemblies of God systematic theology is a three-volume work published in 1953 by a former general superintendent (i.e., leader) of the denomination, Ernest Swing Williams, entitled simply *Systematic Theology*. The tenth chapter of the third volume is dedicated to discussing the "Ordinances of the Church." Five of the six pages in the chapter are given to discuss baptism, while the Lord's Supper receives roughly a paragraph on one page.[12] In this paragraph, Williams explains the meaning of the Eucharist as coming from *eu karis*, which means thanks or gratitude, and he explains the meaning of the sacrament as coming from a military oath.[13] He ends by explaining that theologically, the Lord's Supper is "a visible sign of an inward and spiritual grace" and presents a few Scripture verses to support this explanation.[14] As this section on the Lord's Supper is very brief, it is quite insufficient to deduce whether or not there is more to his eucharistic theology than what is written.

William Menzies's *Bible Doctrines: A Pentecostal Perspective* is essentially an exposition of the Assemblies of God's sixteen-point statement of "fundamental truths," in which the Lord's Supper is contained in

---

9. Pearlman, *Knowing the Doctrines*, 352–53.
10. Pearlman, *Knowing the Doctrines*, 353.
11. Pearlman, *Knowing the Doctrines*, 357–59.
12. E. Williams, *Systematic Theology*, 3:149–55.
13. E. Williams, *Systematic Theology*, 3:153–54.
14. E. Williams, *Systematic Theology*, 3:154.

point 6.[15] It can be said that this volume is a de facto official AG USA systematic theology. According to Menzies, for Christians, the Lord's Supper takes the place of the Israelites' Passover, which is to be celebrated frequently by the church until the Lord returns. Five essential points come from the celebration of the Lord's Supper. First, it is commemorative in that it becomes an occasion to ponder the meaning of the death of Jesus and the cost that he paid for our sins. Second, it is instructive; that is, the celebration is a sacred object lesson of the incarnation of Christ (the physical elements of bread and wine) and the atonement (the consumption of physical elements). This brings Menzies to the third point: it is inspirational when those who participate are reminded that they enter into the benefit of, and identify themselves with, the death and resurrection of Jesus, receiving the victory that he won. Fourth, it is an opportunity to present our thanksgiving for what we receive from Jesus and his death on the cross while enjoying fellowship with him, the Father, and one another through the Holy Spirit. Finally, the Lord's Supper is a proclamation of the new covenant, in which we testify our commitment to carry our cross and recognize our task as his followers.[16]

The last Assemblies of God systematic theology on the Lord's Supper comes from a volume edited by Stanley Horton entitled *Systematic Theology: A Pentecostal Perspective*. The discussion on the Lord's Supper is in a chapter entitled "The New Testament Church," by Michael L. Dusing. Among AG systematics, Dusing's presentation is unusually thorough. It pays special attention to the concept of sacraments and explains why Pentecostals prefer the term "ordinances," due to the "magical connotation" often associated with sacraments.[17] Dusing's explanation of remembrance uniquely captures the threefold eucharistic idea of *anamnēsis*: past, present, and future.[18] While this summary gives a glimpse of Dusing's approach, more detailed aspects of his discussion will be explored further in the next chapter.

---

15. Assemblies of God, "Assemblies of God."
16. Menzies, *Bible Doctrines*, 115–17.
17. Dusing, "New Testament Church," 557.
18. Dusing, "New Testament Church," 562.

Church of God (Cleveland, Tennessee)

The first systematic theology from the Church of God being presented is a volume by Raymond M. Pruitt entitled *Fundamentals of the Faith*. Discussion on the Lord's Supper is found in chapter 32, called "The Membership, Function, and Destiny of the Church."[19] For Pruitt, the ordinances function as a way to express our experience of communion with God in a way that cannot be said with language.[20] The Lord's Supper, for Pruitt, signifies the believers' participation in the life and death of Christ. This participation is done in receiving and feeding on Christ as they figuratively eat his flesh and drink his blood.[21] The celebration is the replacement of the Passover, just as water baptism, in his view, is the substitution for circumcision.[22]

French L. Arrington, Church of God theologian and faculty member at Pentecostal Theological Seminary, published a three-volume systematic theology entitled *Christian Doctrine: A Pentecostal Perspective*. In chapter 11 of volume 3, entitled "The Worship of the Church," where his treatment of the Lord's Supper is found, Arrington begins by stating that "the ministry of the Holy Spirit is indispensable to the worship and life of the church."[23] Calling them "the ordinances," Arrington stresses that both baptism and the Lord's Supper are not just ceremonial in nature; instead, they are "a means of real communion with God and of strengthening grace."[24] Aside from the classic Pentecostal understanding of the meal as remembrance and proclamation of Christ's death, Arrington points out that the Lord's Supper also means sacrifice, as in eucharistic sacrifice—a meaning that is rare in the Pentecostal vernacular—and communion with God and one another through the Holy Spirit.[25]

---

19. Pruitt, *Fundamentals of the Faith*, 361.
20. Pruitt, *Fundamentals of the Faith*, 364.
21. Pruitt, *Fundamentals of the Faith*, 366.
22. Pruitt, *Fundamentals of the Faith*, 367.
23. Arrington, *Christian Doctrine*, 3:201.
24. Arrington, *Christian Doctrine*, 3:208.
25. Arrington, *Christian Doctrine*, 3:213.

The Foursquare Church

The first systematic theology coming out of the Foursquare denomination, entitled the *Foursquare Declaration of Faith*, comes as a teaching manual for adult Sunday school. The volume is separated into teaching materials for two years, and the teaching material on the Lord's Supper is found in year 2, part 1, lesson 8 of the book.[26] The lesson calls the Lord's Supper a "perpetual sacrament" instituted by Jesus, originating at the last Passover he ate with his disciples.[27] There is not much discussion on the meaning of the Lord's Supper except that it is threefold: an act of remembrance, a new covenant, and an act of communion with God and one another. The emphasis of the meaning is put on remembrance, as this particular one gets the most attention out of the three meanings.[28]

The other Foursquare publication, *Foundations of Pentecostal Theology*, was published by two of the editors of the earlier volume reviewed above. For a much newer publication than the previous one, the discussion on the Lord's Supper is still surprisingly short. It briefly discusses the reason a believer should observe the meal; namely, it is an act of obedience, the proclamation of Christ's death, the anticipation of his return, and communion.[29] The remaining part of the presentation explains the different views regarding the nature of the elements of the supper, transubstantiation, consubstantiation, memorialism, and Calvin's receptionism, which is the position taken by the volume.[30] I will discuss the significance of this position in chapter 2.

Discussions by Pentecostal/Charismatic Theologians

I now begin presenting, in chronological order from earlier works to the more recent, discussions on the Lord's Supper by Pentecostal/charismatic theologians. I start with the late Swiss theologian Walter J. Hollenweger, who is recognized as an expert on worldwide Pentecostalism. He dedicates one whole chapter to the discussion of Pentecostal sacraments, entitling the chapter "To Them That Obey Him," in line with the Pentecostal

---

26. Duffield et al., *Declaration of Faith*, 62.
27. Duffield et al., *Declaration of Faith*, 62–63.
28. Duffield et al., *Declaration of Faith*, 65–69.
29. Duffield and Van Cleave, *Foundations of Pentecostal Theology*, 437.
30. Duffield and Van Cleave, *Foundations of Pentecostal Theology*, 437–38.

view of sacraments as an ordinance.³¹ He divides the chapter into three sections, following the most common sacraments most Pentecostals accept: a discussion on the Lord's Supper, water baptism, and foot washing.³² Hollenweger points out that even without a developed theology of the sacraments, there is richness in how Pentecostals celebrate the Lord's Supper and argues that the celebration is part and parcel of Pentecostal worship.³³ Pentecostals see the celebration as an expression of their love for Jesus, putting their hope and trust in him, and as an opportunity for an encounter with Jesus, one that will strengthen their faith to face all sorts of temptation and one that will provide healing for their sickness.³⁴

J. Rodman Williams is the author of the three-volume systematic theology entitled *Renewal Theology: Systematic Theology from a Charismatic Perspective*, and his discussion on the Lord's Supper is found in volume 3. Williams's systematic theology is better described as biblical theology, as the primary source of his work comes from the biblical texts. Referring to the book of Acts, Williams points out that the Lord's Supper holds a vital place in the daily life of the early church.³⁵ For Williams, the Lord's Supper is a Christian Passover. He argues that "even as the Lord passed over the Israelites, saving them from physical death through the sacrificed lamb, so by Christ's infinitely greater sacrifice believers are saved from eternal destruction. As Christians, we celebrate this on every occasion of the Lord's Supper."³⁶ The meaning of the celebration in his view is threefold, namely, remembrance of a historical event, of the new covenant, and forgiveness;³⁷ communion the Lord has with his people, spiritual communion the people have with the Lord, and communion with one another;³⁸ and last about an expectation of the messianic supper in the eschatological kingdom.³⁹

In a chapter entitled "The Spirit and the Lord's Supper," Veli-Matti Kärkkäinen looks at the significance of *anamnēsis*, its relation to the

---

31. Hollenweger, *Pentecostals*, 385.
32. Hollenweger, *Pentecostals*, 385, 390, 395.
33. Hollenweger, *Pentecostals*, 385.
34. Hollenweger, *Pentecostals*, 386.
35. J. R. Williams, *Renewal Theology*, 3:242.
36. J. R. Williams, *Renewal Theology*, 3:244.
37. J. R. Williams, *Renewal Theology*, 3:245.
38. J. R. Williams, *Renewal Theology*, 3:247–51.
39. J. R. Williams, *Renewal Theology*, 3:255.

epiclēsis, the prayer for the invocation of the Holy Spirit to consecrate the bread and wine, and discerning the unity of the Spirit in the celebration of the Eucharist. For him, *anamnēsis* is not just an act of human remembering but a transformative pneumatologically driven event in believers.[40] This kind of remembrance is made possible by the *epiclēsis*. Through petitioning the Spirit's presence, remembering is more than recalling memory (like recalling the memory of a deceased family member); rather, it is a Spirit-driven event.[41]

For Kärkkäinen, the meaning of unity contained in the Eucharist exists at several levels, namely, the unity of the people celebrating locally, the anticipation of the unity of all God's people who are still disunited, and therefore the tasking of the people of God to work toward this unity amid the present disunity.[42] Kärkkäinen also points out that the Spirit is responsible for the healing quality contained in the Eucharist. Through the Spirit, the Eucharist offers renewal to our bodies and spirit.[43] Finally, the advantage of looking at the celebration through the lens of the Spirit is to see the meal in light of the fulfillment of the eschatological promise of renewed creation.[44]

Kenneth Archer, in his article entitled "Nourishment for Our Journey," argues that the classic Pentecostal understanding of ordinance that denies any real grace being mediated through it, thus reducing the Eucharist to strictly a memorial rite, hinders Pentecostals from a fuller understanding of the encounters they have with Christ in the meal. Archer contends that the metaphorical and narrative nature of the sacraments is an event for the Holy Spirit to work redemptively in the lives of the community of faith, therefore strengthening them in their journey (*via salutis*) and reshaping their eschatological identity.[45] Through the sacraments, Archer argues, people are being brought closer to an encounter with the saving work of Christ.[46] At the same time, it is built into the expectation of the believing community that in the sacraments, especially

---

40. Kärkkäinen, "Spirit and the Lord's Supper," 138.
41. Kärkkäinen, "Spirit and the Lord's Supper," 140.
42. Kärkkäinen, "Spirit and the Lord's Supper," 141.
43. Kärkkäinen, "Spirit and the Lord's Supper," 142.
44. Kärkkäinen, "Spirit and the Lord's Supper," 144.
45. Archer, "Nourishment for Our Journey," 81.
46. Archer, "Nourishment for Our Journey," 82.

in the Lord's Supper, they will indeed encounter Christ in the celebration.[47] The sacraments, therefore, provide "nourishment" for the faith of the believers in their journey following Christ together as an eschatological community.[48] Finally, Archer sketches the connections between the Pentecostal fivefold gospel and the sacraments. He connects the idea of Jesus as *Savior* to baptism, Jesus as *Sanctifier* to foot washing, Jesus as *Spirit Baptizer* to Spirit baptism, Jesus as *Healer* to anointing with oil and laying on of hands, and Jesus as *Soon-Coming King* to the Lord's Supper.[49]

In *The Spirit Poured Out on All Flesh: Pentecostalism and the Possibility of Global Theology*, Amos Yong highlights how the Eucharist becomes a transformative ritual through the Holy Spirit. First, it is an embodied ritual, where the community consumes the word of God through the Spirit.[50] In this physical act, God's healing is made available, not only in the patristic *pharmakōn* sense but also, because of the Spirit, as an atonement healing.[51] This is because in the celebration, Christ is present to the believers, and believers are present to him. The Spirit makes "a mysterious interpersonal encounter" possible between Christ and his body.[52] As the body of Christ is present to him, so are they to one another so that the supper is not just an ecclesial act but also an act of solidarity between members.[53] Because of this solidarity, the meal is also political and prophetic, in the sense that through this meal, the Spirit calls the participants to lead a gracious way of life that is different from the world.[54] Finally, because this political and prophetic call is a foretaste of what is to come, the supper then is an eschatological act anticipating the fulfillment of the promise in which members of the body and humanity become Christ's full image and likeness through the Spirit.[55]

Wesley Scott Biddy's essay issues a call to Pentecostals to put sacramentality front and center in their worship practice. He strongly suggests that when the practices of the sacraments, especially the Lord's Supper, are neglected, then Pentecostals are "cheat[ing] themselves every bit as much

47. Archer, "Nourishment for Our Journey," 85.
48. Archer, "Nourishment for Our Journey," 87.
49. Archer, "Nourishment for Our Journey," 90–94.
50. Yong, *Spirit Poured Out*, 163.
51. Yong, *Spirit Poured Out*, 163.
52. Yong, *Spirit Poured Out*, 164.
53. Yong, *Spirit Poured Out*, 164.
54. Yong, *Spirit Poured Out*, 165.
55. Yong, *Spirit Poured Out*, 165.

as some Christians cheat themselves by denying that the *charismata* are available to the Church today."[56] Pentecostals historically have been nervous about seeing the sacraments bestowing any kind of grace, to which his response is if Pentecostals affirm the work of God and his freedom to do what he wants to do through his presence, then Pentecostals should not be wary about him extending his grace like forgiveness through the sacraments.[57] In conversation with Roman Catholic theologian Edward Schillebeeckx, he tries to describe the idea of transubstantiation in the grammar that is acceptable to Pentecostals. The argument Biddy seeks to make is for Pentecostals "to recognize *openly* (1) that divine-human encounters take place in, with, and under *signs*, and (2) that these encounters may rightly be regarded as moments in which God dispenses *grace*,"[58] things that are already embedded in Pentecostal spirituality.

According to Simon Chan, the Eucharist holds an important place among the sacraments because it is the sacrament in which the church finds Christ wholly giving himself his body.[59] In his *Liturgical Theology: The Church as Worshiping Community*, Chan points out that in contrast to baptism, where the emphasis is on the individual believer, the Eucharist, although involving the participation of individuals, is about the church itself—it is in this sacrament that the church and other sacraments find their end and are fulfilled. The reason the Eucharist is more significant than the other sacraments is that in this sacrament the church enters into the life of Christ, who is the head of the church; through the Eucharist, the church truly becomes the body of Christ, in which Christ communes with and among his people.[60] The Eucharist also points to the life God intends to be, a sacramental life oriented toward and around thanksgiving.[61] The implication of this sacrament is that it opens up the profound meaning of sociological categories because these categories are now understood eucharistically as sharing in the life of the triune God

---

56. Biddy, "Re-Envisioning the Pentecostal Understanding," 244–45; emphasis in original.

57. Biddy, "Re-Envisioning the Pentecostal Understanding" 236.

58. Biddy, "Re-Envisioning the Pentecostal Understanding," 250; emphasis in original.

59. Chan, *Liturgical Theology*, 70.

60. Chan, *Liturgical Theology*, 71.

61. Chan, *Liturgical Theology*, 75.

through the redemptive work of Christ, becoming partakers of the divine nature.[62]

Wolfgang Vondey's take on the Lord's Supper found in his *People of Bread: Rediscovering Ecclesiology* revolves around the idea of companionship. Because of Jesus's physical absence, the community of believers is always dealing with a sense of emptiness.[63] The bread serves as a token of Jesus's presence that fills the void. Vondey points out that the breaking of bread at Emmaus that opened the disciples' eyes to Jesus serves as a pointer to the outpouring of the Holy Spirit, who will make Jesus known to the disciples. Vondey points out, "In the breaking of the bread the Church expresses itself as a companion of the faithful, formed by the hospitality of God, transformed through the companionship with God's Son, and empowered by God's Spirit."[64] The breaking of bread was both an opportunity for remembrance *and* anticipation, that is, to remember the instruction Jesus gave them and to anticipate the heavenly banquet.[65] The meal then becomes a place where disciples express hospitality not only to each other but also to the world, which then, in turn, expresses the hospitality of God, who invites the nations to his table.[66]

In his volume *Pentecostal Theology: A Theology of Encounter*, Keith Warrington—contra to Hollenweger, who was reviewed above—does not see that Pentecostals have seen the Lord's Supper as central to their worship. The celebration, which, because of the Zwinglian influence, is more about remembering a past event, is observed in simplicity, emphasizing the death of Jesus in a predictable pattern, although done without written liturgy.[67] Warrington argues that for Pentecostals, the critical feature of the supper is a celebration of his "realized presence" as opposed to the sacramental "real presence."[68]

Because the focus is on the passion and death of Jesus, the celebration—unlike much of Pentecostal worship—is often a quiet and sober occasion where the congregation reflects on the cost Jesus paid for their sins. Another distinctive mark of the Pentecostal celebration of the Lord's

---

62. Chan, *Liturgical Theology*, 78.
63. Vondey, *People of Bread*, 172.
64. Vondey, *People of Bread*, 173.
65. Vondey, *People of Bread*, 175.
66. Vondey, *People of Bread*, 193–94.
67. Warrington, *Pentecostal Theology*, 165.
68. Warrington, *Pentecostal Theology*, 168.

Supper is the emphasis on it being a private event, even if it is done in the context of congregation life. The congregation individually reflects and has a time of introspection while celebrating, accompanied by corporate singing, which often overshadows the celebration itself.[69]

Chris E. W. Green's monograph, *Toward a Pentecostal Theology of the Lord's Supper*, is a Pentecostal's first major published work on the subject. Green reappropriates the word "sacrament" into Pentecostal vernacular. Historically, the word "ordinances" is preferred, mostly because of an anti-Roman Catholic stance. However, the Pentecostal worldview—as seen in the practice of the laying of hands and the use of anointing oil—is inherently sacramental.[70] From this understanding, Green believes Pentecostals should no longer be defining their sacramentality by "what they do *not* believe" and instead begin to articulate what they actually believe.[71] For Green, the Eucharist and its practices relate strongly to mission because the reality they embody and mediate provides the rootedness Pentecostals need in their mission, i.e., the celebration is an acknowledgment that Christ is *missio Dei* himself in the flesh, and the meal becomes a missionary meal whereby the participants become empowered for their mission to be "an ongoing Pentecost" for the world.[72]

In a book entitled *Types of Pentecostal Theology*, Christopher A. Stephenson subjects his *regula spiritualitis, regula doctrinae*—which he proposes to be a broadened and modified understanding of *lex orandi, lex credendi*—to a theoretical test case using the Lord's Supper.[73] He argues that a careful reflection on the meaning of the Lord's Supper deduced from an informed practice can provide content for Pentecostal doctrine. Stephenson proposes that this reflection will lead to an understanding of the meal that is more than just remembrance.[74] Regarding the divine presence in the celebration, Stephenson suggests that Pentecostals should withdraw from joining the debate that focuses on *how*; instead, they should try to focus on discussing the *who*. Stephenson points out, "If according to Pentecostal spirituality it is the Holy Spirit who is active among the people of God to transform them, then for Pentecostals the

---

69. Warrington, *Pentecostal Theology*, 166.
70. Green, *Toward a Pentecostal Theology*, 5, 82–84.
71. Green, *Toward a Pentecostal Theology*, 5; emphasis in original.
72. Green, *Toward a Pentecostal Theology*, 307–8.
73. Stephenson, *Types of Pentecostal Theology*, 115, 120.
74. Stephenson, *Types of Pentecostal Theology*, 121.

question of the Spirit's presence *could take precedence* over the question of Christ's presence in the supper."[75] This is because, in his view, the Eucharist is an opportunity for the church to be immersed in the already-not-yet reality in which she lives and to focus on the present brokenness that is all around so that they can participate in Christ's redemptive work in the Spirit.[76]

Daniel Tomberlin's *Pentecostal Sacraments: Encountering God at the Altar* is another major work on the sacraments by a Pentecostal. Tomberlin defines the term *sacrament* as "a sacred act of worship blessed by Christ the High Priest through which the worshiper encounters the Spirit of grace."[77] He argues that one must look at the gospel stories closely to have a significant understanding of the Lord's Supper. The significance of the supper is found in the fact that all are welcomed, sinners find mercy and receive forgiveness, and disciples are formed.[78] The incarnation, which is the redemptive event of history, is the foundation of the presence of Christ in the bread and cup. Tomberlin contends that "Jesus Christ, the 'enfleshed Word,' offered Himself to be 'broken and poured out' for the redemption of all people. Anyone receiving the Eucharist received nothing less than the flesh and blood of Christ. The bread and cup of the Eucharist are understood to be an extension of the Incarnation."[79] Therefore, for Tomberlin, transformative power is available in communion. Aside from seeing it as medicine for the soul and body of believers, Tomberlin also sees the Eucharist as a "prophetic act of worship" in which confession and reconciliation take place.[80]

Mark Cartledge's volume *The Mediation of the Spirit: Interventions in Practical Theology* is not explicitly written on the subject of the Eucharist. His work was written to see how Pentecostal and charismatic theological views, including that of the Eucharist, can further the discussion of practical theology.[81] Cartledge notes that, unlike in the Roman Catholic tradition, the prayer of *epiclēsis* for Pentecostals is not so much about sanctifying the eucharistic elements; instead, it is about "invoking

---

75. Stephenson, *Types of Pentecostal Theology*, 122; emphasis added.
76. Stephenson, *Types of Pentecostal Theology*, 128.
77. Tomberlin, *Pentecostal Sacraments*, 69.
78. Tomberlin, *Pentecostal Sacraments*, 163.
79. Tomberlin, *Pentecostal Sacraments*, 169.
80. Tomberlin, *Pentecostal Sacraments*, 183–85.
81. Cartledge, *Mediation of the Spirit*, xi.

the Spirit's intervention in healing and restoration."[82] This is an important distinction because of the connection to healing that is found in the Pentecostal understanding of the Eucharist.[83] Cartledge points out that the mediation the Holy Spirit uses is not limited to the spectacular signs and wonders but extends to the "patterned and routine aspects of church life," which includes the Eucharist, and that the routine and the spectacular complete one another, being "the same eschatological and soteriological reality."[84] Therefore, he concludes that the Eucharist is one of the pneumatological processes of receiving salvation and conversion, by which a believer is incorporated and transformed into the body.[85] The Eucharist, therefore, is one of a few "communal matri[ces] for the reception of salvation."[86]

Roman Catholic Literature

Two of the Roman Catholic works presented here represent the thinking of the Second Vatican Council. This is an important note to make as the thinking of Vatican II brought back the sacramental thinking of the patristics into the Roman Catholic doctrines. Henri de Lubac was one of the people who played a crucial role in shaping the Second Vatican Council. In *Corpus Mysticum*, Lubac intends to affirm the essential unity of the Eucharist and the sacrifice of the cross, arguing that the Eucharist is a sacrifice that cannot be understood apart from the sacrifice of Christ. For it to be so, the Eucharist must retain a reference, which is the announcing of Christ.[87] For Lubac, who develops his thinking out of his study of patristic and medieval writings, the Eucharist sacramentally signifies a past action in which the mystery of the passion is "commemorated" and "reproduced" and, therefore, is transformational in nature.[88]

The thoughts of Joseph Ratzinger, also known as Pope Benedict XVI, continue the thrust of Vatican II concerning sacramentality. In *Called to Communion*, Ratzinger grounds the church christologically, noting that

---

82. Cartledge, *Mediation of the Spirit*, 69.
83. Cartledge, *Mediation of the Spirit*, 11.
84. Cartledge, *Mediation of the Spirit*, 102.
85. Cartledge, *Mediation of the Spirit*, 155–56.
86. Cartledge, *Mediation of the Spirit*, 162.
87. Lubac, *Corpus Mysticum*, 58.
88. Lubac, *Corpus Mysticum*, 59.

when Jesus first calls people to himself, he also calls them into a newness life.[89] Therefore, an ecclesiology that does not find its very existence from and in Christ and does not express that existence by living for the world is not adequately Christocentric and evangelical in nature, as that is the only way the reign of God is expressed in the world.[90] Furthermore, Ratzinger insists that the church is the body of Christ construed by the Lord himself when he cleanses us by word and sacrament, thus making us his members.[91] Therefore, in the Eucharist, believers become Pentecost people "through communion with the Body and Blood of Jesus, which is simultaneously communion with God."[92]

O'Loughlin's aim in *The Eucharist: Origins and Contemporary Understandings* is to rethink the theology of the Eucharist first by a thorough historical-critical reconstruction of eucharistic origins and second by paying particular attention to our fundamental nature, people who eat together.[93] Ritual is a big part of our humanity; thus, O'Loughlin seeks to understand what the Eucharist is for Christians by studying how people follow rituals and explaining why they follow them and their implications for their lives.[94] After investigating the ritual aspect, O'Loughlin looks at the idea of memory as a starting point to understand the Eucharist, not in terms of dividing time into past, present, and future, but as something formative to the human self and understanding, in which memory helps us appreciate the Eucharist as a blessing from the Father.[95]

Eastern Orthodox Literature

Metropolitan John D. Zizioulas argues that the relevancy of church doctrine stems from proper ecclesiology and eucharistic theology. Therefore, in *The Eucharistic Communion and the World*, he proposes a eucharistic worldview that reconnects the natural and the supernatural by retrieving the view of the fathers, who never saw a dichotomy between the natural and supernatural. He stresses that in eucharistic liturgical worship, the

89. Ratzinger, *Called to Communion*, 25.
90. Ratzinger, *Called to Communion*, 23.
91. Ratzinger, *Called to Communion*, 161–62.
92. Ratzinger, *Called to Communion*, 28–29.
93. O'Loughlin, *Eucharist*, 13.
94. O'Loughlin, *Eucharist*, 13.
95. O'Loughlin, *Eucharist*, 18, 21.

importance and sacredness of the material world are acknowledged, and that world's significance for the existence of humanity affirmed and declared never to become an object subjugated by humans.[96] Out of all the living beings with a material connection to nature, only human beings are given the responsibility by God to become priests in Christ's recapitulation of the whole creation to him. For Zizioulas, this is how the Eucharist is transformative: through its material connection with the human body, creation enters into communion with God and is recapitulated in Christ through the Holy Spirit in the Eucharist.[97]

In *The Eucharist: Sacrament of the Kingdom*, Fr. Alexander Schmemann warns that dismembering the elements for private analysis negates the Eucharist's power.[98] For him, the purpose of the Eucharist is "partaking of Christ, who has become our food, our life, our manifestation as the body of Christ."[99] He bases his thoughts on the *anaphora*, which is the movement of ascent in the liturgy. This reality is what makes the celebration a divine encounter. Laced into his argument is the pneumatological aspect of the Eucharist, enabling the mystery of Christ's salvation to be communicated to the world.[100]

David Bentley Hart is an American Eastern Orthodox theologian, and in a chapter that discusses the Eastern Orthodox idea of the Eucharist as sacrifice, published in a multiauthored volume, he argues that the theme of *theōsis* is the place to begin to understand the Eastern Orthodox understanding of the Eucharist. The Eucharist is the meeting point of our offering of ourselves and Christ's offering of himself.[101] When the church celebrates the Eucharist, they enter into what he calls a "miraculous exchange" in which the people are made into those who bear God's glory to the world.[102] According to Orthodox tradition espoused by Hart, the Eucharist is an event of Christ's indwelling; in the sacraments, Christ "dwells in us and us in him."[103]

---

96. Zizioulas, *Eucharistic Communion and the World*, 126.

97. Zizioulas, *Eucharistic Communion and the World*, 136–37.

98. Schmemann, *Eucharist*, 196.

99. Schmemann, *Eucharist*, 226.

100. Schmemann, *Eucharist*, 217.

101. Hart, "Thine Own," 143.

102. Hart, "Thine Own," 144.

103. Hart, "Thine Own," 160.

Protestant Literature

To present a "Protestant" view is difficult; thus, this review will give only a sample of current Protestantism, that is, of Gordon T. Smith representing holiness ecclesiology, Geoffrey Wainwright representing Methodism, and Christopher Cocksworth representing Anglicanism. One may ask why not focus on the theology of the Eucharist of John Calvin. I am reserving that discussion for chapter 3, where I present an analysis of the theology of the Eucharist of Eastern Orthodox, Roman Catholicism, and Protestantism.

For Gordon T. Smith, a Christian Missionary Alliance theologian, the Eucharist is a simple act, yet at the same time, very significant because it is an event of an encounter with Christ that sustains members of the body. In *A Holy Meal: The Lord's Supper in the Life of the Church*, Smith points out that just like baptism, the Lord's Supper is an act of union with Christ in which the church identifies with the life of Christ. In the Eucharist, as the community gathers and receives, they come to meet, commune, and identify with Christ, and the outcome is a transformed life that comes from knowing, loving, and obeying him.[104] Smith also points out that the Pentecost event, that is, the outpouring of the Holy Spirit, makes sense of the Eucharist; in the meal, the full experience of the Spirit is made known.[105] The Eucharist enables the church to be Pentecost people, living as witnesses in the power of the Spirit.[106]

In his study entitled *Eucharist and Eschatology*, Wainwright purposes to systematically develop the eschatological character of the Eucharist as displayed by the liturgies and written by the early theologians of the church. Wainwright reasons that the church would become more missional if the celebration is seen in this regard.[107] The eschatological dimension of the Eucharist has been neglected in Western theology, at least since the Reformation.[108] An eschatological Eucharist is missional because it has an inescapable missionary significance insofar as it is the sign of the great feast that God will offer in the final kingdom to express the universal triumph of his saving will and purpose forever.[109]

---

104. Smith, *Holy Meal*, 114.
105. Smith, *Holy Meal*, 116.
106. Smith, *Holy Meal*, 117.
107. Wainwright, *Eucharist and Eschatology*, 3.
108. Wainwright, *Eucharist and Eschatology*, 153.
109. Wainwright, *Eucharist and Eschatology*, 159.

In his volume *Evangelical Eucharistic Thought in the Church of England*, Cocksworth argues that if Evangelicals are to be people of the gospel whose outlook on reality is shaped by Scripture, they must also be, in some sense, Eucharist people.[110] He contends that it is in the Eucharist that Christians come to know the presence and the redeeming work of Jesus.[111] Further, Cocksworth suggests that the experience of the Eucharist is an authentic evangelical criterion by which to judge a religious experience to be genuine as it coheres with the apostolic understanding of the gospel.[112]

Concluding Remarks

The goal of this review has been to see how Pentecostals/charismatics and other Christian traditions have viewed the celebration of the Lord's Supper as a transformative divine encounter experience. In my view, a pneumatological emphasis is vital in bringing out the notion of SET of the Eucharist, and as we have seen, only those writers who emphasized the importance of pneumatology brought this notion to the surface.

METHODOLOGY

This book will employ a method that combines the process of retrieval, comparison, and reconstruction. Gadamer claims, to which I agree, that "understanding is not merely a reproductive but always a *productive* activity as well."[113] In looking at the scriptural texts contextually through a "pneumatological imagination,"[114] this method will demonstrate that the biblical texts were constructed eucharistically and, therefore, will argue that seeing them that way will enable us to see an SET framework in the texts as well. In reading the theology of the Eucharist of other Christian

---

110. Cocksworth, *Evangelical Eucharistic Thought*, 9.
111. Cocksworth, *Evangelical Eucharistic Thought*, xii.
112. Cocksworth, *Evangelical Eucharistic Thought*, 179.
113. Gadamer, *Truth and Method*, 307; emphasis added.
114. Yong, *Spirit, Word, Community*, 119. Yong argues that interpretation is "a subjective reading of an objective fact [that] is always motivated by a problematic recognized by and relevant to the interpreter's situation and goals" (221). His pneumatological imagination functions "to sketch explicitly a hermeneutics of religious experience, a hermeneutics of the Word of God, and a hermeneutics of the ecclesial and theological tradition" (245).

traditions, again using a "pneumatological imagination," this method will probe the interpretation of those traditions, paying attention to their unique vernacular, in order to compare and, therefore, construct an understanding that will demonstrate an SET process—what Gadamer calls "fusion of horizons."[115] For Pentecostals, this fusion of horizons is attributed to the work of the Holy Spirit, as Cartledge contends that in reading Scripture, "the inspired text . . . functions normatively within the community of faith, the church, as the Holy Spirit *mediates between the horizon of the text and of the community.*"[116] Following that, this methodology will then dialogue with the interpretation of the eucharistic texts and the eucharistic theology of other Christian traditions to reconfigure these traditions' views in a specifically Pentecostal pneumatological language, thereby constructing such fusion of horizons. In a similar fashion that a pneumatological imagination in the Pentecostal text-community-Spirit hermeneutical principle allows for a certain "fluidity" in the definition of the community of interpreters—which in my understanding means that the idea of community is elastic enough to allow the accommodation of other reading traditions (what Pentecostals may previously have considered as "the gentiles" [Acts 15]) into "our community"[117]—my method should position Pentecostals in, as Merold Westphal says, "an openness to the possibility that traditions different from our own may have insight into facets of God's truth that we might incorporate into our own understanding."[118] Whether this is accepted or rejected is subject to further scrutiny; I am suggesting, however, that at the very least, this endeavor is plausible because, as a member of the Pentecostal community, what I am offering is an assessment of discerning "God's activity" outside my Pentecostal community in the spirit of the Pentecostal hermeneutics modeled in Acts 15.[119]

To give a brief example of how this works, I will take the way Eastern Orthodox theologian John D. Zizioulas sees how the Eucharist reveals the truth, and, using this method, translate it into a Pentecostal vernacular. First, he sees the Eucharist as revealing Christ's "visitation"

---

115. Gadamer, *Truth and Method*, 317.

116. Cartledge, "Text-Community-Spirit," 134; emphasis added.

117. Cartledge, *Encountering the Spirit*, 130. Cartledge points out that "the community of interpreters will inevitably vary because of time and place and in a sense the concept of 'community' is somewhat fluid."

118. Westphal, "Spirit and Prejudice," 29.

119. Thomas, "Reading the Bible," 119.

and "tabernacle" (John 1:14) taking place within time and space, "allowing partakers to behold the glory of Christ and in communion with him through the Spirit participate with his divine life."[120] Unlike the idea of "real presence" in transubstantiation, "visitation" and "tabernacle" are familiar terminologies for Pentecostals as they convey the idea of an encounter with God in a much more Pentecostal-friendly way. Second, in the Eucharist, truth is understood not merely as historical events moving linearly from past to present but as something that is enclosed by the *anamnetic* (remembrance) and *epicletic* (invocation of the Spirit) nature of the Eucharist, which transforms the celebration into a "Pentecost" event every time.[121] This way of understanding truth is very much in line with the Pentecostal imagination as this is the way Pentecostals interpret history—as we see Peter said on the day of Pentecost, "But this is that which was spoken by the prophet Joel" (Acts 2:16–17 KJV; Joel 2:28).[122] Finally, as opposed to being anthropocentric, the truth found in the Eucharist is Christocentric, having "profound *cosmic* dimensions" as it presents a picture of creation recapitulated by Christ, who is the head of all things.[123] This can be summed up with the idea that is already—at least implicitly—embedded in Pentecostal spirituality, that is, creation shares in the being of God in a participatory relationship because of the reality that "we live and move and have our being" (Acts 17:28) in God.[124] Pentecostals understand the truth not only as cerebral but more so as experiential, which is to say that understanding is finally (although at this point perhaps understood only implicitly) a "sacramental participation in the unfathomable mystery of Christ."[125] This would be the *productive* activity (see Gadamer), where the horizons of other traditions will be translated in a way that can be fused with the Pentecostal horizon.[126]

It needs to be stated, however, that the comparative aspect of this method will serve only as a point of contact. The final purpose of this study is to construct a more coherent and comprehensive renewal theology of the Eucharist that falls within the SET trajectory in an explicitly pneumatological vernacular that is familiar to Pentecostals so that the

120. Zizioulas, *Being as Communion*, 114–15.
121. Zizioulas, *Being as Communion*, 115–16.
122. Cartledge, *Encountering the Spirit*, 130.
123. Zizioulas, *Being as Communion*, 119.
124. Boersma, *Heavenly Participation*, 24.
125. Boersma, *Heavenly Participation*, 154.
126. Gadamer, *Truth and Method*, 317.

cohesiveness of our *lex orandi* and its *lex credendi* and *lex vivendi* can be strengthened, which in turn will contribute constructively to the larger theological conversation already taking place that seeks to advance and expand Pentecostal theology. To do so, I will also employ a comparative analysis of different models of eucharistic theology using key ideas such as commitment and openness and the dialectic between the word and Spirit, which will serve as lenses through which this renewal theology of the Eucharist that is participatory, holistic, inspired and inspiring, and discerning will be constructed.[127]

STRUCTURE OF THE BOOK

This book is made up of six chapters. The outline will be as follows: This introductory chapter provides an overview and a road map of this project. In chapter 2, I will provide an analysis of how Pentecostals have understood the Eucharist and see whether they can be mapped, at least implicitly, into the SET trajectory. In chapter 3, I will examine the various eucharistic theological traditions: Eastern Orthodox, Roman Catholic, and Protestant. Chapters 4 and 5 will be the main thrust of this book. In chapter 4, I will present a rereading of the biblical texts on and relating to the Lord's Supper/Eucharist in light of the SET paradigm. In chapter 5, I will take the rereading of the biblical text and critical analysis of the different traditions in order to create a fusion of the horizons and construct a renewal theology of the Eucharist. Finally, this construction can be meaningful only if it can be lived in the life of the church. Therefore, in chapter 6, I will present some implications and recommendations on implementing this proposal in the church's worship life. I will also point out a few possible further research areas as an outcome of this book.

LIMITATIONS

This book attempts to examine the Eucharist's interpretations as an SET process in the Roman Catholic, Eastern Orthodox, Protestant, and Pentecostal traditions. The first limitation, therefore, is that it is written with the understanding that presenting a view that is truly and authoritatively representative of the theology of each of these traditions is difficult, if not impossible. If one were to scratch below the surface, one could see

127. Cartledge, "Pneumatic Hermeneutic," 186–87.

there is no such thing as a homogenous view of one particular tradition. Take, for example, the Roman Catholic or Eastern Orthodox tradition; although both traditions are more unified in their particular theology, different kinds of literature offering different nuances of their view of the Eucharist have been written by their respective theologians. The Protestant camp proves to be more complicated as there are Lutheran, Reformed, and Methodist strands, to name just a few, each with its own take on the Eucharist. Concerning Pentecostalism itself, it has been suggested that in all its diversity, the movement is better described using the plural form (that is, Pentecostalism/s[128]). Therefore, this book will not claim that its conversation partners are the sole representatives of their traditions; instead, they are samples of their respective traditions. The aim is to see whether the process of SET is present, at least implicitly, in the eucharistic theology of the three older traditions and how it can contribute to Pentecostal eucharistic theology.

Second, as the primary goal of this book is to bring into the consciousness of Pentecostals the place and importance of the Eucharist as a process of SET, this book will not be concerned with the pros and cons debates surrounding real presence (e.g., transubstantiation, consubstantiation,), local presence versus pneumatic presence, or memorialism, et cetera.

Finally, the significance of this research requires further exploration in my Indonesian context. I admit that the conversation partners coming from majority-world countries, Asians, or even Indonesians, which readers may expect from an Indonesian theologian, are very limited, making it another limitation of the study. Although it is not reflected explicitly except in one of the sections in chapter 5, I am, of course, writing this book with my background as an Indonesian Christian, that is, I am a member of a minority group in a Muslim-majority pluralistic society. This is all to say that this renewal theology is unfinished, and a more contextual Indonesian Pentecostal eucharistic theology needs to be investigated at another time.

---

128. Anderson, "Varieties, Taxonomies, and Definitions," 15.

2

Analysis of Pentecostal Eucharistic Theology

INTRODUCTION

THE PRAXIS OF PENTECOSTALS, which contains embedded beliefs and theological values, has been described as sacramental in nature, although in their language, this sacramentality is yet to come out explicitly.[1] Wolfgang Vondey is correct to say that the reason for the uneludicated sacramentality is the eucharistic theology of Pentecostals—and by implication, its ecclesiology is only nascent if not neglected.[2] This underdevelopedness is visible in the way the Eucharist does not occupy a place of importance in the worship life of most Pentecostal churches. Most often, when a Pentecostal church celebrates the Eucharist, it is treated as an addendum to the worship service rather than being the central aspect of it.

Even if this sacramentality is still relatively undeveloped, there is great potential, as Wesley Scott Biddy points out, for developing Pentecostal sacramental theology to mature in a way that will align with its praxis.[3] The purpose of this chapter is to analyze Pentecostal eucharistic

---

1. Vondey, "Pentecostal Sacramentality," 96.
2. Vondey, "Pentecostal Ecclesiology," 42.
3. Biddy, "Re-Envisioning the Pentecostal Understanding," 228.

theologies (plural as there is not one standard Pentecostal eucharistic theology) that are available and to see whether and how the current language and concepts of these theologies can be mapped preliminarily into an SET trajectory. An SET process, as we know, is a contemporary way of modeling a Pentecostal and charismatic spirituality, developed by Mark J. Cartledge, who points out that "Christian spirituality is an indication of a process of searching for God, who once encountered effects change within the life of the searcher, who is then transformed or renewed in order to continue the journey."[4] The process, of course, is not a onetime thing but an endless cycle involving both personal and corporate dimensions. Orthodox theologian John D. Zizioulas points out that the coming of the Spirit in the Eucharist, invoked in the prayer of *epiclēsis*, makes the act of remembrance, or *anamnēsis*, nonlinear and multidimensional, creating a Pentecost event each time the Eucharist is celebrated.[5] Pentecostals understand that the outpouring of the Holy Spirit that took place on the day of Pentecost is not a onetime event but a "repeatable celebration that is essential to the mission of the church."[6] In other words, paradigmatically, it is *the* SET event. Therefore, understanding the Eucharist as creating a repeatable, localized Pentecost event should help Pentecostals live out their call to be the people of God.

This analysis will be carried out by first looking into what can be considered de facto official systematic theology volumes (including also a discipleship manual) of major Pentecostal denominations to see what they have to say about the denominations' understanding of the Eucharist. In this chapter, I will not go beyond these systematic theologies for a historical representation of the Pentecostal denomination's sacramentality, as I do not wish to repeat what Chris Green has done so thoroughly in his monograph.[7] I want to show that these denominations' documents have been viewed to represent what can be considered the official belief of a particular Pentecostal denomination, especially related to the Eucharist.

Second, I will look into more recent academic monographs and journal articles published by Pentecostals to see how the current Pentecostal scholarship views the Eucharist. The one thing that is immediately

---

4. Cartledge, *Encountering the Spirit*, 25.
5. Zizioulas, *Being as Communion*, 115–16.
6. Vondey, "Pentecostal Sacramentality," 94.
7. Green, *Toward a Pentecostal Theology*, 74–177.

noticeable is how different the view, at least in language and concepts, of the systematic theologies of Pentecostal denominations are to the current Pentecostal scholarship. It is safe to deduce that there is, for sure, a great desire to discuss the importance of the Eucharist from a Pentecostal perspective. Following the exposition, I will then engage with these systematic theologies, monographs, and articles, trying to see whether there is a pattern of SET noticeable in their understanding, whether explicit or implicit. I now begin with my discussion on Pentecostal denominations' systematic theology.

SYSTEMATIC THEOLOGY OF PENTECOSTAL DENOMINATIONS

The Assemblies of God USA

As briefly presented in the literature review in the previous chapter, there are four systematic theology volumes representing the eucharistic theology of the US Assemblies of God. In this chapter, however, I will engage with only three of them, namely Myer Pearlman's *Knowing the Doctrines of the Bible*; William Menzies's *Bible Doctrines: A Pentecostal Perspective*; and a multiauthored volume edited by Stanley Horton entitled *Systematic Theology: A Pentecostal Perspective*, where we find the discussion on the Lord's Supper in a chapter entitled "The New Testament Church," written by Michael L. Dusing. I have decided to leave out the material written by Ernest Swing Williams because the content of the material does not provide any additional constructive information that is not already covered in the other three pieces. The brevity of Williams's discussion on the Eucharist is quite insufficient to deduce whether or not there is more to his eucharistic theology than what is written.

I begin with an exposition of Myer Pearlman because being published in the early twentieth century made his work the earliest published Assemblies of God systematic theology. His discussion on the Eucharist is found in a chapter called "The Church" in a section entitled "The Ordinances of The Church." His opening statement, saying, "New Testament Christianity is not a ritualistic religion; at the heart of it is man's direct contact with God through the Spirit," is entirely predictable and quite telling of the AG's vocabulary—or lack of it—to explain worship rituals.[8] This idea of being non-ritualistic is both interesting and difficult to reconcile as a few sentences later Pearlman uses the idea to assert that baptism is the "*rite of entrance* into the Christian church"—a view that is closer to Paul's understanding of baptism (1 Cor 12:13), contra the typical language of the Assemblies of God, used to explain the meaning of baptism at baptism events as an "outward expression of inward faith," and that the Eucharist is the "*rite of communion*."[9] Pearlman's use of the language of "ritual" and "rite" in a misconceived and contradictory manner is quite common among classic Pentecostals, as for them, these words represent "something 'dead,' meaningless or even 'unscriptural' and 'unspiritual,' mechanical religion."[10] The more recent Pentecostal scholarship has begun to see them differently. For example, Albrecht defines *ritual* as elements of worship (that is, rites) that together are created, sustained, acknowledged, and sanctioned by the community, which "express appropriate attitudes, sensibilities, values, and beliefs" of the community.[11]

In Pearlman's view, the Eucharist contains five "keynotes." First, it is commemorative of the sacrifice Jesus made to atone for the sins of the world. He explains this keynote in a strictly Zwinglian memorialist fashion, in which he compares the idea of eucharistic commemoration to how Americans commemorate independence every Fourth of July, remembering that day as an event that gives them the freedom they have. Second, it is an instruction of "sacred object lesson"—a phrase that is quite commonly said by AG-trained pastors to their congregation—that sets forth two aspects of Christ's life, that is, his incarnation and his atonement.[12] Pearlman points out that God's blessing given through the incarnation can be received only because of the atonement.[13] This begs the question of whether resurrection, ascension, and Pentecost are implied or missed out completely, because they are not mentioned. The third keynote for Pearlman is the Eucharist as inspiration. He explains that through faith, the bread and wine give us the privilege to be partakers of Christ's nature and bring us into communion with him. Pearlman says, "As we partake of the bread and wine of the Communion, we are

---

8. Pearlman, *Knowing the Doctrines*, 352.
9. Pearlman, *Knowing the Doctrines*, 353; emphasis added.
10. Albrecht, *Rites in the Spirit*, 21.
11. Albrecht, *Rites in the Spirit*, 22.
12. Pearlman, *Knowing the Doctrines*, 357.
13. Pearlman, *Knowing the Doctrines*, 358.

reminded and assured that, by faith, we may truly receive His Spirit and reflect his character."[14] The fourth keynote is assurance, pointing out that in ancient times covenants that were signed with blood were the weightiest. Thus, the new covenant sealed in Christ's blood gives us that "Divine guarantee" about the seriousness of God to keep the covenant.[15] The last keynote is about responsibility. Pearlman says that when Paul asks about the "sacramental worthiness" (which, considering the word "sacrament" is never a preferred word, is an interesting phrase in and of itself), Pearlman points out that Paul is not talking about the person's unworthiness, as no one is worthy in that sense. Instead, what Paul is talking about is the unworthy actions a person is doing that prohibit them from partaking in the Eucharist with a clean conscience, which for the Corinthians, according to Pearlman, was their drunkenness; hence, they took the table in an irresponsible manner.[16] This analysis seems to be more informed by a classic Pentecostal holiness code that frowns upon the use of alcohol, because New Testament scholarship points out the issue was about the "haves" excluding the "have-nots" from their private meal.[17]

The volume by William Menzies, which is an exposition of the Assemblies of God's sixteen-point statement of fundamental truths, in which the Lord's Supper is contained in point 6, can be considered as a de facto official AG USA systematic theology.[18] Just like Pearlman, Menzies asserts the non-ritualistic and non-sacramentalism of the AG because not being those things is essentially what "Biblical Christianity" is about. On the other hand, sacramentalism, which in his view is not a biblical form of Christianity, "is the belief that special grace is bestowed on participants who engage in certain prescribed rituals. It is usually held by sacramental churches that the grace is received whether or not the participant has any active faith—all one has to do is go through the form." This view of sacramentalism is widely held by many classic Pentecostals with a strong anti-tradition stance; thus, it cannot be viewed as a bona fide theological understanding of sacramentality. It is not surprising, therefore, that for Menzies, baptism and the Eucharist are only memorial occasions and

---

14. Pearlman, *Knowing the Doctrines*, 359.
15. Pearlman, *Knowing the Doctrines*, 358.
16. Pearlman, *Knowing the Doctrines*, 359.
17. Fee, *First Epistle to the Corinthians*, 558.
18. Assemblies of God, "Assemblies of God."

actions that contain no saving power, as the only benefit these acts provide is "a matter of the heart."[19]

As a celebration that is instituted by Christ himself, the Eucharist replaces the Passover of the old covenant. In this celebration, there are four values "in relation to the past"—emphasizing the strict memorialism that Menzies holds. The first of these values is *commemorative*; it is an occasion that presents an opportunity to reflect on the death of Christ. This commemorative value contains a set of subvalues, namely *instructive* as the Eucharist is an object lesson, and *inspirational*, reminding the reality participants will receive through faith. Menzies recommends observing the meal regularly, as in doing so, believers identify themselves with Christ and are "reminded that He died and rose again."[20] The second value is *thanksgiving*, as the term "Eucharist" suggests. The celebration is essentially a thanksgiving meal that gives the opportunity to express gratitude for Jesus's sacrifice while at the same time opening the door for fellowship both with the Lord, who is "the unseen host at every celebration," and with fellow believers.[21] Third, the value of the Eucharist is *proclamation*, as it is an event that proclaims the new covenant instituted by Christ. By celebrating it, believers are making a declaration to the lordship of Jesus and that their purpose in life is to follow and obey him by their willingness to take their cross and carry out the Great Commission. The fourth and final value is the *responsibility* that celebrating the Eucharist brings. When Paul warns the Corinthians of observing in an unworthy manner, this refers to "unworthiness of attitude and behavior [such as] those who harbor sin, whether it be gross and carnal or subtle and personal." These require cleansing and a time of reflection until one can "recognize the body of Christ in each other and partake of the Lord's Supper in unity of love and faith, honoring Christ and God's Word."[22]

As mentioned briefly in chapter 1, the last Assemblies of God systematic theology on the Lord's Supper comes from a volume edited by Stanley Horton entitled *Systematic Theology: A Pentecostal Perspective*. The discussion on the Lord's Supper is found in a chapter entitled "The New Testament Church," by Michael L. Dusing. Out of all the AG systematic theology volumes, Dusing is the only one who considers

---

19. Menzies, *Bible Doctrines*, 111.
20. Menzies, *Bible Doctrines*, 116.
21. Menzies, *Bible Doctrines*, 116–17.
22. Menzies, *Bible Doctrines*, 117–18.

Pentecostal ecclesiology as a theological locus that deserves attention, as historically, the subject has been treated as less important compared to other loci such as soteriology, pneumatology, or eschatology. There are many things to be discovered, according to Dusing, from exploring a theological locus with which many Pentecostals are not already familiar and have neglected in the past.[23]

His discussion on the Eucharist is much lengthier than the others'. Dusing takes time to pay careful attention to explaining the understanding of sacraments. His explanation of remembrance is the only one that captures the threefold eucharistic idea of *anamnēsis*, which is a remembrance that is past, present, and future. He asserts that a proper *anamnēsis* is one that brings "an action which is buried in the past in such a way that its original potency and vitality are not lost, but are carried over into the present."[24] Thus, unlike a strictly memorial remembering, Dusing sees the act of remembrance that generates a past, present, and future sequence in the Eucharist. The celebration is a time to remember the death of Christ in the past. Yet, at the same time, the church is proclaiming Christ not as "a dead hero, but a risen and conquering savior" who is presently reigning and who, in the future, will return and be eternally reunited with his church.[25] According to Dusing, one aspect that is the strength of Pentecostals' understanding of the Eucharist is the fact that Pentecostals celebrate open communion, simply because the celebration is where one finds "true fellowship of believers [where all] are invited to join with the saints in fellowship with the Lord at his table."[26]

An area that Dusing also takes time to explain is the different understanding of the presence of Christ in the Eucharist, beginning with Roman Catholic transubstantiation, Luther's consubstantiation, Zwingli's memorialism, and—purposely put last—Calvin's idea of spiritual presence.[27] The reason for putting Calvin last is that Dusing sees Pentecostals' sacramentality as sitting somewhere between Zwingli and Calvin, contending that it is perhaps closer to Calvin. The rationale for that, according to Dusing, is that "Calvin greatly emphasized the spiritual presence of Christ at his table. This was understood to be a dynamic presence (similar

---

23. Dusing, "New Testament Church," 525.
24. Dusing, "New Testament Church," 562.
25. Dusing, "New Testament Church," 563.
26. Dusing, "New Testament Church," 563.
27. Dusing, "New Testament Church," 563–65.

to the meaning of the Greek term *anamnēsis*) through the power of the Holy Spirit."[28] This allows those who participate in the celebration, who do so in faith, to receive the benefit of Christ's sacrificial death. Dusing's understanding of Calvin or how pneumatology in Calvin's sacramental theology stops right there. There is no mention of the idea of "ascent" that is prominent in Calvin's sacramental theology to describe the mystery of the union between the believer and Christ, or how, for Calvin, the grace given in the Eucharist is always a gift from God through the Holy Spirit.[29]

The Church of God (Cleveland, Tennessee)

For the Church of God (Cleveland, Tennessee), we begin with the volume by Raymond M. Pruitt entitled *Fundamentals of the Faith*. In this volume, the discussion on the Lord's Supper is found in chapter 32, called "The Membership, Function, and Destiny of the Church." Pruitt begins by stating that even as divine image-bearers who are given the privilege to commune with God, humanity remains unable to adequately describe the encounters or explain the nature of the fellowship they have with God and others.[30] Because these experiences of encounter and fellowship are substantial and vital to the life of the believers, according to Pruitt, the more acceptable way to share them with others is through the language of signs and symbols. These signs and symbols do not bestow grace in and of themselves, but they do express outwardly what we have inwardly in our relationship with Christ, and these expressions are the functions of the ordinances.[31]

The Lord's Supper, for Pruitt, signifies believers' participation in the life and death of Christ. This participation takes place as believers receive and feed on Christ when they figuratively eat his flesh and drink his blood. Pruitt emphasizes that "in taking the Lord's Supper, believers do not merely look at the symbols, but receive them and feed upon them."[32] The celebration of the Eucharist is the replacement of the Passover, just as water baptism, in his view, is the substitution for circumcision.[33] The

---

28. Dusing, "New Testament Church," 565.
29. Van Dyk, "Reformed View," 78–79.
30. Pruitt, *Fundamentals of the Faith*, 364–65.
31. Pruitt, *Fundamentals of the Faith*, 365.
32. Pruitt, *Fundamentals of the Faith*, 366.
33. Pruitt, *Fundamentals of the Faith*, 367.

use of the language of feeding on Christ and feeding on the elements is intriguing, to say the least, especially as he contends that the signs and symbols are not means of grace. This begs the question of how one would feed on Christ if the elements do not bestow grace.

Pruitt takes a strong stance when it comes to partaking unworthily by pointing out that those who do so "will be guilty of sinning against the body and blood of the Lord (1 Cor 11:27)" and may end up becoming sick or dead. To partake worthily in the Eucharist, according to Pruitt, is to recognize "in one's heart the significance of this sacrament as it symbolizes for us Christ's sacrifice for our salvation, and the hope of His soon return to receive us to Himself."[34]

The next Church of God systematic theology is by French L. Arrington and is entitled *Christian Doctrine: A Pentecostal Perspective*. In chapter 11 of volume 3, entitled "The Worship of the Church," where his treatment of the Lord's Supper is found, Arrington begins by stating that "the ministry of the Holy Spirit is indispensable to the worship and life of the church."[35] Calling them "the ordinances," Arrington stresses that both baptism and the Lord's Supper are not just ceremonial in nature. Instead, they are "a means of real communion with God and of strengthening grace" because they are "visible signs of the saving work of Jesus Christ" that make the divine promises and the realities of salvation real in the life of the believers. In saying that, however, it does not seem that Arrington is using the idea to imply that sacraments are a "means of grace" in the sense that they are things (the means) through which God gives grace. An act of worship can be considered an ordinance when it fulfills three categories, namely, first, it was an act that Jesus instituted; second, the act is strongly connected to his sacrificial death; third, the act is reenacted in the worship life of the church. According to Arrington, these acts of worship are not "absolutely essential to salvation," and rather than creating faith, they require or presuppose faith; thus, proper participation in these acts is only a response of our inward faith.[36]

Arrington's understanding of remembrance is unclear. On the one hand, he sticks to a strict memorialist understanding of *anamnēsis* that sees it only as recalling of a past event, which in this case is the death of Christ for our salvation, thus the act "serves to remind us frequently of

---

34. Pruitt, *Fundamentals of the Faith*, 368.
35. Arrington, *Christian Doctrine*, 3:201.
36. Arrington, *Christian Doctrine*, 3:208.

our deliverance from the bondage of sin by His death."[37] On the other hand, he does, however, acknowledge that the word *anamnēsis* "is so powerful" that it is efficacious in bringing the blessings of Christ's death into the present.[38] Unfortunately, how this is accomplished, whether pneumatologically by the work of the Holy Spirit or otherwise, is not discussed.

The blessings of Christ in the Eucharist, according to Arrington, are what yield to our thanksgiving. Because of the deliverance given to us through the cross of Christ, we can offer our praise and thanksgiving to God. In Arrington's view, through this meal, we appear before God "with our sacrifices of praise and thanksgiving for the Sacrifice of Calvary."[39] Arrington goes on to say that the thanksgiving brings true fellowship (*koinōnia*), which, as described by Paul, is a "communion of the blood of Christ" in which the participants are fed spiritually by Christ, and communion with one another in the sharing of the saving benefits of the death of Christ.[40] As the participants have fellowship, this celebration then becomes a proclamation of Christ's death. This proclamation, according to Arrington, also acknowledges our in-between-time situation, that is, we live in between Christ's first and second coming, waiting expectantly for the banquet that Christ himself will host in the marriage supper of the Lamb.[41] Because of this, the Eucharist requires faith from the participants for it to be appropriately celebrated. Receiving it in a worthy manner means that people come with a commitment to the lordship of Jesus expressed in love for one another. It should be no surprise, according to Arrington, that some people are being healed or being baptized in the Spirit while partaking in the Eucharist.[42]

The International Church of the Foursquare Gospel

Two volumes coming from the Foursquare denomination will be discussed below. The first one, entitled *Foursquare Declaration of Faith*, is not a systematic theology per se; instead, it is a teaching manual for

---

37. Arrington, *Christian Doctrine*, 3:212.
38. Arrington, *Christian Doctrine*, 3:212.
39. Arrington, *Christian Doctrine*, 3:212–13.
40. Arrington, *Christian Doctrine*, 3:213.
41. Arrington, *Christian Doctrine*, 3:213–14.
42. Arrington, *Christian Doctrine*, 3:214.

ANALYSIS OF PENTECOSTAL EUCHARISTIC THEOLOGY 35

the church's adult Sunday school program. In this discipleship manual's discussion of the Eucharist entitled "We Believe in the Lord's Supper," the Eucharist is mentioned as a "perpetual sacrament" instituted by Jesus himself, originating at the last Passover that he ate with his disciples.[43] The definition of a *sacrament*, according to the manual, "is an outward rite instituted by Christ which is typical of an inward grace or experience of grace."[44] The manual states that the word "sacrament" itself is not found or even used in the Bible; instead, it is a word in Latin that signifies holy ordinance, which was also called "mysteries" not in the sense of their incomprehensibility; instead, they are mysteries because "they typified experiences of grace which were the privilege only of those who belonged to Christ, and whose value could be discerned only by converted persons."[45] Duffield et al., however, prefer the term "ordinance," which is not surprising because, in their view, this word emphasizes that the celebration is something that is instituted by Jesus himself and, therefore, "unquestionably binding upon all believers and churches," giving it the reason to be observed perpetually.[46] However, Duffield et al. stress the fact that mere external observance of this instituted celebration does not automatically say that a believer is obeying Jesus; this outward observance only signals what is already taking place inwardly in the person.[47] Without what takes place inwardly, the observance does not have any significance at all.

With regards to the meaning of the Lord's Supper, a terminology preferred in contrast to the term Eucharist, there is not much discussion on it in this discipleship manual except that it is threefold, namely, as an act of remembrance, a new covenant, and an act of communion with God and one another. Out of the three, the emphasis of the meaning is placed on remembrance because it gets the most attention.[48] There is a twofold pattern in this remembrance directly related to the eucharistic elements, namely, the Lord's broken body, concerning the bread, is given for our healing, and the Lord's blood, concerning the cup, is given for

---

43. Duffield et al., *Declaration of Faith*, 62–63.
44. Duffield et al., *Declaration of Faith*, 62.
45. Duffield et al., *Declaration of Faith*, 62.
46. Duffield et al., *Declaration of Faith*, 62.
47. Duffield et al., *Declaration of Faith*, 63.
48. Duffield et al., *Declaration of Faith*, 65–69.

our pardon.[49] They are all to be received with faith by the believer. Going further on the idea of remembrance, Duffield et al. explain:

> I think this is why Jesus made His great memorial so completely simple. He did not ask us to visit some distant shrine, to accomplish some difficult task or make some great sacrifice. He simply passed around some broken pieces of unleavened bread and a cup of the juice of the grape and said "Do this so that you will not forget Me." . . . The Communion is a memorial service. We celebrate it "lest we forget Calvary."

They also state that "this do in remembrance of me" is not just a recollection of the past; instead, it also contains remembrance connected to the present and the future.[50] Regarding the past, it is to remember that the Lord died so that believers might live. Hence, this remembrance is a "backward look to the supreme act which makes all impartation of divine grace possible."[51] The second remembrance, which is the present, relates to remembering that Jesus is the sustainer of life. The manual states, "He is our food. Not a luxury, but a necessity. We must feed upon him."[52] This aspect of remembrance will bring believers into a deeper spiritual reality, neither because the bread and wine become Christ's physical body and blood, nor because there is some kind of virtue in the elements; instead, the spiritual reality is because partaking the meal in faith "results in the real operation of the Spirit" in the believers, strengthening the inner person and bringing healing to physical bodies.[53] Regarding the future, this aspect of remembrance is an act that renews our hope of Jesus coming again. The manual states, "The Holy Spirit would have us see beyond the symbols of which we partake and know that one day we shall see Him face to face."[54] The celebration, taking place perpetually until Jesus finally comes again, is the church's prophetic act declaring the glorious hope she has in Christ.[55]

The other Foursquare publication, entitled *Foundations of Pentecostal Theology*, was published by two of the editors of the earlier discipleship

---

49. Duffield et al., *Declaration of Faith*, 65.
50. Duffield et al., *Declaration of Faith*, 67.
51. Duffield et al., *Declaration of Faith*, 67.
52. Duffield et al., *Declaration of Faith*, 67.
53. Duffield et al., *Declaration of Faith*, 67.
54. Duffield et al., *Declaration of Faith*, 68.
55. Duffield et al., *Declaration of Faith*, 69.

manual we have discussed above. However, for a much newer publication, and what can be considered to be de facto the official systematic theology volume of the Foursquare, the discussion on the Eucharist is surprisingly too brief—three pages in total in a subsection entitled "The Ordinances of the Church (Sacraments)" contained within the section on "The Doctrine of the Church," which also includes water baptism. It briefly discusses the reason a believer should observe the meal; namely, it is an act of obedience, the proclamation of Christ's death, the anticipation of his return, and communion.[56] The remaining part of the presentation explains the different views regarding the nature of the elements of the supper—transubstantiation, consubstantiation, memorialism, and Calvin's receptionism, which is the position taken by the volume.[57] Regarding Calvin's position taken by the volume, it states, "The elements, when received by faith, mediate to the believer the spiritual benefits of Christ's Death [and] real communion with the Lord is experienced."[58]

Engagement with Pentecostal Denominations' Systematic Theology

In this subsection, I wish to engage with the systematic theologies of the above Pentecostal denominations in the order in which they were discussed, namely the Assemblies of God, followed by the Church of God (Cleveland, Tennessee), and ending with the International Church of the Foursquare Gospel. On first impression, when it comes to constructing a systematic theology, the publications of the Assemblies of God do not seem to attempt to be very creative. Instead, what they seem to be focusing on is merely to expound on their doctrinal position. This results in a deficient theological language to explain the inherently Pentecostal sacramental praxis. The AG and its "Springfield school"—in contrast to the "Cleveland school," which is the terminology Amos Yong used to describe the school of thought of the Church of God coming out of Cleveland, Tennessee, where CG's flagship seminary Pentecostal Theological Seminary is located,[59] seem to be more focused on being apologetic, meaning, that the systematic theology volumes they have published are

---

56. Duffield and Van Cleave, *Foundations of Pentecostal Theology*, 437.
57. Duffield and Van Cleave, *Foundations of Pentecostal Theology*, 437–38.
58. Duffield and Van Cleave, *Foundations of Pentecostal Theology*, 438.
59. Yong, *Hermeneutical Spirit*, 8.

focused and concerned on defending the AG's sixteen fundamentals of faith instead of being more constructive. According to Cecil Robeck, a professor of church history at Fuller Theological Seminary and an ordained Assemblies of God minister, one of the plausible reasons for this is because those who in the past have tried to be creative ended up getting into trouble with the organization and were "systematically . . . silenced" as the expected posture is one that "accept[s], without further question or discussion, the authentic interpretation now given to this Tradition by members of the magisterium."[60] Another plausible reason for the lack of creativity of these volumes is that the writers could be the "magisterium" themselves of whom Robeck is talking so that the views expressed in the volumes are de facto the official theology of the denomination coming out from the magisterium. There is always a tension in conservative traditions between "correct" and "creative" theology, and quite often, we see the former pushing out the latter. It is essential to note the development of the discussion in these three works. Although it cannot be mapped out as a chronological development straightforwardly, Dusing's work, which is the latest among the three, shows that there is a development that can only be the result of awareness of the theologies of other traditions, although this is not explicitly spelled out (more on this in the conclusion). This, however, shows that an openness to other traditions is a possibility in the future development of the Assemblies of God USA.

As stated above, my primary purpose here is to see whether and how the current language of the Assemblies of God's systematic theologies, even in their limitation, can, at least implicitly, be mapped into an SET trajectory. From the first two published systematic theologies, this is clearly lacking. The Eucharist is seen as merely an ordinance to be followed by those desiring to obey the Lord, without much of an explanation, save for a few biblical references, as to whether there is more to the meal than strictly a recollection of past events. It would be arduous, to say the least, to map the belief held about the meal into a process of searching for, encountering, and being transformed by the divine. Dusing, however, begins to show at least signs of sacramentality being more spelled out. The fact that he argues for a position similar to Calvin's, known as receptionism, which we will discuss in the next chapter, begins to hint at an appreciation of the role of pneumatology in the celebration of the

---

60. Robeck Jr., "Emerging Magisterium," 170–71.

Eucharist. However, there is too little material to map this into a celebration that is a process of SET.

Even if the Cleveland school has been known to be more creative in general, this reality is not yet reflected in the Church of God's systematic theologies. There seems to be hesitancy about what to make of the physical observation and elements of the Eucharist. For example, Pruitt does make a point of the importance of the experiences of encounter and fellowship with the divine and fellow believers, and the fact that this encounter is more adequately shared through the language of signs and symbols. However, without going further into how this encounter takes place, whether metaphysically, mystically, or perhaps pneumatologically, he seems to immediately take away the value of the elements as signs and symbols by stressing that they do not bestow grace whatsoever. Arrington's volume shows some development in his discussion. He makes a point to stress that the ordinances, baptism and Eucharist, are not merely ceremonial in nature, but a means to have real communion with God. Concerning how this divine encounter is transformative, there is no explanation other than that it is a way to strengthen the faith of the participants. It is quite intriguing that Arrington neither has much to say about remembrance except as a strict recollection of past events nor mentions any kind of pneumatology working in the celebration, especially because of the fact that he states that in the celebration of the meal in Pentecostal services often there are charismatic manifestations taking place such as Spirit baptism and physical healing experienced by those believers who partake.

We move now to the two systematic theologies of Foursquare, which will be engaged at the same time. It is an interesting observation to make of the contrast between the denomination's discipleship manual, *Foundations of Pentecostal Theology*, and its de facto systematic theology, *The Doctrine of the Church*, in terms of the length of discussion on the sacraments. The discipleship manual never attempts to be constructive; instead, it provides scriptural proof texts to demonstrate the church's beliefs and understanding of the Lord's Supper. In doing so, however, it goes beyond what the systematic theology volume does. For a document targeted mostly at the average churchgoers, the discussion on remembrance it presents is a genuinely eucharistic *anamnēsis* of past, present, future, something that is completely missing from the systematic theology volume. Albeit brief, one thing worth noting about the systematic volume is the receptionism position that is taken by it, which is the same position taken by Dusing from the Assemblies of God, because the position is considered to be the most compatible with Foursquare's beliefs.

At the time of this writing, there is information that some of these systematic volumes are being updated. It is, however, unclear what the discussion of the Eucharist will be like in the updated version, whether it remains the same or expanded. From what we have seen in these volumes, however, there is a noticeable need for Pentecostal systematic theology volumes to develop the discussion on the Eucharist, not least from the perspective of spirituality—which in essence, is Pentecostal theology, so that it can enrich the life of the church. Whether that will be the case remains to be seen. Christopher Stephenson, whose work will be discussed below, puts it well when he says, "Every Christian tradition struggles with the difficulty that its most skilled theologians are not always the ones who make ecclesiastical decisions about the content of official teaching, and Pentecostals are no exception."[61] It would greatly benefit the Pentecostal church if denominations were more conversant with their best theologians, working together to enrich the spiritual life of the church, by incorporating the thoughts of some of the best minds in their denominations in future systematic theology volumes. The next section will present some of those whose ideas could well be included in updated volumes, especially those published by denominations. Denominationally published systematic theology volumes will find more tracking in the life of Pentecostal churches as these volumes are viewed as denominations' de facto systematic theology. Hence, they will be read and more accepted by pastors and leaders of these Pentecostal congregations.

CURRENT PENTECOSTAL DISCUSSIONS ON THE EUCHARIST

In this section, I am going to engage with some of the more current conversations regarding the Eucharist written by Pentecostal scholars. Some were published as journal articles, while others were part of a monograph that contained a discussion on the Eucharist. While this is not an exhaustive list, I am convinced that they are representative of the most current contributions regarding the theology of the Eucharist from a Pentecostal perspective. As we will see later, there is a pattern emerging from their

---

61. Stephenson, *Types of Pentecostal Theology*, 115.

thinking, and for the most part, we can, at least implicitly, notice a SET shape that is implicit in their understanding of the Eucharist.

Kenneth Archer

Kenneth Archer wrote an influential paper entitled "Nourishment for Our Journey: The Pentecostal *Via Salutis* and Sacramental Ordinances," constructing an understanding of Pentecostal sacramentality. Emphasizing the importance of embracing metaphorical language, Archer argues that it is normal for the Holy Spirit to use what is being conveyed metaphorically through the sacraments in order for the Spirit "to work redemptively in our lives by strengthening the community in her journey (*via salutis*) thus (re)shaping Pentecostal identity as the eschatological people of God."[62]

Archer points out the paradox that exists in Pentecostal theology and praxis. On the one hand, Pentecostals would be very quick to deny any real grace mediated by the Eucharist and affirm the strictly memorial aspect of it; on the other hand, this denial is understood as not in line with the expectation of the community of believers that in the sacrament the Holy Spirit gives believers the opportunity to encounter the risen Christ. Archer argues that the reduction of the Eucharist to a mere memorial and cognitive rite impedes the community's ability to sense the presence and power of the Spirit.[63] This cognitive way is in contradiction to the Pentecostal *via salutis*, which, according to Archer, is a dynamic action driven by the Spirit. The sacraments have a role in this journey of salvation. They act as signs that bring people closer to the salvific work of Jesus, bringing with them "transformative grace."[64]

Archer is quick to remind his readers that even if the sacraments mediate transformative grace, they are not, by any means, "magical actions." By the work of the Holy Spirit, the sacraments become effectual means of grace when they are received by faith by individuals who belong to a community of faith.[65] The sacraments are significant to the way Pentecostals do theology, what Archer calls the "narrative-praxis" approach to theology. Narrative, or "testimony," is a contextualized theological

---

62. Archer, "Nourishment for Our Journey," 79.
63. Archer, "Nourishment for Our Journey," 84–85.
64. Archer, "Nourishment for Our Journey," 82.
65. Archer, "Nourishment for Our Journey," 86.

account that takes place within a worshipping community. At the same time, praxis brings together the living-out aspect of the community's faith and its theologizing into one "reflective activity." A narrative-praxis approach then allows our testimony (i.e., theological reflection) to be critically engaged without negating how our religious experiences shape our beliefs and vice versa in a mutually informing way.[66] In this back-and-forth reflection and critical engagement, the sacraments become the placeholders that act as "prophetic narrative signs involving words and deeds through which the community can experience the redemptive living presence of God in Christ through the Holy Spirit."[67]

Since life in Christ for Pentecostals is not just about salvation, but more about a journey participating in the divine life, an idea that is not unlike the Eastern Orthodox idea of *theosis*, the sacrament is an absolute necessity for Pentecostals to continue in that salvific journey as they provide the framework for the Holy Spirit to keep the community in the right path of the *via salutis*.[68] In other words, Archer points out that the Eucharist is the "sustaining nourishment" for the *via salutis* that at the same time continues the transformation of their identity as an eschatological community whereby they travel "in the Spirit forward or backward in time—back to Sinai, back to Calvary, back to Pentecost—forward to Armageddon, the Great White Throne of judgment, the Marriage Supper of the Lamb."[69]

Engagement with Kenneth Archer

While not explicitly mapped out as such, the way Archer sees the sacraments in his proposal is very much an SET process. There are a few key takeaways from his paper. First, Pentecostals need to let go of the tendency to be "literal"—which I believe is an unfortunate inheritance of fundamentalism—and, as a way to truly embrace pneumatology, be very comfortable with metaphors. The metaphorical language provides richness to their spirituality while at the same time saving Pentecostals from the idea of "magical" faith that many of them seem to fear so much. This brings us to the second takeaway. Pentecostals see truth not only in

---

66. Archer, "Nourishment for Our Journey," 81.
67. Archer, "Nourishment for Our Journey," 86.
68. Archer, "Nourishment for Our Journey," 85.
69. Archer, "Nourishment for Our Journey," 86–87.

an intellectual and propositional sense but through the affective as well. Testimony, which is a regular part of Pentecostal worship, is the prime example of this affective knowledge being expressed. Pentecostals "know" in their heart that they have encountered God and that he has spoken to them. I will discuss more of this affective knowledge in the conclusion of this chapter. For now, what I want to point out is that embracing metaphorical language will help move Pentecostals from the strictly cognitive way of understanding the Eucharist, which is debilitating to its spirituality, and enrich their narrative-praxis reflection while they go through the experience of *via salutis*. Viewed as such, the Eucharist for Archer then is indeed a process of SET.

Simon Chan

Simon Chan argues that the Eucharist needs to be front and center in the Pentecostal church because it is what defines the meaning of church. In the Eucharist, the church is given a foretaste of the marriage supper of the Lamb, and the celebration makes the church the eschatological community that it is. Chan understands that the ultimate goal of *missio Dei* is the communion of saints, to which the anticipation of this goal is found in the celebration of the Eucharist.[70] This is where Pentecostals have some homework to do; that is, they need to rethink their praxis that is already implicitly sacramental in nature and express it theologically in a more explicit way.[71]

According to Chan, the challenge is not to simply adopt the theology of older traditions, because such an attempt will end up making the adaptation not recognizable as "Pentecostal"; instead, the challenge is to "'corporatize' [the] Pentecostal experience" that will contribute to the development and evolution of its doctrine yet remain consistent to its core beliefs.[72] This task is vital for Pentecostals if they are to retain the early-day vigor of their movement. According to Chan, this can be carried out by developing a Pentecostal spiritual theology that first begins with a willingness to examine critically the Pentecostal community's fundamental beliefs, which he contends will yield to a greater understanding that life in the Spirit is communal rather than an individualistic

---

70. Chan, *Grassroots Asian Theology*, 45.
71. Chan, *Pentecostal Ecclesiology*, 117.
72. Chan, *Pentecostal Ecclesiology*, 94.

enterprise. This self-examination of beliefs should finally reconsider the current Pentecostal praxis in a way that will make the Eucharist the theological and ritual hub of its liturgical worship.[73] The reason for this, Chan argues, is that in the Eucharist, every element of the community's worship finds its appropriate place and is united as a whole in a logical manner, both concerning its pneumatic aspect and its kerygmatic aspect. The pneumatic aspect happens when, by the power of the Spirit who is invoked in the *epiclēsis*, the bread and wine, which are everyday mundane things, and the act of eating and drinking, which are everyday human experiences, are being "transfigured" in the celebration of the Eucharist.[74] The outcome of this pneumatic aspect is that the church gets renewed in her identity, which is a charismatic eschatological body that she became on the day of Pentecost. The kerygmatic aspect happens because, in the Eucharist, the mystery of the Christian faith—Christ has died, Christ is risen, Christ will come again—is "celebrated, remembered, reenacted, reappropriated and applied, [and] proclaimed."[75] The Eucharist is, therefore, an act of worship of the church that helps Pentecostals preserve their distinction in the acts of praise and their proclamation.

For Chan, making the Eucharist front and center in their worship life presents Pentecostals with both a challenge and an opportunity. The challenge is to make the celebration that is faithful to the understanding of the historical church but, at the same time, make it so that it is recognizable as genuinely Pentecostal. This is understood as the Eucharist making the church a charismatic body of Christ through the Spirit as he is called upon in the *epiclēsis*.[76] The process of retrieving the historical understanding of the Eucharist needs to be consistent with the core of Pentecostal spirituality.[77] At the same time, the Eucharist also presents an opportunity for Pentecostals with regard to the worship life of the church; where the tendency is an individualistic worship experience, the Eucharist reminds the church that what is both at heart and the ultimate end goal of *missio Dei* is the communion of the saints, which is celebrated and anticipated each time the word is preached and the sacrament served. Chan explains that "in eating and drinking the church proleptically

---

73. Chan, *Pentecostal Theology*, 32–37.
74. Chan, *Pentecostal Theology*, 38.
75. Chan, *Pentecostal Theology*, 38.
76. Chan, *Pentecostal Theology*, 38.
77. Chan, *Pentecostal Ecclesiology*, 94.

participates in the marriage supper of the Lamb," proclaiming this reality prophetically while making the church what it really is: through the Eucharist, in *the* church, *me* is transformed into *we*.[78]

One way to emphasize the Pentecostal-ness of the Eucharist is to emphasize the healing that is offered in the celebration. Healing is very dear and near to the Pentecostal framework, and throughout the history of the church, the Eucharist as *pharmakon* is seen as offering healing not only to our physical and spiritual dimensions, but also to relationships in the community and cosmic healing. This holistic healing is what is contained in the theme of *Christus Victor*, and it reminds the church that the Spirit always relates to our materialness.[79]

The Eucharist, according to Chan, also presents Pentecostals an opportunity to be genuinely Trinitarian in their worship because it is a celebration that is both pneumatologically Christocentric and christologically pneumatic.[80] A Christology that is absent of pneumatology becomes christomonistic, and pneumatology not grounded in Christology is in danger of becoming pneumatomonistic; both are insufficient. Another important fact about the Eucharist is that it does not allow room for an over-realized eschatology; in the meal, partakers are always brought "back to earth," remembering that we still groan while awaiting the wedding supper of the Lamb and all its fullness.[81] Therefore, the rediscovery of Pentecostal's implicit sacramentality is not some fad, which is often the sort of thing Pentecostals fall into; rather, it is opening up something that is already in the Pentecostal DNA, which brings with it the implication of the rediscovery, which is an opportunity for genuine life transformation of the worshipping community.[82] It is in the Eucharist that Pentecostals can be Pentecostal as the Spirit continues the experience of the day of Pentecost in each celebration taking place, making the church the body of Christ that is ready to be offered to the world.[83]

---

78. Chan, *Grassroots Asian Theology*, 45.
79. Chan, *Grassroots Asian Theology*, 109.
80. Chan, *Pentecostal Ecclesiology*, 121–22.
81. Chan, *Pentecostal Ecclesiology*, 122.
82. Chan, *Pentecostal Ecclesiology*, 118.
83. Chan, *Pentecostal Ecclesiology*, 137.

Engagement with Simon Chan

Throughout most of his writing, Simon Chan advocates for the centrality of the celebration of the Eucharist to take place in Pentecostal worship, and this book certainly follows in those footsteps. My attempt to map out Chan's understanding of the Eucharist in an SET paradigm will begin backward, that is, with the transformation aspect. The fact that Chan points to the outcome *missio Dei* as the communion of saints, which is the total transformation of creation anticipated in the Eucharist as it points toward that "transformation," is vital to note, especially as Pentecostals are a community very much oriented toward the hope of eschatological fulfillment. The anticipation of this total transformation is found in the Trinitarian "encounter" that Chan brings to mind, one that is both pneumatologically Christocentric and christologically pneumatic. As he points out, this Trinitarian encounter keeps Pentecostals grounded as it prevents an over-realized eschatology, maintaining the tension of already-not yet. Yet it does so in a hopeful "search," that in the Eucharist, the benefits of *Christus Victor*, while not fully realized, are given as a foretaste, as those who seek are often given the taste of *pharmakon* that the Eucharist is, bringing healing to our physical, spiritual, relational, and cosmic dimensions. The historic position that Chan adopts is closer to the Orthodox tradition than the Roman Catholic, and there is at least one concern that can be an obstacle to Pentecostals. The fact that it is difficult to separate the theology of the Eastern Orthodox Church from its ecclesial life begs the question of how one would join a theology that comes from a very closed ecclesiology.

Chris E. W. Green

Chris E. W. Green is one of the few Pentecostals who dedicated his research to the Lord's Supper. His monograph, which came from his doctoral dissertation, is a comprehensive presentation that makes the case for the sacramentality of Pentecostalism. Green is convinced that the Eucharist must be placed preeminently in the Pentecostal liturgy without it being isolated or isolating the typical Pentecostal practices.[84] Green sees the Eucharist as an opportunity to encounter Christ, who then would open the Scriptures for the church and inspire the church to take on its mission

---

84. Green, "Then Their Eyes Were Opened," 224.

in the world.[85] Reading Scripture that would bring a Christ encounter, that is, to have our eyes opened to see Christ through the breaking of bread, is the only way to read the Scripture "in a Christian way."[86] This "Christian way" of reading Scripture, for Green, means that the end goal of reading is a community of believers that lives and passes on to others the character and wisdom of Christ himself, living for one another and the world, serving both in the way Jesus did during his earthly ministry.[87] Accomplishing that requires both reading Scripture "eucharistically" and celebrating the Eucharist "scripturally" so that the church feasts on the Word himself in both an audible and edible sense. This is the only kind of hermeneutic that opens the eyes of the church to the way the Father exegetes (John 1:18).[88] Therefore, in his view, if the Pentecostal church is to find Jesus in the Scriptures, there need to be two things that are taking place. The Pentecostal church must find a way, first, to celebrate the Eucharist in a faithful manner so that the celebration allows the church to be "eucharistically formed," and second, to take on habits that are virtue forming, which are found in the celebration and the liturgy and spirituality of the Christian traditions.[89] The issue of how Christ is present in the Eucharist will always be a contentious point for different traditions. To focus on this issue alone would not be constructive to the Pentecostal church; what matters the most is that Christ is present, and this presence is needed for the church to read Scripture in the right way, which will be transformative to the body.[90]

In his proposal to develop a Pentecostal theology of the Lord's Supper, Green points out that the Eucharist is an event that can be celebrated rightly only because of the outpouring of the Spirit on the day of Pentecost. The work of the incarnate Christ made Pentecost possible; the ongoing sacramental ministry of Christ taking place after his ascension is possible because of the day of Pentecost; by virtue of that reality, the Eucharist then also becomes an ongoing Pentecost because the only way Christ can act in the lives of the believers partaking the Eucharist

---

85. Green, "Then Their Eyes Were Opened," 223.
86. Green, "Then Their Eyes Were Opened," 225.
87. Green, "Then Their Eyes Were Opened," 226.
88. Green, "Then Their Eyes Were Opened," 226–27.
89. Green, "Then Their Eyes Were Opened," 223–25.
90. Green, "Then Their Eyes Were Opened," 234.

is because of the work of the Spirit.[91] Within this reality, then true communion will take place.

The implication of an experience of a genuine *koinōnia* is redemptive because it provides the church with the occasion for continuous spiritual formation with the goal of forming Christlikeness made possible by an encounter with the Spirit of Christ that brings the story of Christ alive in people.[92] The *koinōnia* that will be carried on by the members of the community, who will be committed to making every effort to live as a genuine community, is what validates the thanksgiving offered in the Eucharist.[93] Communion will ensure that thanksgiving, something that is natural for Pentecostals, will not be individualistic; instead, thanksgiving will be offered as a community, recognizing that when one member suffers, we suffer with them too.[94]

His proposal requires what Green calls "liturgical exactness" that he is convinced will orient and invigorate the Pentecostal worship.[95] If Pentecostals are anxious with the idea of "liturgy" for fear that it will bring with it the danger of dead tradition, Green argues that the liturgy, as a matter of fact, creates a space for a Spirit-led discernment that opens up to the people the intention of Christ for them at that particular moment.[96]

In the Eucharist, the people are reminded of two promises given by the Father, which are Christ and the Spirit.[97] This fulfillment of promise happens when the people encounter the risen and reigning Christ through the pneumatic operation of the Spirit so that "believers come face-to-face with the spiritually present living Christ."[98] The Eucharist facilitates the face-to-face experience of Christ through the Spirit because, as a "visible word," it allows a divine-human dialogue.[99] Regarding this idea of the visible word, Green explains, "At one level, it is merely the semiotic import of the elements themselves. In other words, the 'word' is what the meal means for the participants. At another level, however, this

---

91. Green, *Toward a Pentecostal Theology*, 292–93.
92. Green, *Toward a Pentecostal Theology*, 248.
93. Green, *Toward a Pentecostal Theology*, 249.
94. Green, *Toward a Pentecostal Theology*, 249–50.
95. Green, *Toward a Pentecostal Theology*, 249, 252.
96. Green, *Toward a Pentecostal Theology*, 261.
97. Green, *Toward a Pentecostal Theology*, 262.
98. Green, *Toward a Pentecostal Theology*, 264.
99. Green, *Toward a Pentecostal Theology*, 264.

word is Christ himself! He is the meal's meaning, the significance, and the signifier."[100]

Engagement with Chris E. W. Green

Through Green, we see another Pentecostal scholar issuing a call for Pentecostal churches to put the Eucharist front and center in the worship life of the church, insisting that the church should do so in a way that is distinguishable as Pentecostal. Green's insistence on having liturgical exactness calls for the thoughtful planning of the church service, which is needed so that Pentecostals can escape the emotionalism that often plagues their worship life. Green relates the idea of the Eucharist as an opportunity to encounter Christ that would open the Scriptures for the church, referencing the post-resurrection encounter that was told in the Gospel of Luke. In his proposal, Green also stresses the importance of pneumatology in making the Eucharist a truly charismatic event. Although Green is not primarily concerned with the charismatic spirituality of SET, in my view, the process is present in his proposal. He insists that a eucharistic reading of Scripture that brings about a Christ encounter is the only way of reading that can be considered Christian reading. This eucharistic "encounter" begins with a "search," which is the act of reading and preaching the Scripture that takes place before partaking the meal, which then through the pneumatic operation of the Spirit in the meal would bring a Christ encounter, meaning believers having their eyes opened by the breaking of bread. This then would make the reading of the text a Christian reading. As Christ is found and encountered through the spoken and visible word, there will be a "transformation" in believers' lives in such a way that two things will happen: First, a genuine fellowship among believers, where Christlikeness is formed. As this happens, then believers will be inspired to be sent into the world, taking on the mission of Jesus. However, what is unclear is whether, for Green, the process of "search" that brings the people to an experience of "encounter" that adds to "transformation" in the Eucharist precedes or necessitates faith. For example, in his reading of the biblical texts, Green maintains that Scripture teaches that the Eucharist becomes a real celebration "only as we faithfully respond to the Word of God."[101] At another place, Green maintains that "the reality of

---

100. Green, *Toward a Pentecostal Theology*, 264–65.
101. Green, *Toward a Pentecostal Theology*, 242.

Christ's and the Spirit's shared presence in the Supper does not wait on our believing [in] it," which would be how I see it as well.[102]

Christopher A. Stephenson

In subjecting his theory *regula spiritualitis, regula doctrinae* to the Eucharist, a theory that is his appropriation of *lex orandi, lex credendi*, Christopher A. Stephenson contends that an informed practice of the meal can lead to a deeper understanding of the Eucharist that is beyond mere memorialism.[103] Stephenson proposes that his *regula spiritualitis, regula doctrinae* is potentially more adaptable than *lex orandi, lex credendi* to Pentecostal spirituality and theology for two reasons. First, it can seize the practices and formative experiences of the Pentecostal community and systematically express them as doctrine in relation to practices. Second, unlike *lex orandi, lex credendi*, which he believes can be and in the past has been taken by some people as an either/or approach, *regula spiritualitis, regula doctrinae* provides a better both/and understanding of the connection between and mutual informing of spirituality and doctrine.[104] For Pentecostals, this fact is in line with the reality on the ground, that community practices have always been part of how they interpret, view, evaluate, and adjust their beliefs.[105]

The dialectic between practice and beliefs in *regula spiritualitis, regula doctrinae* is what can help Pentecostals move away from a strictly memorialist understanding of the Eucharist into a celebration that both opens and provides an opportunity for the Spirit to transform the community. Stephenson points out that this moving away from memorialism can and should happen through a process in which Pentecostals are mining from their own sources and practices.[106]

One of the ways to mine from Pentecostal sources is to go back and reflect on the doctrine of divine presence in the Eucharist, by once again asking the question *what* is present rather than joining the ongoing arguments about the *how*. Because Pentecostals believe firmly that the Third Person of the Trinity is the one who effects changes and transformation

---

102. Green, *Toward a Pentecostal Theology*, 285.
103. Stephenson, *Types of Pentecostal Theology*, 115.
104. Stephenson, *Types of Pentecostal Theology*, 115–16.
105. Stephenson, *Types of Pentecostal Theology*, 117.
106. Stephenson, *Types of Pentecostal Theology*, 121.

in the believers, then Stephenson contends that moving towards greater awareness that it is the Holy Spirit who is present in the Eucharist could and should take precedence over how Christ is present in it.[107] Stephenson points out that concerning the meal, the synoptic texts talk about Jesus preparing his disciples for his absence by telling them that he will not be with them again until they eat together with him in the kingdom of God.[108]

This idea of Jesus's absence and the Spirit's presence is the eschatological orientation of Pentecostal spirituality. This fact is what invigorates the hope of the coming kingdom of God in all its fullness, and therefore, according to Stephenson, it should be the key to developing a doctrine of the Eucharist that is in line with this Pentecostal distinction.[109] Seen this way (Jesus's absence, Spirit's presence), each time the Eucharist is celebrated, it will be an event that rekindles the hope for the reality of the kingdom of God to be fully revealed. However, at the same time, it is also an event that will highlight the broken reality in which the church still exists.[110]

For Pentecostals, who often fall into the trap of an over-realized eschatology, seeing the Eucharist in this way maintains the tension inherent in the already-not-yet reality of the church. Jesus is still absent, but the Spirit is present and is given to the church as a down payment to mediate his presence and provide us with a foretaste of what is to come while we anticipate the return of Jesus as king.[111] A doctrine of the Eucharist that highlights Jesus's absence, which, according to Stephenson, is a pneumatological view of the Eucharist, would then call Pentecostals to be more aware of the present-day reality in which they are, which is still full of brokenness and suffering, and respond in a way that takes and address evil more seriously through concrete social actions.[112] Highlighting Jesus's absence would help Pentecostals to imitate Jesus in the self-surrender model that he adopted while on earth, which, for Stephenson, does not cancel the christological dimension of the supper; rather it highlights Christology in a way that demands the participants to be

---

107. Stephenson, *Types of Pentecostal Theology*, 122.
108. Stephenson, *Types of Pentecostal Theology*, 123.
109. Stephenson, *Types of Pentecostal Theology*, 123–24.
110. Stephenson, *Types of Pentecostal Theology*, 124.
111. Stephenson, *Types of Pentecostal Theology*, 126.
112. Stephenson, *Types of Pentecostal Theology*, 126–27.

self-giving to others by participating in the ongoing redemptive work of Jesus in the power of the Spirit.[113]

Engagement with Christopher Stephenson

Stephenson is to be commended for constructing a systematic theology that is explicitly tested on the Pentecostal understanding of the Eucharist. Built into the celebration is an implicit process of SET, which I will map while directly engaging his proposal. While I am not entirely convinced the *regula spiritualitis, regula doctrinae* terminology is significantly different than *lex orandi, lex credendi*, or whether the former tends to be better at being both/and when it comes to the relationship between spirituality and beliefs compared to the latter, I think he is correct that there should be a back-and-forth, mutually informing relationship between doctrine and spiritual life because this is the "search" aspect of spirituality. This brings the worship life of the community to a time of "encounter"—which, in his view, is with the Spirit who is present in the Eucharist. The encounter with the Spirit in the celebration, while remembering the absence of Jesus, should bring awareness in the church that they need to respond by concrete actions to address the brokenness around them. This is the "transformation" brought into the lives of believers. While Stephenson admits that highlighting the presence of the Spirit and the absence of Christ should not be at the expense of Christology, there is a question of whether that may be unpreventable in the way he presents it. Rather than emphasizing the absence, it may just be better to state the presence of Christ in, or through, the Spirit, which would make the encounter Trinitarian while still highlighting the already-not-yet and the call of the church's eschatological hope to be taking part in addressing the present brokenness and reality. Because when it comes to the divine presence, Stephenson focuses on the *how* question rather than the *what* question, it is unclear how he sees Christ as present in the elements, whether as means of grace, nourishment, or otherwise.

In my view, it is the Trinitarian encounter embodied in the physicality of the eucharistic elements, as opposed to highlighting Jesus's absence, that will bring the transformation of believers, invigorating the hope of the coming kingdom of God, living it out in a surrendered life modeled by Jesus.

---

113. Stephenson, *Types of Pentecostal Theology*, 127–28.

Daniel Tomberlin

In his book *Pentecostal Sacraments: Encountering God at the Altar*, Daniel Tomberlin points out that the essence of Pentecostalism spirituality is its embodiedness, shown by the fact that the baptism of the Holy Spirit—a central feature of Pentecostalism—means the whole of our physicality is interpenetrated by, and immersed in, the Spirit.[114] Viewed from its embodiedness, Spirit baptism, which is about an encounter with the divine, is sacramental in nature, making Pentecostalism, therefore, a theology that is essentially sacramental.[115] Tomberlin defines the word *sacramental* as "God's grace . . . mediated, not through association with the blessed object, but through the prayers of blessing and intercession of God's people."[116] This sacramentality has existed since the early days of Pentecostalism. It can be seen by their use of anointing oil and laying on of hands on the sick, water baptism, foot washing, and the celebration of the Eucharist that took place in revival meetings.[117] In its early days, Spirit baptism was understood by many as an event that brought the "real presence" of Jesus into the lives of the believers.[118]

Throughout its history, Pentecostals have used different models of discipleship. However, one that stood out as the primary method is its worship experience. In essence, this is participating in the sacramental life. This model of discipleship is not unlike the model of liturgical churches, where teaching is being passed down through the liturgical life of the church. Because of this, Tomberlin points out that understanding participation in the sacramental life as essential to the *via salutis* must be made more explicit if Pentecostals are to be faithful to the biblical tradition.[119] What makes Pentecostal worship distinct, if compared to different church worship traditions, is the fact that it emphasizes the redemptive experiences brought by the Holy Spirit, who is encountered personally. These redemptive experiences, which take place at the altar, include salvific and sanctifying experiences, healing, and Spirit baptism.[120] Just like in other Christian traditions, the worship life of the believers in

---

114. Tomberlin, *Pentecostal Sacraments*, 59.
115. Tomberlin, *Pentecostal Sacraments*, 60.
116. Tomberlin, *Pentecostal Sacraments*, 65.
117. Tomberlin, *Pentecostal Sacraments*, 61.
118. Tomberlin, *Pentecostal Sacraments*, 61.
119. Tomberlin, *Pentecostal Sacraments*, 76.
120. Tomberlin, *Pentecostal Sacraments*, 84.

Pentecostal churches can lead to shortcomings. What needs to take place in these communities is the cultivation of holistic worship, still with a focus on the altar but with a robust emphasis on the word and sacraments so that the worship experience does not fall into mere emotionalism.[121]

Moving to the specific discussion on the Eucharist, Tomberlin points out that, in essence, Christian worship is an act of remembering that is "an active re-presentation."[122] If Pentecostals are to experience the whole salvific story of Christ, it is not enough to rely on songs and sermons; full participation in the ongoing divine drama of salvation comes only from observing the Eucharist. Tomberlin points out:

> When Christians gather at the Table of the Lord, it is to remember the sacrificial death of Christ and, thus, the past event becomes present. It is not simply to recall a past redemptive; it reminds believers that they are participants in an ongoing redemptive event. To remember Christ's passion through the Eucharist is to *re-live* the event, to *reenact* the drama, and to participate in the story.[123]

According to Tomberlin, intentional incorporation of the celebration of the Eucharist into Pentecostal worship should not be too difficult. The use of metaphors such as "drinking" and swallowing "God liquidized" when receiving Spirit baptism by early Pentecostals shows that Pentecostals affirm that God's energies can be transferred into tangible things, and, therefore, should have no difficulty seeing the Eucharist as an act of worship that is touchable.[124] Tomberlin maintains that the antecedent of this idea of divine energies can be found in Eastern Orthodoxy, especially in the teaching of fourteenth-century Greek Orthodox theologian Gregory Palamas, although it is highly doubtful that Pentecostals are familiar with any of Palamas's teachings.[125] This understanding of the transfer of divine energies is how Pentecostal understanding of real presence is, according to Tomberlin, "Christo-Pneumatic," meaning that the eucharistic participants and the elements of bread and wine are being interpenetrated by the "dyadic relationship" of the Son and the Spirit.[126]

---

121. Tomberlin, *Pentecostal Sacraments*, 85.
122. Tomberlin, *Pentecostal Sacraments*, 164.
123. Tomberlin, *Pentecostal Sacraments*, 165.
124. Tomberlin, *Pentecostal Sacraments*, 174.
125. Tomberlin, *Pentecostal Sacraments*, 69.
126. Tomberlin, *Pentecostal Sacraments*, 179.

Tomberlin then points out the implications of the Eucharist celebration that should be noted by Pentecostals. First, he shows a reading of the Gospel of Matthew, in which Jesus's feeding miracles are all connected to his healing ministry.[127] Then Tomberlin stresses that the Eucharist, as a salvific meal offered to humanity, is the ultimate feeding miracle because in it, Christ, through his own body on the cross, offers himself for the salvation of humanity.[128] Pentecostals often refer to the meal as "God's medicine" and have always affirmed the understanding of the Eucharist as a healing meal—an understanding in agreement with the ancient church—and through this view Pentecostals should see it as sacramental, that is, the meal *is* a means of grace.[129]

Another aspect of the Eucharist that needs to be embraced by Pentecostals is the fact that the meal is a prophetic act. First of all, if the active presence of the Spirit is the heart of Pentecostalism, then the Eucharist, as a means of grace, should be a prophetic act in which repentance takes place.[130] Unlike other traditions that practice closed communion, Pentecostals should always allow people to come to the table of grace. Second, this prophetic aspect should make Pentecostals realize that the Eucharist is a celebration of confession and reconciliation, meaning when a person participates, they are required to be in an unbroken fellowship with their fellow neighbors. Participating in the Eucharist should then make a person recognize if they are in a strained relationship and be compelled to seek reconciliation.[131] Finally, the Eucharist is prophetic because it is a foretaste of the wedding supper of the Lamb, and participating in the meal brings believers into the eschatological reality of the new heaven and new earth that the meal anticipates.[132] Because Pentecostalism is a movement based on the hope of the last things, the celebration of the Eucharist should be front and center in Pentecostal worship. While imbued with this hope in the celebration, Pentecostals should also lament the fact that, at present, the bread and the cup represent the broken communion that exists within the body of Christ. Pentecostals, therefore, must be fully

---

127. Tomberlin, *Pentecostal Sacraments*, 180.
128. Tomberlin, *Pentecostal Sacraments*, 181.
129. Tomberlin, *Pentecostal Sacraments*, 182.
130. Tomberlin, *Pentecostal Sacraments*, 183.
131. Tomberlin, *Pentecostal Sacraments*, 185.
132. Tomberlin, *Pentecostal Sacraments*, 187.

committed to and involved in works that foster unity among those who confess Jesus is Lord so that all may sit in fellowship at the Lord's table.[133]

Tomberlin then gives suggestions to pastors on how to integrate the Eucharist into the worship service. The first thing is to ensure that the celebration is a conduit for believers to encounter the Holy Spirit. Because for Pentecostals, this encounter takes place sacramentally at the altar when they respond to the altar call, Tomberlin suggests that worshippers are to receive the Eucharist at the altar, meaning they should come forward in the same way they respond to an altar call, rather than the pew.[134] This would also aid people who would not come otherwise to come to the altar. The idea of coming to the altar is not so much about receiving the bread and the cup; instead, the primary purpose is to encounter God through Christ and the Spirit.[135]

Engagement with Daniel Tomberlin

In building his theology around the altar, altar call, and Spirit baptism, Tomberlin succeeds in constructing a theology of the sacraments, which includes the Eucharist, that is genuinely Pentecostal. His presentation can indeed be arrayed or clustered in an SET system of spirituality, with the Spirit whose presence is called upon as the main actor in the process. The "search" aspect is found in what he calls "active-representation," remembering that this presents believers with the opportunity of full participation in the ongoing divine drama of salvation. This participation is the "encounter" aspect. As believers encounter God at the altar through the Eucharist, a place where worship is transformed into something touchable through what he calls a "Christo-Pneumatic" interpenetration of the elements, so could the lives of the believers also be transformed. Tomberlin spells out the outcome of this transformative encounter as lamenting the current disunity of the body of Christ and commitment to being involved with efforts that will foster unity and fellowship with fellow followers of Christ. Because he insists on using the word "sacraments/sacramental," I think Tomberlin can go a bit further in appropriating the historical church's understanding of such concepts to a Pentecostal vernacular. However, I believe his practical proposal on combining the

---

133. Tomberlin, *Pentecostal Sacraments*, 190.
134. Tomberlin, *Pentecostal Sacraments*, 190.
135. Tomberlin, *Pentecostal Sacraments*, 191.

Pentecostal altar call and the Eucharist celebration is commendable and, so far, the one that will make incorporating the celebration of the Eucharist in every worship service look recognizably Pentecostal.

Wolfgang Vondey

In his essay "Pentecostal Sacramentality and the Theology of the Altar," the starting point of Wolfgang Vondey in developing his version of Pentecostal sacramentality is an insistence that we read the Pentecostal story in a sacramental way. He argues that such a reading will "reveal an inherent sacramentality marked by four distinct moments: (1) the creation of a sacramental environment, (2) a call to personal participation in the divine-human encounter, (3) personal and communal response, and (4) transformation and manifestations of the effects of the encounter."[136]

In developing their sacramentality, Pentecostals, according to Vondey, have an opportunity to bolster both their Trinitarian identity and ecclesiology. The reason for this is that while sacramental theology begins with christological assumptions, especially regarding the mystery of salvation—which is thoroughly found in the sacramental theology of the historic church—it is at the same time also "governed by a pneumatological principle rooted in the visible birth of the church through the Spirit of Pentecost."[137] The result of bolstering this Trinitarian identity is a sacramental theology that is fundamental to the mission of the church because here is where communion as the ultimate goal of *missio Dei* begins to take place.[138]

Vondey goes back to the day of Pentecost, as he sees this day to be "the liturgical fountainhead for the manifestation of the life of the Spirit" that is inherent and fundamental to the church as it participates in *missio Dei*.[139] The location that is symbolically used to represent this environment, in which active participation and transformation of all people take place, is the Pentecostal altar.[140] Whether Pentecostals typically acknowledge this or not, the altar and the call to approach it—a genuinely

---

136. Vondey, "Pentecostal Sacramentality," 95.

137. Vondey, "Pentecostal Sacramentality," 98.

138. Vondey, "Pentecostal Sacramentality," 94; cf. Chan, *Grassroots Asian Theology*, 45.

139. Vondey, "Pentecostal Sacramentality," 94.

140. Vondey, "Pentecostal Sacramentality," 98.

Pentecostal ritual—is a sacramental reality; it is in that place that the congregation take themselves to meet God.[141] The telos, or goal of this ritual, one that involves the altar as the entry point into a sacramental reality that offers the congregation an actual encounter with the presence of God, is none other than the transformation of the person. This is so because, in the worship life of the community, Pentecostals have always understood the altar and the call given to approach it as a place of new beginnings and healing. The altar and the call to approach it, therefore, are part of a sacramental reality, and the response of the congregation to approach is their acceptance to enter into that sacramental reality.[142]

Even if the sacraments do not yet occupy a primary space in Pentecostal sacramentality, they can be integrated more easily into the extended sacramental journey of the community through an understanding of the sacramental reality of the altar and the call to approach. The reason for this, according to Vondey, is that the altar presents what he calls "a pneumatological entrance to the construction of the liturgy," in which liturgical experience is not seen as structures but as a construction that requires the invocation and working of the Holy Spirit.[143] In light of this, the sacraments and the actions connected to them become a location in which the presence and work of Christ as the gift of the Father are manifested to the church. All this is held together by the altar as a place at which the divine-human encounter takes place in the Pentecostal liturgy and is established by the manifestation of the Spirit who "leads towards, makes possible, and carries further the meeting of the human being with God [where] the Holy Spirit is the origin, medium, and goal of all sacramentality."[144] This then offers an opportunity to see the efficacy of the sacraments in a more Pentecostal way, that is, not in the elements or rituals themselves; rather, they are found in the divine-human encounter mediated by the Holy Spirit and made tangible in the transformation of the community as a missional and eschatological community.[145]

---

141. Vondey, "Pentecostal Sacramentality," 99.
142. Vondey, "Pentecostal Sacramentality," 100.
143. Vondey, "Pentecostal Sacramentality," 101.
144. Vondey, "Pentecostal Sacramentality," 102.
145. Vondey, "Pentecostal Sacramentality," 104.

Engagement with Wolfgang Vondey

I would now like to point out some key takeaways from Vondey's presentation. Vondey builds his Pentecostal sacramental theology by using what is very familiar to Pentecostals, which is the altar. I believe this is very helpful because it is easily recognizable by his Pentecostal hearers, so his proposal should find tracking in the Pentecostal mind. This would then help make way for his proposal of reading the Pentecost story sacramentally. The "four moments" created by the reading fit nicely into an SET trajectory. Through the praise and worship event, the creation of a sacramental environment at the altar qualifies as a place of "search"; the "encounter" takes place in the altar call to personal participation in the divine-human encounter moment, which would also include the reception of communion elements; the individual and collective response, followed by manifestations of the effects of the encounter, both spectacular and mundane, is where "transformation" takes place. His insistence for Pentecostals to strengthen their Trinitarian identity and ecclesiology, through an enhanced understanding of sacramental celebrations such as the Eucharist that is more connected to the Pentecostal "altar" where the presence and work of Christ as the gifts of the Father become a reality, would result in a much richer spiritual life of the church; and as they do that then mission will be primarily understood as *missio Dei*, rather than classically understood as missions activities.

CONCLUSION

I want to begin my conclusion by offering some general comments on the systematic volumes published by the denominations as a whole. As I see it, these volumes were the first of their kind, namely an attempt to do systematic theology from a Pentecostal perspective, not unlike the three volumes of *Renewal Theology* written by J. Rodman Williams. For its time, I believe these volumes were a much-needed work as there were none that offered a kind of apologetics work needed to show what was happening within the Pentecostal/charismatic movement, especially in light of the many negative criticisms the movement received. These volumes, then, are clearly helpful and vital to pastors and students of theology with a Pentecostal/charismatic background who, at the time, may have had to use generic evangelical systematic theology textbooks.

As a systematic theology, however, these works, in general, lack in many things, and I will name two: First, I do not see them engaging much with systematic theologians, whether present or past. Such engagement would, I believe, enrich these volumes tremendously, and without such, I think what we are left with, at best, is a biblical theology as opposed to a systematic theology. Second, Pentecostals/charismatics praxes are inherently steeped in the affective. As I mentioned above in my engagement with Kenneth Archer, the Pentecostal testimony is a prime example. Pentecostals "know" in their heart that they have encountered God and that he has spoken to them. Of course, to be genuine, this affective knowledge must be grounded christologically within a Trinitarian framework.[146] Hence, I see their methodology as still very much grounded in the tradition of "intellectualism" that is characteristic of evangelical theology. I am, of course, not advocating anti-intellectualism. Still, I believe a theological method that provides an excellent reflection on the experiential nature of the Spirit is more "Pentecostal/charismatic" in terms of methodology. For example, the process of acquiring truth through *yada* (the Old Testament word "to know"), which Cheryl Bridges Johns points out is more than just a cognitive knowing but knowing by the heart through "active and intentional engagement in lived experience," needs to be considered more significantly.[147] These would then offer a more significant opportunity to discuss the theology of the Eucharist charismatically as well. If denominations are hesitant to engage the theology of other traditions, this is where the work of the Pentecostal theologian above could contribute to the conversation and enrich the volumes that would find most tracking with Pentecostal pastors and denominational leaders.

With regard to the more current reflections on the theology of the Eucharist written by Pentecostal theologians, I want to trace a common thread and point out a noticeable pattern in their writing. I can point out four things. First, all the theologians discussed issue a call to the Pentecostal church to take the celebration of the Eucharist more seriously and to incorporate it more fully into the life of the church. Without it, the worship life of the Pentecostal church, especially as it is one that values highly the affective, can fall into sterile intellectualism and, in the end, be debilitated. Life in the Spirit is embodied, and this embodiedness is expressed best in the Eucharist.

---

146. Cartledge, *Practical Theology*, 61.
147. Johns, *Pentecostal Formation*, 35.

The second common thread is these theologians also point out that taking the Eucharist seriously will foster a Trinitarian worship life. The telos of a Spirit-filled eucharistic worship will deepen the Trinitarian identity of the Pentecostal church, who is the body of Christ, as it offers the congregation an actual encounter with the presence of Christ through the Spirit, bringing transformation to all persons.

With this transformation in mind, the third common thread found in most, if not all, of these theologians is the miracle of healing that is being offered in the Eucharist, yet seeing it grounded in the reality of already-not-yet. Thus, the Eucharist also reminds Pentecostal churches that the healing provided in the meal, they must also take to the world as agents of Christ's healing the world, through their work in confronting evil, addressing social injustices, and dismantling sin structures, while anticipating the wedding supper of the Lamb.

The fourth and final common thread is a greater understanding of mission as *missio Dei* that the Eucharist brings. The God Christians worship, who is Father, Son, and Spirit, is a communion. In the Eucharist, the church could understand more that the goal of *missio Dei* is the reconciliation of all things in communion. Therefore, through a eucharistic Spirit-filled worship life, the Pentecostal church could be empowered to be agents of reconciliation in the world as they gain greater awareness of the ministry they have been given as new creations (2 Cor 5:16–20). Insofar as this empowerment goes, in a Spirit-filled eucharistic worship, it takes place in a distinctively Pentecostal way, as some of the theologians above put the altar where transformation into new creation takes place. All these threads display a familiar trajectory in their thinking and demonstrate the inherent richness of Pentecostal theology of the Eucharist, which is distinctively Pentecostal, yet not without any commonality with the eucharistic theology of other church traditions, which discussion we will find in the next chapter.

3

Analysis of Ecumenical Eucharistic Theology

INTRODUCTION

As there are many expressions of Christianity in the world, it is not surprising that the celebration of the Eucharist—the thanksgiving meal of the church—is celebrated in various ways in different Christian traditions in different cultures. It would be natural that different denominational groups would stress aspects of the celebration differently, not just when it comes to the issue of the elements but on a host of other problems as well that shape how this celebration is observed. What is unnatural and somewhat ironic, however, is how divided the church is as a result of the variances of this celebration—a meal that is supposed to promote unity among Christians who offer their worship to God the Father through Jesus in the Spirit "has attracted not only enormous devotion and great energy, but also unparalleled levels of sustained argument and in-fighting" because differences—old and new—take precedence, resulting in Christians excluding and even condemning one another.[1] It may seem that in the Eucharist, a meal in which we both celebrate the reign of God and proclaim ourselves as a people who

---

1. O'Loughlin, *Eucharist*, xv.

live in that reign, Jesus's prayer that all who claim to follow him "may be one" (John 17:21) gets unanswered.

Despite the divisiveness we find in this celebratory meal, the fact remains that it is a gift Jesus himself has given to the church. As such, continued efforts to foster unity in this act of worship must take place in order to appreciate the celebration as a gift. Because worship is central to Pentecostals—and as we have seen in the last chapter, quite a few Pentecostal theologians see that in the Eucharist, the church could better understand that the goal of *missio Dei* is the reconciliation of all things in communion—I am convinced that we can contribute to the church's inherent desire to be united in this act of worship by especially looking at the meal from the lens of pneumatology.[2] Christian Missionary Alliance theologian Gordon Smith, in his book *A Holy Meal: The Lord's Supper in the Life of the Church*, makes an excellent point, stating, "Each dimension of the meaning in the Lord's Supper—each grace received—is but another facet of the gift that is given to the church through the ministry of the Spirit. The study of the Lord's Supper is, then, a consideration of the ministry of the Spirit as it is manifested in the life of the community of faith," because the underlying idea is as "we participate in the Lord's Supper in the Spirit, and as we leave, we pray that we will return to the world in the fullness of the Spirit."[3] A reflection on the Eucharist that is "in the fullness of the Spirit" requires us to think theologically about this meal and see where, amid differences, we can have, or at least, somewhat identify common ground. It is only by allowing ourselves to venture outside of our own particularity in order to appreciate the universality of our faith that we can be connected to "the wider historical and contemporary tradition of Christianity."[4]

I believe it would be a worthy endeavor to explore this meal from a pneumatological perspective for two reasons: First, because the Holy Spirit is what unites the church (Eph 4:1–6). Second, because the Spirit is the one who is bringing the church to worship in truth (John 4:24; cf. 14:26, 15:26). As the adage says, the purpose of theology is doxology (that is, worship), and throughout her history, the church has understood the Eucharist to be the highest expression of worship. Because of that, pneumatology as a theological locus is an appropriate lens through which to

---

2. Cartledge, *Mediation of the Spirit*, 114.

3. Smith, *Holy Meal*, 10.

4. Cartledge, *Mediation of the Spirit*, 130.

explore the theology of the Eucharist, which will lead to a greater understanding of spirituality. The aim of this chapter, therefore, is twofold: first, to investigate the role of pneumatology in different eucharistic traditions of the church, and second, by way of looking into their pneumatology, to trace an implicit process of SET in the understanding of these eucharistic traditions, because this essentially is the spirituality process of Pentecostal, if not all Christian, traditions.[5]

The Chapter's Approach

I am dividing this chapter into three major sections. The first section explores the pneumatology found in the eucharistic theology of John D. Zizioulas as a representative of Eastern Orthodoxy. In this section, my goal is to show that for Eastern Orthodoxy, it is clear that the *epiclēsis* makes the Eucharist; that is, it is because of the work of the Holy Spirit that the *anamnēsis* or "remembering" becomes a multidimensional charismatic event that reenacts the event of Pentecost. The day of Pentecost is what propels the disciples to become the church, and in the reenacting of this day, a process of SET can be traced.

In the second section, I investigate the role of the Holy Spirit in Roman Catholic eucharistic theology. I do this not by looking at one particular theologian but by piecing together some of what has been written by Roman Catholic thinkers on the subject matter, namely, by Bouyer, Congar, Lubac, Dulles, and O'Connor. The *epiclēsis* takes a slightly different role in the Roman Catholic Church; the Holy Spirit was, up until Vatican II, somehow overshadowed by the pope, the Virgin Mary, and the practice of eucharistic adoration.[6] However, even if the language of the Holy Spirit is not prominent in the Roman Church, as we will also see later, it is actually understood that it is the Holy Spirit himself who is working in the background, sanctifying the gifts on the altar even to the point of making transubstantiation—a unique feature of Rome's eucharistic theology—possible. The Holy Spirit, seemingly overshadowed as he is, for example, by the practice of adoration of the Eucharist, is still the heart of the matter. The process of SET in the Roman Catholic Church is more visible, being embedded in the liturgical language of the Eucharist.

---

5. Cartledge, *Encountering the Spirit*, 25.
6. Congar, *I Believe*, 1:160.

In the third section, I explore the role of pneumatology in the eucharistic theology of the Protestant Reformers, namely, Zwingli, Luther, and Calvin. Limiting myself to this demarcation is important because realizing the complexities and various nuances of what can be put under the category of "Protestant," which can make the task of defining Protestant eucharistic theology impossible, these three Reformers can be sufficiently regarded as representatives of Protestantism in general. Here, we will see how the three Reformers see the Eucharist differently. The main thrust of this section is, first of all, to show that pneumatology offers a way for Protestants to be "eucharistic people" amid those differences because a pneumatological lens is what enables the Protestant church to create a sympathetic historical and theological climate, which is required in order for the Eucharist to be central in the worship life of the Protestant church.[7] Second, because the Holy Spirit is the person responsible for making "eucharistic people," then pneumatology is the driving force of the SET process.

Given the fact that this book is ultimately a Pentecostal project, it also seeks to continue the ongoing dialogue the Pentecostal tradition has with those that are outside as its way to participate with "the Spirit [in] achieving his agenda for the Church."[8] Therefore, after each section of this chapter, I will provide concluding remarks specifically related to that section either by way of showing key takeaways available for Pentecostal eucharistic theology or the contribution that Pentecostal theology can offer, both in light of the SET paradigm. I will then conclude this chapter by restating some of the connecting threads that we have seen throughout the discussion. We begin now with the first section.

THE PNEUMATOLOGY OF ZIZIOULAS'S EUCHARISTIC THEOLOGY

The goal of this section is to investigate the role of pneumatology in the eucharistic theology of the Eastern Orthodox Church by considering closely the work of Metropolitan John D. Zizioulas, who is one of the most widely read Orthodox theologians in the West. The work of Zizioulas, which will be the main conversation partner of this section, is a volume under the title *The Eucharistic Communion of the World* published in

---

7. Cocksworth, *Evangelical Eucharistic Thought*, 8–9.
8. Warrington, *Pentecostal Theology*, 324.

2011 and made up of eight separate essays that were previously published in non-English journals. There is, however, an underlying theme that keeps reappearing in these essays about the eschatological nature of the Eucharist, which is the result of pneumatology.

I am aware that Zizioulas's theology, especially his idea of personhood, found in his most known work, *Being as Communion*, has come under criticism by some because they claim that what he presents is actually a modern reading of the patristic sources that results in wrong conclusions about personhood.[9] That conversation, however, is not pertinent to our present discussion as the goal of this investigation is to see whether the pneumatology of Eastern Orthodoxy can enrich the eucharistic theology in my Pentecostal tradition. In this section, I contend that for Eastern Orthodoxy, pneumatology is what makes the eucharistic *anamnēsis* possible. That is, it is because of the coming down of the Spirit—who is invoked in the prayer of *epiclēsis*—that "remembering" becomes a multidimensional event that is charismatic in nature, making the remembrance a Pentecost event taking place each time, as opposed to a remembering of historical events that is merely linear.[10]

Investigating this idea of "remembering" is beneficial for Pentecostal eucharistic theology for at least two reasons. First, exploring the relationship between the Spirit and the Eucharist, especially with regards to the *epiclēsis* that is practiced and understood in the Eastern Orthodox Church, provides an opportunity to enrich the pneumatology of Pentecostal theology—a theological locus that is close to Pentecostals but still continued to be developed.[11] Second, the epicletic-anamnetic reality that is found in the Eastern Orthodox Church, especially in its eucharistic theology—what Grumett calls "an intense eschatological sensibility"[12]— is not that foreign to Pentecostals because, at its heart, it is reminiscent of our "this is that" way of interpreting and understanding history.[13] Zizioulas's ideas on the Eucharist in this volume can be summed up as a proposal for "a *Eucharistic* ontology, *Eucharistic* Christology, [and] *Eucharistic* pneumatology" that is worth careful reflection by theologians

---

9. Turcescu, "'Person' versus 'Individual.'"

10. Zizioulas, *Being as Communion*, 115–16.

11. Kärkkäinen, "Spirit and the Lord's Supper," 136.

12. Grumett, Review, 246.

13. Cartledge, *Encountering the Spirit*, 130; Vondey and Green, "Between This and That," 246–47.

coming from traditions that are mostly non-sacramental.[14] This section will attempt to exposit those ideas.

This section will begin by highlighting why Eastern Orthodoxy sees pneumatology as vital in its eucharistic theology and briefly relate that to the Orthodox understanding of the unity of the work of the Holy Spirit in the sacrament of baptism, confirmation, and Eucharist. It will then explain the understanding of "remembering" according to Eastern Orthodoxy. A brief presentation on how Zizioulas sees the biblical evidence to support this understanding of "remembering" follows. The section will then proceed to present how pneumatology impacts the celebration of the Eucharist and highlight some of its implications. Finally, it will conclude by pointing out a few reasons that considering the eucharistic theology of the Eastern Orthodox is important for Pentecostals. The day of Pentecost is what propels the disciples to become the church. Therefore, I will argue that a process of SET can be traced from the understanding of the Eucharist as Pentecost.

Pneumatology in the Sacraments

Zizioulas regrets the fact that recently, there has been an overemphasis on Christology at the expense of pneumatology due to Western influence making its way into Eastern Orthodox eucharistic theology. This issue, Zizioulas argues, is creating a deficiency in eucharistic theology; therefore, to go back to an original Orthodox understanding of pneumatology is a critical theological task that Zizioulas seeks to undertake. For him, the celebration of the Eucharist must be contained within a pneumatological framework in order for it to have an eschatological understanding of the presence of Christ. It is the Spirit who holds together Christ's presence and the gathering of the assembly because the descent of the Holy Spirit on the day of Pentecost is what turns the gathered into an eschatological community (Acts 2:17).[15] This eschatological reality in the present is described as *new time*; not a replacement of our current reality—*old time*—but reality brought and held together by the Holy Spirit, which makes it possible for the gathered community to perceive and receive, in the Eucharist, the in-breaking of the future renewed creation

---

14. Nelson, Review, 366.
15. Zizioulas, *Eucharistic Communion and the World*, 74.

filled with the glory of God.[16] The same eschatological reality brought by the Holy Spirit is also what unites the three sacraments, namely, baptism, confirmation, and the Eucharist. To try to see them outside of this unity and their eschatological dimension would be, according to Zizioulas, theologically problematic.[17] In and through the Holy Spirit, these three sacraments form a unity because, in them, the entire history of salvation is eschatologically realized.[18]

Anamnēsis

In Zizioulas's understanding, the *anamnēsis*, or the multidimensional remembering that takes place in the Eucharist, is a pneumatologically driven event of remembering Christ "in the fullest sense" that allows his presence to be real.[19] It is only because of the work of the Holy Spirit that the church can remember Christ in a way that he asked them to do (i.e., "do this in remembrance of me"), which is not just a remembering of past events, but most importantly a remembering that anticipates the *eschaton* in the present. A genuine *anamnēsis*, where "in the present, the past becomes a new reality, [and] the future becomes a reality that is already," is impossible apart from the invocation of the Holy Spirit in the *epiclēsis*.[20] A "remembrance" that focuses only on remembering the sacrifice of Christ on the cross is, according to Zizioulas, theologically deficient.[21] This should be taken into consideration by Pentecostals, whose idea of remembrance is somewhat limited to a historical remembering that they received from a Zwinglian understanding that historically is known to be the result of pragmatism rather than of deep theological reflection.[22] Fortunately, recent Pentecostal theologians are beginning to be aware that this limited understanding of "remembrance" does not account fully for the command Jesus gave his disciples to "remember him."[23] This kind of remembrance, Zizioulas points out, does not provide "enough room for

16. Schmemann, *Eucharist*, 219.
17. Zizioulas, *Eucharistic Communion and the World*, 114.
18. Zizioulas, *Eucharistic Communion and the World*, 115.
19. Zizioulas, *Eucharistic Communion and the World*, 8.
20. Zizioulas, *Eucharistic Communion and the World*, 6.
21. Zizioulas, *Eucharistic Communion and the World*, 6.
22. Kärkkäinen, "Pentecostal View," 117, 122.
23. Bricknell, "Ordinances," 207.

pneumatology" as history here is perceived to be moving only linearly toward the end of time, causing the celebration of the Eucharist—viewed only from a Christo-monist perspective—that is, seeing everything in the celebration only in light of what Christ did—to be incomplete.[24]

The fuller way to see history is to locate "remembrance" within "the realm of pneumatological action" that does not negate the salvific history but considers the actual value of the past work of Christ in light of the coming and the work of the Holy Spirit. It is in this way of looking at history—when the eschaton, through the power of the Holy Spirit, penetrates the here and now—that the Eucharist retains its mystery and, most importantly, Trinitarian significance.[25]

The Testimony of Scripture

We now proceed to look at the testimony of Scripture that, according to Zizioulas, supports this understanding of remembering. Zizioulas argues that the intersection of the past and the *eschaton* that takes place in the Eucharist can be found in the pneumatology of the early church, especially the one that is testified in the Fourth Gospel and alluded to in the book of Revelation. In the Gospel of John, a later document compared to the letters of Paul, the theology of the Holy Spirit has already accounted for the experience of the church; thus, the description it gives on the Lord's Supper already accounts for it as a eucharistic experience.[26] This lived-out eucharistic experience of the church comes out in the speech Jesus gives to his disciples the night before his crucifixion. According to Zizioulas, a careful reading of the text will yield three observations: first, the Holy Spirit is and will be that Comforter "until he comes"—referring to Paul's declaration in the Eucharist (1 Cor 11:26); second, it is the Holy Spirit who will teach and remind the church all that Jesus said and did (John 14:26); and third, it is the Spirit who will be the one announcing and proclaiming of the things to come (John 16:13).[27]

In the book of Revelation, we find Jesus, the one who has already come and is present (the implication being who was and is and is to come, at the same time), saying to his followers, "I am coming soon" (Rev

---

24. Zizioulas, *Eucharistic Communion and the World*, 9.
25. Zizioulas, *Eucharistic Communion and the World*, 9.
26. Zizioulas, *Eucharistic Communion and the World*, 7.
27. Zizioulas, *Eucharistic Communion and the World*, 8.

22:7). In this present reality, it is in the eucharistic *epiclēsis* that makes what Jesus says become a reality, that is, where the historical and the eschatological dimensions are joined together in *prayer* without the need to have to turn them into an "objective reality."[28] This is an important fact to point out, as it is the prayer that makes the "eschatological sensibility" in the Orthodox worship life dynamic rather than static, as commonly assumed by the West.[29]

The eucharistic reality—which is the joining of dimensions that we see in the Gospel of John and the book of Revelation that is the result of the *epiclēsis*—is what enables Paul's proclamation of Christ's death and the joy of the resurrection found in the celebration of the community as narrated by Luke to coexist together side by side. That is the reason Luke points out that when the Eucharist is celebrated, it is done so "with glad and sincere hearts" (Acts 2:46). Only the resurrection and the second coming could justify this atmosphere of rejoicing. Because the Holy Spirit is present as he is called upon, the proclamation of the death of Christ is always seen in the light of his resurrection, ascension, and second coming. In Zizioulas's words, "The proclamation of the Lord's death in 'joy' and 'until he comes' is in tension with a history always dependent upon the Spirit in 'these last days'—seen by the Church since Pentecost as it undertakes the remembrance of the whole of salvation history through its Eucharistic *epiclēsis*."[30] We can see, therefore, that Zizioulas sees in the church of the New Testament the Eucharist as the moment in which the last days enter into the present history and are lived in the experience of the church.[31]

Pneumatological Implication for the Life of the Church

I now proceed to discuss the impact of pneumatology on the celebration of the Eucharist in light of the life of the ministry of the community in the Eastern Orthodox Church. The pneumatology of the Eastern Orthodox eucharistic gathering requires the participation of all people and ministries, as this is how the image of the eschatological community that transcends all human divisions—whether natural (for example, age,

---

28. Zizioulas, *Eucharistic Communion and the World*, 10.
29. Grumett, Review, 246.
30. Zizioulas, *Eucharistic Communion and the World*, 11.
31. Zizioulas, *Eucharistic Communion and the World*, 12.

race, or sex) or social (for example, rich, poor, the difference of vocation, etc.)—takes place.[32] In the celebration, the assembled community receives the Holy Spirit as a gift of unity, making all to be one body in Christ. As Kallistos Ware explains, the result of the coming of the Spirit at Pentecost is the reversal of the curse of the tower of Babel, bringing "unity and mutual comprehension," and by which individuals are now transformed into persons who are "united in heart and soul" (Acts 2:44, 4:32).[33] This unity of persons, however, is not understood as uniformity. Frank Macchia, for example, points out that the Pentecost event is not just a reversal of Babel but also a fulfillment. If read through the lenses of Acts 17:24–27, especially v. 27, the Pentecost event "reverses the *threat*" of Babel but in a way that respects the unique journeys of cultural groups, in which differences are embraced.[34]

Therefore, as the Spirit is invoked, the community can "remember" the variety of the gifts he distributes for the purpose of ministry. Christ is the source of ministry, and it is he who incorporates the many, but the Spirit who is at the same time the bond that unites all into one manifests the charisms in different ways.[35] The mystery of this life in the Spirit, in which the gifts are made real in the church, according to Zizioulas, is "revealed *par excellence* in the Eucharist."[36] This is true in the local setting as well as in the universal church.

The way the church—who are the people of God scattered and dispersed—experiences unity in the Eucharist is through the *koinōnia* of the Holy Spirit. This *koinōnia* is to be understood in two ways. First, it is the Holy Spirit who makes the presence of Christ real in the community and the life of each person. Without being located "in Spirit" (1 Cor 14:16), the presence of Christ that Paul calls "*koinōnia* in the body" and "*koinōnia* in the blood" (1 Cor 10:16) is meaningless.[37] The Spirit is the one responsible for making "the objective communion in the body and blood of Christ into a personal and existential reality."[38] Second, because of the transformation that takes place, the church then becomes a

---

32. Zizioulas, *Eucharistic Communion and the World*, 75.
33. Ware, *Orthodox Way*, 94.
34. Macchia, "Babel and the Tongues," 45; emphasis in original.
35. Ware, *Orthodox Way*, 95.
36. Zizioulas, *Eucharistic Communion and the World*, 21–22.
37. Zizioulas, *Eucharistic Communion and the World*, 20.
38. Zizioulas, *Eucharistic Communion and the World*, 20.

charismatic community in which she can reveal and make her charismatic character into reality.

The eschatological community that is formed in the celebration of the Eucharist—a community in which there is a recapitulation of the divine economy and the imaging of the kingdom—exists within a framework. That framework is the liturgy, and it creates a kind of scaffolding that supports this eschatological mystery.[39] It is in the work of the people (*leitourgia*) that the gift of the Spirit is conferred upon all people—which, in the Orthodox understanding, would be all baptized people. It is evident that the liturgy is an important place for Zizioulas, demonstrated by his claim that the academic theologian who takes up the study of the Eucharist "should be a liturgiologist"; at the same time, Zizioulas calls liturgiologists to also be theologians, especially those concerned about and well versed in ecclesiology.[40] Having said that, the discussion on the nature of liturgy in this volume seems inadequate. In fact, the liturgical concept with which Zizioulas deals is said to be the product of early twentieth-century scholarship that has now been surpassed.[41] This fact, of course, does not cause too much of a concern for our present discussion because what I am looking for is a general Orthodox understanding of liturgy that makes such a framework as I mentioned earlier possible. In general, the Orthodox understand the liturgy to be a symbol of the "new time" that the Holy Spirit brought on the day of Pentecost.[42] This new time is not a replacement of the old time; instead, it is a time of an in-breaking of the kingdom; the liturgy sacramentally (as opposed to empirically) makes this new time in this world real. Zizioulas further explains this idea of new time, saying, "In the Eucharist, history and time (usually understood either as an evil human obligation or as the antechamber of eternity) intersect with eternity and consequently, eternity ceases to be 'before' or 'after' time and becomes exactly the dimension into which time can open. In this way, we become contemporaries of the whole history of God's pre-eternal plan for our salvation in a unity of past, present, and future that allows the full acceptance and sanctification of time and history."[43] In the liturgy, the Eucharist presents the

---

39. Zizioulas, *Eucharistic Communion and the World*, 75.
40. Zizioulas, *Eucharistic Communion and the World*, 74.
41. Belcher, Review, 208.
42. Schmemann, *Eucharist*, 219.
43. Zizioulas, *Eucharistic Communion and the World*, 127.

image of the kingdom of God by giving the church "a manifestation, a prefiguration and a foretaste of the Kingdom of God."[44]

At this point, it is appropriate to bring into our discussion the Orthodox idea of "real presence." In Eastern Orthodox teaching, the transformation of the Eucharist requires the descent of the Holy Spirit. Unlike in the West, however, Eastern Orthodoxy does not believe that something palpable happens to the gifts themselves. Orthodox eucharistic theology is against that sort of teaching because they consider it meddling with "magic."[45] What they seek in the liturgy, and most of all in the *epiclēsis*, is two things. First, they seek a sacramental (in contrast to a palpable) transformation of the elements into the body and blood of Christ. That is why, in the East, the bread and wine do not become objects of reverence, contemplation, and even adoration. The transformation of the gifts "is a mystery that cannot be revealed and explained in the categories of 'this world'—time, essence, causality, etc., [and] revealed only in faith."[46] Second, and more importantly, what they seek in the *epiclēsis* is the sacramental transformation of all the community members. As Zizioulas puts it, "The Spirit does not come down only 'upon these gifts here set forth' but also 'upon us' (the celebrants and the Eucharistic gathering)."[47] Thus, the communion and partaking of the body and blood of Christ are also the communion in the Holy Spirit, and the real presence of Christ is then broadened and enlarged by the gathered assembly, which is now the body of Christ. The celebration of the Eucharist as a communion of the Holy Spirit then becomes a double "communion of the holy," that is, communion in the holy things and the communion of saints.[48] The Eucharist then becomes a sacrament that images the mystery of love because its eschatological character is linked to the eschatological character of love, which is the epitome of experience in the kingdom.[49] The implication of all this, then, is that the epicletic-anamnetic reality of the Eucharist creates a "Pentecostal, eschatological community *par excellence*" that testifies the in-breaking of the *eschaton* into the here and now, as all charisms

---

44. Zizioulas, *Eucharistic Communion and the World*, 81.
45. Schmemann, *Eucharist*, 222.
46. Schmemann, *Eucharist*, 226.
47. Zizioulas, *Eucharistic Communion and the World*, 76.
48. Zizioulas, *Eucharistic Communion and the World*, 75.
49. Zizioulas, *Eucharistic Communion and the World*, 76.

and ministry are presenting to the world a foretaste of the kingdom that is to come.[50]

Evaluation

I now conclude this section by pointing out some reasons that considering the eucharistic theology of the Eastern Orthodox is important for Pentecostals. First of all, it is clear that the pneumatology we find in the Eastern Orthodox Church is rich and can inform the pneumatology of Pentecostals. We know there is consensus that Pentecostal theology is about an encounter with a mystery mediated by the experience with the Holy Spirit.[51] Pentecostals will attest there is more to reality than meets the senses; consequently, they are also quick to admit that theological enterprise is not just about rationalistic propositions or doctrines but more experiential in nature. If Pentecostals have always been nervous about the idea of "magic," as we have seen, there is nothing that should cause alarm in the pneumatology of Eastern Orthodox, and the idea of Christ's "real presence" the Eastern Orthodox espouses is not at all connected to the idea of magic. Pentecostals are generally very concerned about being the body of Christ, and I contend that the Eastern Orthodox idea of real presence could enrich our understanding of what it means to be the body.

Second, as Tomberlin points out, Pentecostals often have trouble creating a worship experience that "manifest[s] the Spirit's power, [with] charismatic manifestations [that] demonstrate the Spirit's order."[52] It is the challenge of the Pentecostal community to realize that lack of order can actually stifle the work of the Spirit. As I mentioned before, in the Orthodox tradition, the liturgy is understood as providing the space for the Spirit to move to create that eschatological community. This fits with the Pauline concern of creating a worship experience that is orderly and, at the same time, powerful (1 Cor 11:34, 14:40). Pentecostals need not incorporate the Orthodox liturgy into our practice; however, the ideas and objectives contained in this older tradition can undoubtedly serve as a model for us. An orderly yet powerful worship experience can be created only by thoughtful and intentional reflection. Pentecostals do not need to resist making our version of liturgy based or modeled on older

---

50. Zizioulas, *Eucharistic Communion and the World*, 121.

51. Cartledge, *Encountering the Spirit*, 16; Warrington, *Pentecostal Theology*, 20.

52. Tomberlin, *Pentecostal Sacraments*, 156.

traditions. Green is right when he says, "When we reject liturgical forms received from the historical Christian tradition, we end up inevitably *replacing* them, and what we craft as replacements often fail drastically (both aesthetically and theologically)."[53] I would add that the replacement we create fails linguistically as well. Fortunately, conversations in this line of thinking are becoming quite common among Pentecostal theologians. We now proceed to the discussion on the pneumatology of Roman Catholic eucharistic theology.

PNEUMATOLOGY IN THE ROMAN CATHOLIC EUCHARISTIC THEOLOGY

This section investigates the role of the Holy Spirit in Roman Catholic eucharistic theology. It is a challenging task as, unlike Eastern Orthodoxy, piecing together the role of pneumatology in the Roman eucharistic celebration is not as straightforward as one may think. Latin theologians such as Yves Congar admit that although the teaching of the Holy Spirit has always been present in the church, it seems to have been forgotten in the worship life, "overshadowed by the Pope, the Virgin Mary and the cult of the Blessed Sacrament."[54] This can be seen in the fact that before the Second Vatican Council, the prayer of *epiclēsis*, a prominent feature in Eastern Orthodox liturgy, was missing from the Roman canon and was given its proper place only after Vatican II.[55]

The teaching on transubstantiation—the belief that through consecration, the communion elements of bread and wine become the body and blood of Christ—is central to Roman Catholic teaching. I will discuss this teaching in more detail below. Still, it is necessary to mention at this point that in the Roman Catholic teaching, this change takes place after the words of institution, an act that leans more heavily on Christology and the role of the priest as a sacramental reality acting *in persona Christi*. Upon looking at the literature, however, one will see that the church does acknowledge the Holy Spirit as the one working in the background through the sacrament of the priesthood, sanctifying the gifts on the altar. I contend, therefore, that although the pneumatological language is not indisputably defined, the church believes it is the Holy

---

53. Green, "Saving Liturgy," 109.
54. Congar, *I Believe*, 1:160.
55. Dulles, "Eucharist and the Mystery," 234–35; Congar, *I Believe*, 3:234–35.

Spirit, linked to the office of the priest, that makes the office a "charism" that makes transubstantiation possible. This reality is what I intend to unpack in this section.

This section is divided into four subsections. First, I will begin by briefly discussing the state of pneumatology of the Latin Church prior to and after the Second Vatican Council. I will proceed to a discussion explaining the Roman doctrine of transubstantiation. Third, I will then go back to a discussion of the *epiclēsis* and the role of the Holy Spirit in the Eucharist, according to the Roman Church. Finally, I will end by offering some contact points and lessons that could be learned by Pentecostals from the Roman Church, including a suggestion of why a renewed understanding of the doctrine of transubstantiation could be useful in enriching Pentecostal theology. I now proceed to the first section.

Pneumatology in the Roman Church

The doctrine of the Holy Spirit, just like the doctrine of the church—and the whole of theological loci, for that matter—can flourish only if it is experienced and realized in the life of the community, so much so that theory is always dependent on praxis.[56] For quite some time, however, the teachings of the Roman Catholic Church did not seem to offer a place to support robust pneumatology. The Holy Spirit, it seems, had been pushed aside, as seen by what was said by Karl Adam, quoted by Yves Congar: "The structure of Catholic faith may be summarized in a single sentence: I come to a living faith in the Triune God through Christ in his Church. I experience the action of the living God through Christ realizing himself in His Church. Thus, we see the certitude of the Catholic faith rests on the sacred triad: God, Christ, Church."[57] Furthermore, the liturgical language of the Latin Church is pronouncedly patriological and christological, yet when it comes to the person of the Holy Spirit, he seems to be overshadowed by the pope, the Virgin Mary, and the eucharistic adoration.[58]

This seemed to take a drastic positive turn after Vatican II, a turning-point council in the history of the Latin Church that was opened by Pope John XXIII, who said, "Throw open the windows of the church and

---

56. Congar, *I Believe*, 1:172.
57. Congar, *I Believe*, 1:159.
58. Congar, *I Believe*, 1:160.

let the fresh air of the spirit blow through."[59] According to Congar, an influential Vatican II figure in reviving theological interest in the Holy Spirit, one of the council's most significant achievements was bringing the *epiclēsis*—which had been missing before the council—back into the new eucharistic prayers, ascribing to the Spirit as the "active agent of the sacrament of the body and blood of the Lord."[60] Through his reading of the findings of the Catholic-Orthodox Joint International Commission, Avery Dulles maintains that after the Second Vatican Council, the difference between the Western and Eastern Church regarding the *epiclēsis* can today be regarded as pastoral and theological rather than dogmatic and has to do more with the difference between the doctrine of the procession of the Holy Spirit that each holds, rather than to doctrine related to the Eucharist.[61] This is a significant development in the work toward the unity of the church.

Transubstantiation

We now proceed to discuss transubstantiation, which is a doctrine central to the eucharistic theology of the Roman Church regarding the change of the substance of the consecrated bread and wine offered during the Mass into the body and blood of Jesus. The notion of the elements becoming the body and blood of Christ goes back much further in the history of the church.[62] It was St. Thomas Aquinas, however, who was the first to describe—as opposed to explain (the Roman Catholic Church would stress)—the process and change that take place using Aristotelian concepts and terminology.[63] I will not go into a discussion of Aristotelian concepts and terminology in detail as it does not serve the purpose of this book.[64] It is essential, however, to point out that Aquinas's use of the language of "form," "substance," and "accident" functions differently for him than for Aristotle.[65] Aquinas uses his reshaped version of Aristotelian

---

59. University of Notre Dame, "Pope St. John XXIII," para. 5.

60. Congar, *I Believe*, 1:170.

61. Dulles, "Eucharist and the Mystery," 235–36.

62. For a historical account of the idea, see Salkeld, *Transubstantiation*, 57–73.

63. O'Connor, *Hidden Manna*, 280.

64. For a brief explanation on the subject, see Hunsinger, *Eucharist and Ecumenism*, 73–76.

65. Salkeld, *Transubstantiation*, 82.

categories because of the intellectual understanding of the times that was in line with Aristotelian interests.[66] Aquinas argues that because Christ is fully human (while also fully divine), the human flesh has become the "conjoined instrument" of God's work of salvation, and it is through that same human nature that God continues to disclose this salvific reality and its effect.[67] I see this as something of which Pentecostals will want to take heed, especially because of the embodiedness of our faith.

For Aquinas, Christ's salvific action, rather than something far and remote, is a spiritual reality that operates solely through grace and faith's response to it, but that is at the same time made in person-to-person, body-to-body contact. Christ's spiritual contact becomes a physical contact in the sacraments.[68] Because physical contact with Christ, especially in his glorified state, bears salvific importance, this necessitates the mystery of the real presence in the Eucharist.[69] Christ heals and saves because he is present, body and soul, to his people. The reception of the elements represents the life-giving touch of Christ that actually absorbs the bodies of the recipients into his own body. As Christ's body is the stronger one, in this act of eating and drinking, it is the food that assimilates the eater as opposed to the other way around.[70]

This idea of real presence is strongly connected to the idea of the Eucharist as sacrifice. The Roman Catholic Church emphasizes this doctrine. Still, it is not exclusively a Roman Catholic idea because it has existed in the church since the second century when Clement of Alexandria began to describe its meaning.[71] The idea of the Eucharist as sacrifice is not to say that the sacrifice of Christ is being repeated in each of the celebrations. On the contrary, as Christ becomes present in the Eucharist through the Spirit, he is drawing the people to himself, making them participants in his own sacrifice. O'Connor explains that the Roman Catholic Church teaches that

> the Last Supper and Calvary and the Mass are all the same sacrifice, not because the historical acts of the past are repeated or re-presented but because of the intrinsic unity that all these

---

66. Salkeld, *Transubstantiation*, 80.
67. O'Connor, *Hidden Manna*, 277–78.
68. O'Connor, *Hidden Manna*, 277–78.
69. O'Connor, *Hidden Manna*, 279.
70. O'Connor, *Hidden Manna*, 278–79.
71. Young, "Eucharist as Sacrifice," 63–65.

actions, past and present, possess in the one Priest and Victim. The twofold Consecration symbolically represents what is past, but it makes actually present Christ who is what he is now because of those past actions. The killing and offering of the Victim has passed; the Victim who was killed and offered remains, now alive but Victim still. The past is irretrievable, but it always lives on in those it has affected.[72]

Having discussed the idea of sacrifice being connected to the understanding of real presence, I will now unpack it briefly. Reformed theologian George Hunsinger says one of the greatest achievements of Thomas Aquinas was to be able to "hold together . . . a robust definition of 'real presence' with an equally robust definition of 'local presence.'"[73] Aquinas teaches that Christ is not present in the sacrament in the sense that he is locally contained in it.[74] The glorified body of Christ, which is still a real human body, exists locally in heaven "at the right hand of the Father," and to say that he is really present in the Eucharist is to say he does so "without leaving heaven."[75] Aquinas relates the mystery of "real presence" to the mystery of the incarnation, in which we witness God's immeasurable greatness, taking the minuteness of humanity without becoming little.[76] Congar elaborates on the continuity that lies between the Eucharist and the incarnation, where just as the latter came into reality through the work of the Holy Spirit, so also the consecration and sanctification of the gifts that sanctify the believers and incorporate them into Christ.[77]

With that in mind, I want to end the discussion of transubstantiation by talking about the change that takes place in the Eucharist. Roman Catholic teaching readily admits the mystery of this event. The change takes place in "a mighty spiral of ascent," that is, Christ lifting up the creaturely realities of the elements and absorbing them into himself instead of coming down to enter into the bread and wine.[78] Using Aristotelian terminology, Thomas describes (as opposed to trying to explain) the change taking place. When the element changes, it does so not in the perception but in the "pliability" of the material. It is the same

72. O'Connor, *Hidden Manna*, 308.
73. Hunsinger, *Eucharist and Ecumenism*, 23.
74. Hunsinger, *Eucharist and Ecumenism*, 24.
75. O'Connor, *Hidden Manna*, 283.
76. O'Connor, *Hidden Manna*, 284.
77. Congar, *I Believe*, 3:229–30.
78. O'Connor, *Hidden Manna*, 291.

pliability of the grain that is shaped into bread that in the Eucharist has been reconfigured by the Holy Spirit in such a way that it becomes the physical body of Christ.[79] Again, it is essential to emphasize the change in the element's properties is not discernible. The change in the properties—which Thomas calls "accidents," but in the official teaching of the church is called "appearances"—that now have been touched by the Holy Spirit are representing the eschatological reality in which the whole of creation has been redeemed and transformed.[80] The elements become the "here-and-now signs of what the Lord's power can do—and is doing,"[81] the halfway point between the reality as we presently experience it and what it will become when the process of renewal and transformation is made complete.[82]

The most pressing question left for us would be how these truths are to be understood. For that, the church relies on mystery; as Lubac says, "The 'miracle' of the Eucharist [does] not easily make sense."[83] What occurs in the celebration and when the bread and wine are changed into the body and blood of Christ is precisely "the Mystery of transubstantiation."[84] This is affirmed by the formal teaching found in the catechism of the Catholic Church, which maintains that the conversion of the elements is due to "the efficacy of the Word of Christ and of the action of the Holy Spirit."[85] With that, I now move to the third section, which is a discussion on the *epiclēsis* and the role of the Holy Spirit in the Eucharist according to the Roman Church.

The *Epiclēsis*

Even though the Spirit's role is not as obviously pronounced in the Latin Church as in the Eastern Orthodox Church, the Spirit is not absent. As Avery Dulles points out, "When the church celebrates the Eucharist . . . the Holy Spirit is engaged in the action performed on the altar [that is,

---

79. O'Connor, *Hidden Manna*, 279–80.
80. O'Connor, *Hidden Manna*, 295.
81. O'Connor, *Hidden Manna*, 296.
82. O'Connor, *Hidden Manna*, 296–97.
83. Lubac, *Corpus Mysticum*, 243.
84. O'Connor, *Hidden Manna*, 286.
85. Interdicasterial Commission, *Catechism of Catholic Church*, §1375.

by the priest] and in the minds and hearts of the faithful."[86] Dulles goes on to point out that this teaching on the Holy Spirit's agency is not exclusive to the Eastern Church, even though the *epiclēsis* was absent from the liturgy until Vatican II.[87] However, countering some Eastern Orthodox theologians who see the Roman Church as pneumatologically deficient in its defense, Dulles asserts that the church remains in a continuous state of *epiclēsis in the Eucharist*.[88] In the Eucharist, the church encounters the Father in the very act of sending his Son and breathing forth the Holy Spirit, whose task is to divinize those who receive the bread and wine in faith as they are drawn into the Trinitarian life of God.[89] Even though the West and the East differ in their formulation of eucharistic prayer, they are, as Congar argues, essentially the same because the goal is to realize the mystery of the Christian faith, which is "to extend to the Body of Christ, the Church, the salvation, deification, and membership as sons that Christ himself has gained for us through his incarnation, his death, his resurrection and glorification through the Spirit, and finally the gift of Pentecost."[90]

That is why, according to Congar, the eucharistic prayers are complete if they show the continuity between the celebration and the incarnation, what the Holy Spirit accomplishes through the gifts in the believers as recipients, the mystery of Christ who died and rose again, the calling upon God to consecrate the elements, and the proclamation of the history of salvation.[91] Congar continues,

> There was (and there is), in fact, only *one* Eucharist—the one celebrated by Jesus himself the night he was betrayed. Our Eucharists are only Eucharists by the virtue and the making present of *that* Eucharist. [Therefore, regarding the words] "This is my body" [a]lthough they were only spoken once, they give, and will continue to give until the end of the world, their existence and their virtue to all sacrifices.[92]

---

86. Dulles, "Eucharist and the Mystery," 234.
87. Dulles, "Eucharist and the Mystery," 234–35.
88. Dulles, "Eucharist and the Mystery," 235–36.
89. Dulles, "Eucharist and the Mystery," 236–37.
90. Congar, *I Believe*, 3:229.
91. Congar, *I Believe*, 3:229–31.
92. Congar, *I Believe*, 3:233.

When talking about the role of the Holy Spirit in the Latin Church, we cannot help but make some comparisons with its Eastern counterpart. While the Greeks emphasize the changes to the bread and wine taking place through the prayer of the priest invoking the Holy Spirit, the Roman Church emphasizes the words of institution spoken by the priest to act out what Christ instituted. In the Latin Church, the priest's act of instituting—not done by his own accord or ability, of course, but because in the Spirit he has become a sacramental reality—is done by taking place or playing the part of Christ (*in persona Christi*), and in his name (*in nomine Christi*).[93] This may not sound overtly pneumatological, but because the priest leading the celebration *in persona Christi* is a sacramental reality, he is actually representing a spiritual reality.[94] This is part of the charism of the priesthood the priest receives at ordination, the laying on of hands and the invocation or *epiclēsis* of the Holy Spirit invoked upon the priest enables him to have the power to invoke the Spirit upon the elements within his sacramental ministry. Thus, the main difference between the priests of the East and the West is that the priest in the former invokes the person who is acting, and the latter plays the part of the person instituting.[95] There is no denial in both, however, that the efficacy of the sacraments can be attributed only to the power of the Holy Spirit, *virtus Spiritus Sancti*, which means that celebration of the Eucharist calls for an active coming of the Spirit over the celebration.[96] This spiritual reality is certainly true not only in the Eucharist but in all of the other sacraments of the church. I now proceed to our last subsection, where I want to point out a few things Pentecostals can learn from the Roman Church.

Evaluation

Broadly speaking, two models of spirituality exist in Christianity; one is the way of perfection (*imitatio*), while the other is participation (*participatio*); the Western Church leans toward the former, while the Eastern Church leans toward the latter.[97] Even as an offspring of Western Christianity, we know, however, that Pentecostalism's paradox is that its

93. Congar, *I Believe*, 3:234.
94. Congar, *I Believe*, 3:235.
95. Congar, *I Believe*, 1:169.
96. Congar, *I Believe*, 3:250.
97. Lossky, *Mystical Theology*, 197.

understanding of spirituality is more Eastern than Western.[98] Therefore, the idea of the Eucharist as sacrifice—a more Western idea—can help Pentecostals to be reminded of the reality of our life as a sacrifice and that the life of discipleship is a life of obeying Christ (*imitatio Christi*) that is already emphasized in the traditional Pentecostal understanding of the Lord's Supper as ordinance.[99]

Regarding the presence of Christ, Tomberlin reminds us, "Christ's presence in the bread and cup is firmly based on the Incarnation."[100] This sense of embodiedness, however, is lacking in a typical Pentecostal celebration of the Lord's Supper. The doctrine of transubstantiation is, I believe, a good reminder of the embodiedness of the Pentecostal faith. It is known that many Pentecostals are keen on using anointing oil, prayer cloths, and other material things. Still, perhaps because of their historical anti-Roman Catholic posture, the idea of "real presence" has been distasteful. There are some practices of the Latin eucharistic celebration, mainly those found in the cult of the sacraments, that would be questionable to some Pentecostals for sure. I, for one, had a few experiences of the tangible feeling of the presence of God when I had the opportunity to visit Roman Catholic churches and spend time in the eucharistic adoration chapel. I see this, of course, as one example of the mediation of the Holy Spirit, which is understood as not limited to the spectacular signs and wonders but also "patterned and routine aspects of church life," all presenting us with an "eschatological and soteriological reality."[101] Therefore, as I have already mentioned earlier, the beauty of the "real presence" in the Roman Catholic doctrine is that it symbolically shows that the world, in its materiality, is taken up by Christ to participate in his glory and, therefore, in the glory of the eschatological reality.

Finally, the Eucharist has rightly been called *pharmakon* or medicine by the church fathers.[102] I will construct and expound a renewal understanding of this in chapter 5. For now, what I want to point out is this: what is true for the fathers is undoubtedly true for Pentecostals. It is not uncommon in the Pentecostal celebration of the Lord's Supper to hear

---

98. Land, *Pentecostal Spirituality*, 18.
99. Bricknell, "Ordinances," 206.
100. Tomberlin, *Pentecostal Sacraments*, 162.
101. Cartledge, *Mediation of the Spirit*, 102.
102. Kärkkäinen, "Spirit and the Lord's Supper," 142.

that healing is available at the table of the Lord.[103] The healing that the Lord gives, although it does not exclude physical healing, is undoubtedly much more extensive than that. If the nearness of the kingdom that Jesus brought in his ministry is still present post-resurrection, then the contact with Christ's flesh in the Eucharist manifests that nearness. The doctrine of "real presence" can actually present an opportunity for Pentecostals to rethink their doctrine of healing.[104] Simon Chan argues that healing in a holistic sense, which is physical, spiritual, relational, and cosmic, can and should be the criterion of mission that is also holistic, and it is in and through the Eucharist—transfigured created things—that the Spirit continues to do his work to bring this healing.[105] Regarding this doctrine of healing, Kimberly Alexander points out what it should contain:

> The healing ministry of Jesus is not separate from the work of social justice; it was and is, in fact, part and parcel of it. Jesus touched the outcasts and healed them, thus fulfilling his mother, Mary's, prophecy that her son would exalt those of low degree. For Pentecostals to minister healing effectively in the 21st century, they must embrace a ministry of healing that addresses all areas affected by sin and the Fall: the healing of the earth, the healing of divisions of race and gender, the oppression of the weak by the strong, the exploitation of the poor by the rich. Empowered by the Spirit, Pentecostals must bring healing to every area made sick by structural sin.[106]

And as Cartledge points out, this healing begins in the Pentecostal household of faith that will offer prayer, which I contend to be eucharistic prayer, that will result in social actions that include care of the poor, the liberation of the oppressed, and deal with the "sin-sickness, alienation, and frailty" that marks everyday society, so that the body of Christ can eucharistically be the hands and feet of Jesus in his ongoing healing ministry.[107] Therefore, the time has come for Pentecostals to not simply reject the Latin teaching on the Eucharist, no matter how strange on the surface it may look. What is required of the Pentecostal church is the gift of charity, which is the greatest of all the gifts of the Spirit, enabling us to be graceful and generous in trying to understand the teaching of other

---

103. Kärkkäinen, "Pentecostal View," 127.

104. Green, *Toward a Pentecostal Theology*, 275.

105. Chan, *Grassroots Asian Theology*, 109.

106. Alexander, "Pentecostal Healing Community," 203–4.

107. Cartledge, *Testimony in the Spirit*, 184–85.

traditions, and how this teaching could be received into the Pentecostal tradition.

PNEUMATOLOGY IN THE EUCHARISTIC THEOLOGY OF ZWINGLI, LUTHER, AND CALVIN

In this section, I investigate the role of pneumatology in Protestant eucharistic theology. After the Reformation, perpetuated by theological and historical forces, the Eucharist has yet to take back its rightful place in the worship life of the Protestant church.[108] But as Cocksworth argues correctly, Protestants—and I include Pentecostals in this broad category as Pentecostals are also offspring of the Protestant Reformation—"must be also, in some sense, Eucharist people" for the simple reason that they are people who claim the centrality of Scripture, and, as he also argues, the way to continue to move towards a proper acknowledgment of the importance of the Eucharist is to create a sympathetic historical and theological climate.[109] In this chapter, I contend that it is in pneumatology that we can create such a climate and find congruity in different streams of eucharistic theologies. Focusing on the Holy Spirit can foster progress towards putting back the centrality of the Eucharist among Pentecostals because it is through a pneumatological lens that we can find "authenticity" from outside our own tradition.[110] Realizing the complexities and various nuances of what can be put under the category of "Protestant," this task could be overly ambitious and almost impossible to carry out. To avoid falling into such a trap, I will use the natural demarcation of the Protestant Reformation—namely Zwingli, Luther, and Calvin—and consider it to provide a big enough Protestant tent. I will work this out by presenting the eucharistic theology of each of the Reformers, highlighting especially its pneumatology. I will treat Zwingli, Luther, and Calvin each in its own section and in that order. The reason for this is that Calvin's pneumatology is the most pronounced out of the three. I will end the discussion by highlighting the pneumatological convergences in these theologies and how they create the sympathetic climate that Cocksworth mentioned.

---

108. Cocksworth, *Evangelical Eucharistic Thought*, 9–10.
109. Cocksworth, *Evangelical Eucharistic Thought*, 8–9.
110. Cartledge, *Mediation of the Spirit*, 130.

Pneumatology in the Eucharistic Theology of Ulrich Zwingli

The Swiss pastor Ulrich Zwingli is one of the earliest of the major reformers. In his theology of the Eucharist, he is known for advocating what is known as a representational memorialism of the Lord's Supper. For Zwingli, the sacrament is primarily a sign that points beyond itself to something much more substantial: the reality of the risen and ascended Christ.[111] He argues against taking the word "is" in Jesus's words "this is my body" literally, and contends that the correct way to understand the word is metaphorically or figuratively. In his own words, Zwingli argues that when Jesus said, "'This is my body,' [it] means, 'The bread signifies my body,' or 'is a figure of my body.' For immediately afterward in Luke 22, Christ adds: 'This do in remembrance of me,' from which it follows that the bread is only a figure of his body to remind us in the Supper that the body was crucified for us."[112] Nevertheless, for Zwingli, the sacrament signifies something that is holy and indicates a spiritual reality; it is, however, only a sign that points beyond itself to the reality of the risen Christ in a similar way that the written word "pencil" points to and signifies a pencil.[113]

What enables this signifying, for Zwingli, is the Holy Spirit himself. He understands that the Spirit is the one who plays an active role in the sacrament, just as he plays an active role in every aspect of the life of the community. Because of that, it would be a mistake to see Zwingli's idea of memorialism as merely a commemorative act, meaning that the celebration is only an act of "calling to mind" the person of Jesus Christ. Zwingli does not see that the elements are nothing more than a reminder of the death and passion of Christ. Pneumatologically, there is more that is going on in his understanding of the celebration of the Lord's Supper, because for Zwingli, the risen Jesus, through the sovereign activity of the Holy Spirit, is present among his people who are partaking in the Lord's Supper.[114] It is just that he is only willing to say that in and of themselves, the elements are nothing more than a representation of the body and blood of Christ. The presence of the risen Christ is not to be identified with the eucharistic elements but with the elements being a signifier of

---

111. Van Dyk, "Reformed View," 68–69.

112. Zwingli, "On the Lord's Supper," 225.

113. Van Dyk, "Reformed View," 70.

114. Bromiley, "Introduction," 183.

a larger reality, and this is the reason that, for Zwingli, they are called a sacrament.[115]

We may be inclined to ask, what then is the purpose of the Lord's Supper—or baptism for that matter—according to Zwingli? The answer is that in the observance of the sacrament, the person is given the opportunity to attest and make a proclamation about their faith, as Zwingli, in his own words, says, "But that we might publicly attest it with praise and thanksgiving, joining together for the greater magnifying and proclaiming of the matter in the eating and drinking of the sacrament of his sacred passion, which is a representation of Christ's giving of his body and shedding of his blood for our sakes."[116]

Finally, in the pneumatology of his theology of the Lord's Supper, Zwingli sees God being active not only in bringing the spiritual presence of Christ but, more importantly, also in working out of the internal ministry of the Holy Spirit. It is here that the act of attesting and proclaiming in the Lord's Supper gains its significance, but also interestingly where Zwingli's doctrine actually—and peculiarly, one might say—sides with the *ex opere operato* doctrine of sacramental efficacy that focuses on the sacraments deriving their efficacy from the work of Christ, because in a sense both are more concerned with "the divine transcendence and sovereignty" of God.[117] On that note, we now proceed to the section on Luther.

Pneumatology in the Eucharistic Theology of Martin Luther

To say that the writing of the German Reformer Martin Luther is peculiar would be an understatement. Most of his writings, including those regarding the Lord's Supper, are concerned with challenging the "misunderstanding" and "abuses" that he sees as taking place in the Roman Catholic Church. Therefore, these writings are mostly polemical in nature. Because Luther typically sought to deal with these misunderstandings and abuses on a case-by-case basis, his writings were directed to a particular issue that he found and, when seen as a whole, may look somewhat fragmented.

---

115. Bromiley, "Introduction," 179.
116. Zwingli, "On the Lord's Supper," 234.
117. Bromiley, "Introduction," 183.

One major misunderstanding against which Luther spoke was the power held by the priests in the understanding of the function of the Eucharist. He argues that the words of institutions (i.e., 1 Cor 11:23–26) are what possess the definitive power in transforming the communion elements into the body and blood of Christ.[118] Luther says, "[On] these words [of] the Apostle . . . we must rest; on them we must build as on a firm rock. . . . For in these words nothing is omitted that pertains to the completeness, the use, and the blessing of this sacrament; and nothing is included that is superfluous and not necessary for us to know."[119] Here, Luther is not willing to accept that human agency adds additional layers of meanings or dimensions to the Lord's Supper.[120]

Just like in baptism, the water and the word of God are conjoined, so for Luther, the bread and wine are bound to the word of God, and it is this very fact that makes it a sacrament, as he says, "If you take away the words, you have only the bread and wine."[121] Therefore, for the sacrament to be appropriately administered, the priest must first proclaim that "the sacrament is the body and blood of the Lord under the bread and wine [for] the forgiveness of sins."[122] The efficacy of the sacrament, for Luther, does not depend on the condition of the recipient—worthy or unworthy—because it does not alter the word of God.[123]

The purpose of the Lord's Supper, according to Luther, is twofold, namely for one to receive the experience of justification and sanctification that Christ offers, for according to him, in the celebration, one experiences "forgiveness of sins and the Holy Spirit" because in them, and by acknowledging in faith the need to obtain "remedy and salvation," one is justified and sanctified.[124] In his sermon on the catechism, Luther explains, "I go to the sacrament in order to take and use Christ's body and blood, given and shed for me. I use the sacrament for the forgiveness of sins,"[125] and then later continues, "The sacrament is not given to those who are sick as a poison but as a remedy. See to it, then, that you seek

---

118. Wandel, *Eucharist in the Reformation*, 99.
119. Luther, "Babylonian Captivity," 154.
120. Wandel, *Eucharist in the Reformation*, 99.
121. Luther, "Sermons on the Catechism," 234–35.
122. Luther, "Sermons on the Catechism," 236.
123. Luther, "Sermons on the Catechism," 235.
124. Luther, "Sermons on the Catechism," 238.
125. Luther, "Sermons on the Catechism," 235.

the sacrament for *your betterment* when you find yourself in an hour of peril of life, when the flesh drives you, the world entices you, and Satan assails you." Contrary to the practice of his time that discourages people from participating—something he calls "a trick of the devil"—he strongly encourages believers to come and receive communion for their benefit.[126]

Luther's idea of real presence is commonly known as consubstantiation, an idea that Christ's body and blood are present simultaneously with bread and wine while both maintain their substances. Lutheranism rejects the view of the Eucharist as "making present" Christ's sacrifice on the cross, and his consubstantiation offers an incarnational analogy that is an alternative to the doctrine of transubstantiation.[127] Although it is not spelled out straightforwardly, this analogy is, in a sense, pneumatological because, for Luther, the relationship between substances in the Eucharist, just as in the incarnation, is a participation (*koinōnia*) that is dependent on the mystery of mutual indwelling. As Hunsinger explains,

> Just as the divine nature dwelt in Christ bodily, so also did his life-giving flesh come to dwell, so to speak, in the consecrated bread, and vice versa. Regardless of whether reason could understand it, both entities in the relation were simply there in their entirety. Consequently, just as one could point to the human Jesus and say without equivocation, "This man is the Lord," so also could one take the consecrated bread and say without equivocation, "This is the body of Christ." The predications were true by participation, and for Luther the idea of participation invalidated the idea that one substance was transformed into another. Real presence meant that Christ's life-giving flesh was substantially present in, with, and under the bread, whose substance remained that of bread.[128]

So, for Luther, the phrase "This is my body" is to be taken as Christ's body being present in the Eucharist truly—which means essentially and substantively—but not locally, meaning neither present quantitatively nor according to ordinary qualities of being locally present.[129] According to Luther, the words of Jesus were a figure of speech "such that when two

---

126. Luther, "Sermons on the Catechism," 238; emphasis added.
127. Hunsinger, *Eucharist and Ecumenism*, 28.
128. Hunsinger, *Eucharist and Ecumenism*, 29.
129. Hunsinger, *Eucharist and Ecumenism*, 30–31.

realities were present so that the one was contained in the other, either could be used to refer to the other."[130]

Pneumatology in the Eucharistic Theology of John Calvin

In contrast to Luther, Calvin's pneumatology is much more developed. The efficacy of the sacraments is dependent on the Holy Spirit. He says, "But the sacraments properly fulfill their office only when the Spirit, that inward teacher, comes to them, by whose power alone hearts are penetrated and affections moved and our souls opened for the sacraments to enter in. If the Spirit be lacking, the sacraments can accomplish nothing more in our minds than the splendor of the sun shining upon blind eyes, or a voice sounding in deaf ears."[131] Calvin's pronounced pneumatology is also seen in how he regards the efficacy of the person presiding. It is "God [who] accomplishes within what the minister represents and attests by outward action . . . by invisible grace through the Holy Spirit."[132]

The pneumatology of Calvin's eucharistic theology is also pronounced in Calvin's understanding of the presence of Jesus. This comes out in a few ways: First, the role of the Holy Spirit is more prominent than what is usually common in Western eucharistic theology. Second, in contrast to Luther, who thinks primarily of a movement from heaven to earth, Calvin introduces the complementary idea of a movement from earth to heaven—a view sometimes known as *receptionism*—and it is the Holy Spirit who propels this movement and mediates the communion taking place between heaven and earth. By the power of the Spirit's ineffable operation, Christ is really present to believers in the Eucharist, spiritually nourishing them with himself, while they are also made really present to him in heaven.[133]

For Calvin, Christ is not present literally in the elements; instead, his presence is spiritual, and those receiving the elements will, in faith, spiritually receive the body and blood of Christ. Calvin explains, "For why should the Lord put in your hand the symbol of his body, except to assure you of a true participation in it? But if it is true that a visible sign is given us to seal the gift of a thing invisible, when we have received the

---

130. Hunsinger, *Eucharist and Ecumenism*, 32–32.
131. Calvin, *Institutes*, §4.14.9.
132. Calvin, *Institutes*, §4.14.17.
133. Hunsinger, *Eucharist and Ecumenism*, 34–35.

symbol of the body, let us no less surely trust that the body itself is also given to us."[134]

In Calvin's understanding, the purpose of the Lord's Supper is threefold. First, in the celebration, God's goodness, the source of all gifts and graces, is declared and affirmed.[135] Because we are embodied beings, God, being the good Father, provides for us in our embodiedness. Calvin says, "To fulfill the duties of a most excellent Father concerned for his offspring, he undertakes also to nourish us throughout the course of our life. . . . Through the hand of his only-begotten Son, [he] give[s] to his church another sacrament, that is, a spiritual banquet, wherein Christ attests himself to be the life-giving bread, upon which our souls feed unto true and blessed immortality."[136] This, then is the cause of our thanksgiving (that is, Eucharist) offered to the Father.

Second, this eucharistic celebration points beyond itself to none other than Jesus Christ. This is where Calvin stresses the strong connection between the Scripture, the sacrament, and Christ, as he explains, "Therefore, let it be regarded as a settled principle that the sacraments have the same office as the Word of God: to offer and set forth Christ to us and in him the treasures of heavenly grace."[137] Again, this is all possible because of the active Holy Spirit, who is the bringer of communion between Christ and the believer initiated in baptism and confirmed and sustained in the Eucharist.[138]

Third, the Lord's Supper is an act of the Father nourishing his children with the good gift of the Holy Spirit himself (Luke 11:13). Through faith, Christ is present among the people, uniting them with him through the gracious initiative of God, who gives them the gifts of the Holy Spirit despite whether the recipient or the minister is worthy or not.[139] Faith is the key to receiving the gifts of the Holy Spirit, and this is also to say that the Lord's Supper is not within the control of the church, the minister, or the people. Instead, the grace in the Lord's Supper is always a fresh gift of God the Holy Spirit.[140] Calvin explains, "But when the source of life be-

---

134. Calvin, *Institutes*, §4.17.10.
135. Van Dyk, "Reformed View," 75.
136. Calvin, *Institutes*, §4.17.1.
137. Calvin, *Institutes*, §4.14.17.
138. Van Dyk, "Reformed View," 76.
139. Van Dyk, "Reformed View," 79.
140. Van Dyk, "Reformed View," 79.

gins to abide in our flesh, he no longer lies hidden far from us, but shows us that we are to partake of him. But he also quickens our very flesh in which he abides, that by partaking of him we may be fed unto immortality. . . . From this also these things follow: that his flesh is truly food, and his blood truly drink, and by these foods believers are nourished unto eternal life."[141] The Holy Spirit brings about the life-giving communion as Christ abides in our flesh through the Spirit. As Calvin explains,

> The presence of Christ's body in the Lord's Supper: "To summarize: our souls are fed by the flesh and blood of Christ in the same way that bread and wine keep and sustain physical life. . . . Even though it seems unbelievable that Christ's flesh, separated from us by such great distance, penetrates to us, so that it becomes our food, let us remember how far the secret power of the Holy Spirit towers above all our senses, and how foolish it is to wish to measure his immeasurableness by our measure. What then, our mind does not comprehend, let faith conceive: that the Spirit truly unites things separated in space."[142]

Evaluation

I would like to conclude this section of the chapter and proceed to highlight the pneumatological convergences in these theologies. Although the Holy Spirit's active role in the Eucharist is nuanced differently by each of the Reformers, there is congruity that we can trace. For Zwingli, the Spirit is the one who enables the signifying of the celebration to happen, making it a spiritual reality working internally in the hearts of the people where Christ is present. For Luther, it is the Holy Spirit who enables the body and blood of Christ to be simultaneously present with the bread and wine, and most importantly, the Eucharist becomes a means to receive the Holy Spirit as the remedy. For Calvin, whom we have seen is the one with the most pronounced pneumatology, the Holy Spirit, who makes Christ's presence a reality, is also a nourishment given to the people by the Father. As Tomberlin points out, in the early days, Pentecostals saw, and by that affirmed, the early Christian understanding of the Eucharist as therapeutic, calling it "God's medicine."[143] I contend that this, along with the Reformers' understanding of the Holy Spirit, is the location of

---

141. Calvin, *Institutes*, §4.17.8.
142. Calvin, *Institutes*, §4.17.10.
143. Tomberlin, *Pentecostal Sacraments*, 182.

that sympathetic climate in which Pentecostals can and should become, as Cocksworth earlier pointed out, Eucharist people, who will minister healing by addressing all areas affected by sin and the fall.[144] If in the Eucharist people can find healing—which is better understood as healing not just our physical ailments but also our humanity—then Pentecostals should be compelled to come and find such healing there.

Finally, concerning the presence of Christ that the three Reformers have pointed out, albeit differently, Pentecostals also need to see this as a sympathetic theological location. Pentecostals strongly affirm that an encounter with his presence is life changing. As Green points out, "To be in Christ's presence is to be *transformed*, for he is always present in transformative power."[145] This is because the presence of Christ that is encountered in the Eucharist is both his presence in our midst and the foretaste of the fullness of his eschatological kingdom.[146] This transformative presence will make us participants in Christ's humanity on this side of reality right now. Thus, if Pentecostals are to be genuinely missional people, it would benefit them to notice that the transformation that turns them into such people happens in the encounter with the risen and ascended Christ taking place at the Eucharist—a subject that I will explore more fully in chapter 5 of this book.

CONCLUSION

Regarding the Holy Spirit, St. Basil the Great says, "Everything that needs holiness turns to him. All that live virtuously desire him, as they are watered by his inspiration and assisted toward their proper and natural end. . . . He is the source of holiness, an intellectual light for every rational power's discovery of truth, supplying clarity, so to say, through himself."[147] If nothing else, this gives us the reason for examining the Eucharist using a pneumatological perspective. In studying the Eucharist, it is ultimately the Spirit from whom we want to learn. Using lenses given by the Holy Spirit, the process of investigation can lead to insights and findings that are at once orthodox yet generous as we are enabled to "welcome,

---

144. Alexander, "Pentecostal Healing Community," 204; Cocksworth, *Evangelical Eucharistic Thought*, 8–9.

145. Green, *Toward a Pentecostal Theology*, 267; emphasis in original.

146. Cocksworth, *Evangelical Eucharistic Thought*, 208.

147. Basil the Great, *On the Holy Spirit*, §9.22.

affirm, and celebrate a greater range of theological perspectives."[148] This is precisely the reading of the theology of the Eucharist of other Christian traditions that uses a "pneumatological imagination," which will enable the construction of an understanding that will correlate with the SET process—what Gadamer calls "fusion of horizons."[149] As I mentioned earlier, for Pentecostals, this fusion of horizons can only be the work of the Holy Spirit, who "*mediates between the horizon* of the text and of the community."[150]

In this chapter, I have attempted to show the richness of Eastern Orthodox pneumatology that presents great potential for Pentecostals to develop our own understanding of the Holy Spirit that will, in turn, enrich our conclusion of what it means to be the body of Christ. In trying to understand the doctrine of transubstantiation of Roman Catholicism, I attempted to show how this doctrine can potentially provide a greater understanding of the embodiedness of our faith and the Eucharist as the physical body and blood of Christ being *pharmakon* for our holistic healing. Finally, despite the different understandings held by the Protestant Reformers, I have also attempted to show that pneumatology is the conducive agent for bringing back the celebration of the Eucharist front and center in the life of the Protestant church, which includes Pentecostals. This is a stepping stone toward what can be developed in the subsequent chapters as I construct a renewal theology of the Eucharist within the framework of Pentecostal spirituality that shows "a process of searching for God, who once encountered effects within the life of the searcher, who is then transformed or renewed in order to continue the journey."[151] I will say, however, that the significance of this chapter in trying to appreciate the different eucharistic traditions lies in the fact—repeating what Gordon Smith said, which I noted earlier—that the study of the Eucharist is the study of the ministry of the Spirit. I hope it is in the fullness of the Spirit that the conversation taking place in the next chapters should continue. As Spirit-filled people, one of the ways Pentecostals can do that is to exercise the gift of charity, the greatest of all the gifts of the Spirit, that will enable us to have a "pneumatological imagination." In the next chapter, I will attempt to listen to how traditions have read the biblical

---

148. Cartledge, *Mediation of the Spirit*, 167.
149. Gadamer, *Truth and Method*, 317.
150. Cartledge, "Text-Community-Spirit," 134; emphasis added.
151. Cartledge, *Encountering the Spirit*, 25.

texts on the Eucharist as a way to reread them through a pneumatological imagination and construct an understanding that will correlate with the SET process—what Gadamer calls "fusion of horizons."[152] As I have mentioned in the introduction chapter, for Pentecostals, we know that this fusion of horizons can only be attributed to the work of the Holy Spirit, as Cartledge contends that in reading Scripture, "the inspired text . . . functions normatively within the community of faith, the church, as the Holy Spirit *mediates between the horizon* of the text and of the community."[153]

---

152. Gadamer, *Truth and Method*, 317.
153. Cartledge, "Text-Community-Spirit," 134; emphasis added.

4

Rereading the Biblical Text

INTRODUCTION

IN THIS CHAPTER, MY purpose is to show that the Pentecostal text-community-Spirit hermeneutic allows an amalgamation of how other Christian traditions read the eucharistic text into Pentecostal reading to construct, expand, and specifically locate the Pentecostal understanding of the Eucharist within an SET framework.[1] The eucharistic texts that will be examined below are 1 Cor 10:14–22, 11:23–34, Matt 14:13–21, 26:26–30; Mark 14:12–26, Luke 22:14–20, 24:13–35; and John 6:11–14, 51–58. Using a "pneumatological imagination"[2] inherent in text-community-Spirit (which in Yong's terminology is "Spirit-word-community"), the aim is to come to a reading of the text that possesses an ecumenical awareness—which to me is essentially an understanding of the "community" of interpreters that has been expanded and enlarged—thus allowing incorporating how other traditions interpret the "text." In reading these texts, my main goal is to show their eucharistic provenance; that is, the narratives were redacted in a way that informs the worship gatherings of the early church in

---

1. Cartledge, "Text-Community-Spirit"; Cross, "Proposal to Break the Ice"; Dabney, "Saul's Armor."

2. See 20n114.

order to relive and reenact the experience of their encounter with Jesus eucharistically. This will be elaborated and unpacked below, but as Wainwright suggests, it is certainly a plausible way to understand how Jesus is present in the gathering of two and three (Matt 18:20).[3]

For our discussion purpose, I understand "pneumatological imagination" as the result of the freedom afforded by the Third Person of the Trinity (2 Cor 3:17) to construct a process of retrieval, comparison, and reconstruction, that allows me to arrive at the point of understanding that, as Gadamer says, "is not merely a reproductive but always a *productive* activity as well."[4] I contend that this productive activity that includes probing the interpretation of other traditions in order to compare and, therefore, reconstruct an understanding will reinform comprehension of the Eucharist that will correlate with the SET process of Pentecostal spirituality—which in and of itself is always a dialectical process, creating what Gadamer calls the "fusion of horizons."[5] In one sense, I maintain that this is similar to the dialectical process Cartledge sets up to create a practical theology model that considers seriously the orthopraxy found in charismatic spirituality. This dialectic takes place between the "lifeworld," which is the concrete setting of the particular situation that is being examined, and the "transcontextual system," which is the framework used to analyze such a situation. The result of this dialectic is an integration of the system and the lifeworld that resulted in a holistic transformation.[6]

For Pentecostals, this fusion of horizons is, of course, attributed to the work of the Holy Spirit that is experiential, hence an imagination that is pneumatological. Cartledge contends correctly that in reading Scripture, "the inspired text . . . functions normatively within the community of faith, the church, as the Holy Spirit *mediates between the horizon* of the text and of the community."[7] In addition, I will contend that the Holy Spirit mediates the horizons of interpreting communities, allowing a dialogue that will provide a fusion between them and resulting in an enlarged understanding of "community."

In what follows, I will show that the Eastern Orthodox use of Scripture as primarily to be experienced in the context of the liturgical worship

---

3. Wainwright, *Eucharist and Eschatology*, 76.
4. Gadamer, *Truth and Method*, 307; emphasis added.
5. Gadamer, *Truth and Method*, 317.
6. Cartledge, *Practical Theology*, 17–23.
7. Cartledge, "Text-Community-Spirit," 13; emphasis added.

is similar to, and therefore may inform how Pentecostals see Scripture as normative as a source of guide and teaching to live in the world. I will also show that it is possible to see the Roman Catholic understanding of "living tradition" as having similarity to, and therefore can inform the understanding of "community" in text-community-Spirit. I will discuss this further below, but suffice it to say that this expansion of the community does not betray the Pentecostal spirit. Instead, it is actually one of the ways to shed the burdening "Saul's Armor" we have borrowed and develop our third-article theology as suggested.[8] This enlarged understanding of community is precisely how the Pentecostal text-community-Spirit hermeneutical principle allows for a certain "fluidity" in the definition of the community of interpreters—where the idea of community is elastic enough to allow the accommodation of other reading traditions (what Pentecostals may previously have considered as "the gentiles" [Acts 15]) into "our community,"[9] providing "an openness to the possibility that traditions different from our own may have insight into facets of God's truth that we might incorporate into our own understanding,"[10] while given with the opportunity to discern "God's activity" outside the Pentecostal community in the spirit of the Pentecostal hermeneutics modeled in Acts 15.[11] I will then focus specifically on how other traditions read the text eucharistically and conclude by arguing that if Pentecostals are zealous of becoming a community that is devoted to the apostles' teaching, the fellowship, to the breaking of bread and the prayers (Acts 2:42), then Pentecostals should read the text eucharistically as well. Before doing so, however, I will discuss the hermeneutical principles that have been proposed by a few Pentecostal scholars.

PENTECOSTAL HERMENEUTICAL PRINCIPLE(S)

The work of interpretation does not take place in a vacuum; instead, it takes place, as Kenneth J. Archer puts it, "within the contextual horizon of the reading community."[12] It could also be argued that the work of interpretation that a particular community undertakes does not happen

---

8. Dabney, "Saul's Armor," 145; Cross, "Proposal to Break the Ice," 70.
9. See 21n117.
10. Westphal, "Spirit and Prejudice," 29.
11. Thomas, "Reading the Bible," 119.
12. Archer, *Pentecostal Hermeneutic*, 127.

in a vacuum either; rather, it always necessitates, even requires, the interaction with the reading of other communities as well. In my view, this is precisely what participating in the ever-widening *koinōnia* of the Trinity that marks a pneumatic hermeneutic is all about, one that involves a process of discernment which, as Cartledge points out, "appeal to the wider ecumenical Christian discussion and ask how different contemporary communities, presumably with differing reading traditions, approach particular issues of interpretation."[13] Before we do that, however, we need to begin by looking into the Pentecostal hermeneutical principles that have been presented by several Pentecostal scholars, such as John Christopher Thomas, Kenneth J. Archer, and Amos Yong.

Hermeneutical Approach of John Christopher Thomas

John Christopher Thomas suggests that the Pentecostal hermeneutical method fits the approach found in the interpretive process of the Jerusalem Council demonstrated in Acts 15.[14] The council, Thomas points out, came to a decision regarding the inclusion of the gentiles through a way of reading Scripture that sets them on a trajectory moving from their present context to the original context of the text; that is, they first made an appeal to their experience that they see as the work of the Holy Spirit prior to moving towards considering Scripture.[15] For Thomas, the Pentecostal method of interpretation consists of three components, namely, the community of believers, the work of the Holy Spirit, and the Scripture text itself.[16] He points out that community is what helps keep "uncontrolled subjectivism or a rampant individualism" from happening, as the shared experience of individuals in a community should be ideally subjected to communal accountability, discernment, and evaluation. The work of the Holy Spirit takes place within a community, giving members an experience of the Spirit who manifests divine acts in the community and is then enabled to testify about such work.[17] The role of the Spirit is understood to be more than just providing illumination; it is one that moves the community towards creating a context to interpret Scripture

13. Cartledge, "Pneumatic Hermeneutic," 186–87.
14. Thomas, "Reading the Bible," 118.
15. Thomas, "Reading the Bible," 113.
16. Thomas, "Reading the Bible," 117.
17. Thomas, "Women, Pentecostals and Bible," 52.

that will guide the life of the community.[18] With these two at work (that is, community and Spirit), the text of Scripture can then be grappled with in order for the community to come to a conclusion about the text, in the form of validation or repudiation, that, in the end, gives direction to their life.[19] The way these three components work together is never static; rather, they continue to be in a trialectic relationship with one another, which can be seen in the way the Jerusalem Council came to a decision regarding the inclusion of gentiles. Thomas notes that there are several implications for using this hermeneutical method in the ongoing life of the church. For this discussion, the most important one is the fact that this process of interpretation presents a way for the Pentecostal community to continue wrestling with issues that are part of a dynamic and living community in the Spirit.[20]

Hermeneutical Strategy of Kenneth J. Archer

The hermeneutical strategy that Kenneth J. Archer proposes seeks to be both faithful to the Pentecostal community's tradition and conscious of the methods related to the interpretation of text brought by academia.[21] Archer creates a strategy that—similar to that developed by Thomas—involves three components, namely text-Spirit-community. The strategy employs a narrative approach that Archer says "embraces a tridactic negotiation for meaning between the biblical text, the Holy Spirit, and the Pentecostal community" that will produce a theological interpretation from a discourse between these three elements.[22] In this process of negotiation, each of the three elements provides what Archer calls "contribution." Through the process of semiotics, a process that looks at how signs contribute to meaning and how a transaction of meaning then takes place between the reader and the text, the biblical text as a full-fledged "interdependent dialogical participant" in this negotiation contributes to the making of meaning by giving cues in how the text wants to be read and heard.[23] The text is understood as a respected dialog partner, but the

18. Thomas, "Reading the Bible," 119.
19. Thomas, "Women, Pentecostals and Bible," 54.
20. Thomas, "Reading the Bible," 120.
21. Archer, *Pentecostal Hermeneutic*, 156.
22. Archer, *Pentecostal Hermeneutic*, 157.
23. Archer, *Pentecostal Hermeneutic*, 161, 163.

text does not control the negotiation between itself, the community, and the Spirit; rather, it contributes to the conversation taking place between the three and in the making of meaning.[24]

The meaning of the text—if it is to be meaningful in a real sense—must be embodied in the lives of people. The role of the reading community, therefore, becomes essential because it contributes to the making of meaning that is in line with the context of the community. The critical question to ask is, in what way does the text speak to a community situation? The community then becomes a "filter and foil" for understanding what the text seeks to communicate. In Archer's Pentecostal hermeneutical strategy, the interpreting community provides the space and context in which the word of God is to be heard. Scripture becomes and speaks the word of God that needs to be heard, believed, and obeyed in a community at a particular place and time.[25] According to Archer, this would be achieved by favoring the narrative critical approach along with a reader's response over the historical-critical method because, as opposed to the latter, the two former allow not just for the text to be interpreted by the community but also, and more importantly, for the text to interpret the community.[26] The narrative critical approach connects the Pentecostal community to the story of Scripture. It provides an opportunity for the community to be taken and shaped by that story while preventing it from being reduced to propositions that miss its transforming big story.[27]

According to Archer, describing the contribution of the Holy Spirit is more difficult because the way the Spirit contributes is through the community and the text; that is, the "voice" of the Spirit is always heard in and through the community and Scripture itself.[28] Therefore, explaining the Holy Spirit's contribution must be done through what the Spirit is speaking in and through the community and the text. To do this, the community will first have to invite the Spirit's presence and be open to the Spirit to manifest himself in the community through testimonies, charismata, preaching, teaching, serving the poor, and all other acts of ministry, to empower, guide, and transform the individual members of

---

24. Archer, *Pentecostal Hermeneutic*, 163–64.
25. Archer, *Pentecostal Hermeneutic*, 165.
26. Archer, *Pentecostal Hermeneutic*, 166.
27. Archer, *Pentecostal Hermeneutic*, 168.
28. Archer, *Pentecostal Hermeneutic*, 182.

the community.²⁹ This manifestation, or experiences of the Spirit, then shapes how the community reads Scripture and is understood as the way the Spirit works in and through the community. The Spirit also works in and through the text of Scripture itself. This is in line with how Pentecostals hold a high view of Scripture, which means Scripture is understood as a testimony about God that is authoritative and trustworthy.³⁰ As a consequence, Pentecostals also see Scripture as normative and a source of guidance and teaching to live in the world. The Holy Spirit works through Scripture in the hermeneutical process, speaking to the community and giving a new understanding that is rooted in Scripture but has room to go beyond it.³¹

Trinitarian Theological Hermeneutics of Amos Yong

The theological hermeneutics that Amos Yong proposes also consists of three things, namely the act (the Spirit), the object (the word), and the contexts (the community), all three remaining in a continuous interplay among themselves. Although consisting of the same elements as the previous models, Yong starts with the Spirit as he sees that it is the Spirit who mediates, forms, and transforms both the word and the community.³² The work of the Spirit in the activity of interpretation requires the interpreters to "be open to the unpredictable movements of the Spirit who 'breaks in to' (or 'breaks through') the interpreter's situation and enables interpretive activity to commence in and through the same Spirit."³³ This breaking into needs to happen so that a process of conversion in the interpreter can take place and eventually drive what Yong calls a "pneumatological imagination," bringing with it creativity that works in two ways: first, truth is encountered as something that is retrieved and reappropriated, and second, truth is encountered as the result of new significations and

---

29. Archer, *Pentecostal Hermeneutic*, 183.

30. Archer, *Pentecostal Hermeneutic*, 184. Archer never specifically mentions Karl Barth. Admitting my very limited knowledge of Barthian theology, this seems to be similar to what Macchia points out in a back-and-forth dialogue between him, Yong, Irvin, and Del Colle, saying that "all [is] fallible but infallible in living witness" in the sense that infallibility of Scripture is found in its testimony of the infallible Christ (Yong et al., "Christ and Spirit," 58).

31. Archer, *Pentecostal Hermeneutic*, 185.

32. Yong, *Spirit, Word, Community*, 275.

33. Yong, *Spirit, Word, Community*, 222–23.

appropriations.[34] If these encounters with truth do not take place when grappling with the text, then the text one encounters would be only dead letters as opposed to something transformative.

Yong also points out that theological hermeneutics that sees itself only as an activity of pneumatology will risk (and have actually ended up) making false claims in the name of the Spirit. In the process of theological hermeneutics, when the word is said to be an object of interpretation, this is understood only in what he calls "a weak sense" because the word is not something that the interpreters can shape and handle as an object according to the way they want.[35] Quite the opposite, the word is actually the one that, through the Spirit, interprets the interpreters, demonstrated most clearly in the person of Jesus, who is the living Word of God.[36] Thus, to say the "word" being the object as in Scripture being "word" is in a sense to say that it functions as an object of interpretation that is not dead letters only to be read but is a text that is always alive and able to be experienced.[37] This hermeneutical principle says Scripture is not *the* word of God because to say that would be to say that those who do not have access to the written word, for example, because of illiteracy or lack of translation, cannot access the divine Word; rather, Scripture is a testimony of the living Word of God (that is Jesus) present, active, and made alive by the Spirit.[38] This does not mean that Yong's hermeneutical principle negates the authority of Scripture; rather, it is to say that Scripture's authority does not take place in isolation but always takes place in relation to the multitude of human reality, which is the reason that Scripture becomes normative in theological interpretation in the first place.[39]

The act of reading the Bible in Yong's theological interpretation employs a kind of reasoning that is practical (as opposed to theoretical) that is the outcome of and steered by "the convictions, concerns, habits, dispositions, virtues, practices and faithful living of the Christian community."[40] Just like the previous two hermeneutical methods, Yong also prefers narrative interpretation because of the conviction that stories

---

34. Yong, *Spirit, Word, Community*, 223.
35. Yong, *Spirit, Word, Community*, 256.
36. Yong, *Spirit, Word, Community*, 257.
37. Yong, *Spirit, Word, Community*, 260.
38. Yong, *Spirit, Word, Community*, 261.
39. Yong, *Spirit, Word, Community*, 263.
40. Yong, *Spirit, Word, Community*, 276.

are what shape a person's identity, and the identity of the community comes from the amalgamation of shared stories of individuals that testify to their shared identity as members of a community.[41] Although *community* comes in third place, for Yong, it is only in the context of a community that Spirit and word can go together. It is important to note that Yong also understands the idea of the community not only as the local community, for example, the Pentecostal community, the local church, or even the universal church; rather, he understands the community as the whole of the human community. Although one may question whether the whole of the human community can really be a community, in my view, this way of looking at "community" can be reconciled with the christological vision Paul gives in Eph 1:10, in which all things will be recapitulated in Christ. Therefore, the theological interpretation he espouses is not just about the church's endeavor for the sake of the church but, more importantly, for the world so that a fuller understanding of the church's relationship to the world can be gained. In his view, "truth is not only transformative, pragmatic, coherent vis-à-vis the Church's ministry and traditions, but also vis-à-vis the Church's situation in the world."[42]

EASTERN ORTHODOX AND ROMAN CATHOLIC HERMENEUTICS

Having presented the Pentecostal/charismatic text-community-Spirit hermeneutics in its various nuances as offered by the three different theologians, I now proceed to the next task, which is twofold: First, to show that the Orthodox use of Scripture as primarily to be experienced in the context of liturgical worship has similarities to, and therefore can inform, how Pentecostals see Scripture as normative, as the source of guide and teaching to live in the world. Second, to show the understanding of "community" in the Pentecostal hermeneutical principle has much in common with the Roman Catholic understanding of *living tradition*.

In what follows, I will present an exposition on how these two Christian traditions understood what the text is, how it came about, and how it is to be interpreted, and then demonstrate compatibility between their understanding and the Pentecostal/charismatic hermeneutics. I intend to show that the Pentecostal hermeneutical principle has the opportunity to

41. Yong, *Spirit, Word, Community*, 277.
42. Yong, *Spirit, Word, Community*, 297.

mine the Eastern Orthodox and Roman Catholic way of understanding Scripture in tradition, allowing for pollination to take place. As this is a Pentecostal project, my main concern is a constructive pollination taking place on our side as opposed to theirs because I am more concerned with what we can receive from their way of reading and interpreting the text rather than insisting on a cross-pollination—for example, on what they can learn from us, although this is certainly possible, or on being apologetic about Pentecostalism classical understanding of Scripture. I now begin with the exposition of the Eastern Orthodox tradition.

Eastern Orthodox Approach to Scripture

The Eastern Orthodox truly understands that the work of interpretation does not take place in a vacuum. That is one of the reasons that we do not see many Orthodox biblical scholars focusing on writing commentaries on the books of the Bible.[43] Rather than merely exegetical, they understand the interpretation and use of Scripture as primarily to be experienced in the context of the liturgical worship of the church community, an idea that was already present since the time of the church fathers, which they continue to maintain.[44] This is not to say that today's Eastern Orthodox biblical scholars do not see the value of modern critical tools that are available; instead, for them, these tools are valuable inasmuch as they can contribute to the main concern they have in engaging the biblical text, which is to interpret it as the life-giving word encountered in the context of worship.[45]

Following the tradition of the patristics, Eastern Orthodoxy sees the relationship between Scripture and tradition as inseparable. The Eastern Orthodox sees the two neither as either/or nor both/and. Instead, Eastern Orthodoxy sees Scripture as being *in* tradition because Scripture itself *is* tradition. This means that Scripture was birthed and shaped within the community of believers (that is, tradition), whereby the Bible, specifically the New Testament, constitutes the normative element of that community.[46] Eastern Orthodoxy views Scripture, tradition, and church as three interdependent parts that form a comprehensive unity. The church—a

---

43. Breck, *Scripture in Tradition*, 1.
44. Stylianopoulos, "Scripture and Tradition," 26.
45. Breck, *Scripture in Tradition*, 2.
46. Breck, *Scripture in Tradition*, 3–4.

community of believers and the temple of the Holy Spirit—is the place in which Scripture and tradition materialize and become the revelatory norming norm for the life of the community.[47] This idea of a living tradition is clearly explained by Orthodox biblical scholar John Breck, who says, "Tradition has been aptly described as the life of the Holy Spirit within the Church, the presence of the divine, sanctifying Life within the Body of believers."[48]

Eastern Orthodoxy understands that there is a dialectic relationship between Scripture and tradition, whereby it is through Scripture that all traditions are deemed authentic and living tradition is regulated. At the same time, we know that the canon came about from within the church as a believing community, so while Scripture dictates what is genuine tradition, it is from the living tradition that Scripture emerges and is eventually canonized.[49] This dialectic relationship is alive because of the presence and work of the Holy Spirit, who is the Spirit of truth. He is responsible for guiding the inspired writers and the canonization of the text in the church and preserving the transmission of this truth as tradition to future generations. Without the work of the Third Person of the Trinity, Scripture and tradition amount to merely the product of human endeavor, which does not have the right to claim authority or possession of the ultimate truth. Following the patristics, Eastern Orthodox interpreters attest that it is only the Spirit who enables the canon of Scripture containing normative truth to emanate from the church and who gives the church the ability to interpret it as well. This process of the hermeneutical circle, one that is enabled and validated by the Spirit, is how they understand Scripture in tradition.[50]

The church fathers do not see the Bible as *sui generis* but something that is birthed and formed within a community of faith.[51] The implication of this way of seeing Scripture for the hermeneutical principle of Orthodoxy, a principle that continues the legacy of patristic hermeneutics, is that the primary goal of interpretation is not exegesis but "remembrance" or *anamnēsis*, which is more than just a simple recalling of events that happened in the past. Instead, through the work of the Holy Spirit, the

---

47. Stylianopoulos, "Scripture and Tradition," 21.
48. Breck, *Scripture in Tradition*, 4.
49. Breck, *Scripture in Tradition*, 11.
50. Breck, *Scripture in Tradition*, 11–12.
51. Breck, *Scripture in Tradition*, 3.

act of interpretation is also an act of reliving the past events within the community of faith, bringing fulfillment to the word.[52] In an anamnetic interpretation, Jesus's life and mission and his saving power are manifested in the experience of the community when it celebrates the Eucharist. This is how the church retains her memories and nurtures herself, and in the end, will open herself up to be used by God to fulfill his purposes in history.[53] All of this shows the Orthodox tradition's insistence that the primary agent in translating the message of God in his written word is God himself in the person of the Holy Spirit, who dwells within the universal community of God's people.[54]

Critical Engagement with the Eastern Orthodox Approach

Pentecostal engagement with Eastern Orthodox theology, with the intention to extract from a tradition still very much grounded in the patristic understanding, is nothing new and has been done before.[55] There are undoubtedly several ways that Pentecostals differ from the Eastern Orthodox Church, most notably concerning the main topic of our discussion, which is the Pentecostal view of open communion versus their closed practice. Despite that difference, in my opinion, an engagement with Eastern Orthodoxy is important for Pentecostals, especially in our effort to continue to develop our "third-article theology." As I have argued, the Pentecostal imagination afforded an idea of community that is elastic enough for us to be open to incorporating an understanding of other traditions into ours.[56] This is part of our engagement with the great tradition.

The Eastern Orthodox way of seeing the goal of interpretation not stopping at exegesis but interpreting Scripture as the life-giving word and in the context of worship is a helpful reminder that what Pentecostals seek to interpret is also a text that is always alive and able to be experienced and not dead letters.[57] This is because Orthodoxy sees the relationship between Scripture and tradition as inseparable. A dialectic relation,

---

52. Breck, *Scripture in Tradition*, 12.
53. Stylianopoulus, "Scripture and Tradition," 24–25.
54. Breck, *Scripture in Tradition*, 43.
55. A good example would be Rybarczyk, *Beyond Salvation*.
56. Westphal, "Spirit and Prejudice," 29.
57. Yong, *Spirit, Word, Community*, 260.

creating a movement back and forth between Scripture and tradition (since it is through Scripture that all traditions are deemed authentic and the living tradition is regulated in principle), is similar to how Pentecostals see community becoming a "filter and foil" for understanding what the text seeks to communicate.[58] This is how interpretation moves from exegesis to *anamnēsis*, and reading stops from being merely a recalling of events that happened in the past. Instead, through the work of the Holy Spirit taking place in the life of the community, the members can experience the Spirit manifesting divine acts in the community, who enables them to testify about such work.[59]

Roman Catholic Understanding of Tradition

Following the above discussion on Eastern Orthodox hermeneutics that continues the trajectory of the patristic tradition, in this subsection, I will begin by highlighting the Roman Catholic understanding of *living tradition*. Cardinal Henri de Lubac, one of the significant figures in the Second Vatican Council, points out that during the period when the church was very "tradition-minded," rather than talking much about it, they just lived tradition, in the sense that it is as they *live* tradition that they *read* the Scriptures.[60] To live tradition is understood as seeing themselves as being part of a continuous community of faith from past to present and future.[61] In trying to understand Roman Catholic hermeneutics, it is helpful, therefore, to begin with paying attention to the essential words of Max Thurian, quoted by Congar, who says:

> Tradition is thus a universal and ecumenical reading of Scripture by the Church in light of the Holy Spirit. This ecclesiastical reading alone will lead us to the fullness of God's Word. It is true that a theologian, an exegete or a historian may possess particular talents for the interpretation of the text. But these talents are only efficacious when placed in the understanding of the whole Church, guided by the Holy Spirit. This implies the need to place exegesis and theology in tradition and in the present-day ecumenical activity, since a complete understanding of

---

58. Archer, *Pentecostal Hermeneutic*, 165.
59. Thomas, "Women, Pentecostals and Bible," 52.
60. Lubac, *Splendor of the Church*, 15.
61. Congar, *Meaning of Tradition*, 78.

Scripture depends upon a reading that is not only historical, but traditional and ecumenical.[62]

The hermeneutical principle that remains present in the Roman Catholic tradition is what is known as an *allegorical reading* (this is also present in Eastern Orthodoxy, but that fact is not the purpose of this subsection). To read in allegory is to read the text of Scripture, paying attention to the mysteries of Christ and of the church. An allegorical reading is not understood to be ahistorical; rather, it sees this reading as firmly rooted in history because the reading provides an uncompromising retelling of the salvific story that forms the foundational dogmatic of the church.[63]

Because of the emphasis on looking for the mysteries of Christ and of the church contained in the text, this allegorical meaning has also been understood as *spiritual meaning*, a term that is preferred, as in the progression of history, the meaning of the word "allegory" has been perceived as ambiguous.[64] At the same time, there is, however, a drawback in using the term "spiritual meaning," as this can be seen as only the individual's interiorization of Scripture.[65] Spiritual meaning is primarily the meaning of Scripture for the church. Since the mystery of the faith is not something that can be accessed merely through empirical observation or contemplation, spiritual meaning is a reminder that the word of God "acquires true fulfillment and total significance" when its meaning brings the "transformation which it effects on the one who receives it," which can happen only if the meaning *is* spiritual.[66]

This does not mean that spiritual meaning is to be pitted against literal meaning that comes from the use of modern critical tools because the Spirit of God is also working in the latter process. The interpreter, however, will fail to see that the Spirit is at work when the task of interpretation using modern critical tools fails to "penetrate to the deepest level" of meaning, which is encountering the mystery of Christ and of the church.[67] It is in recognizing that the literal meaning also has to be viewed spiritually that a person who reads the Bible, a book of human

---

62. Congar, *Meaning of Tradition*, 94–95.
63. Lubac, *Scripture in the Tradition*, 12.
64. Lubac, *Scripture in the Tradition*, 20.
65. Lubac, *Scripture in the Tradition*, 17.
66. Lubac, *Scripture in the Tradition*, 21.
67. Lubac, *Scripture in the Tradition*, 19.

authors, finds the mysteries of the Holy Spirit (*Spiritus Sancti sacramenta*) and at the same time enjoys the companion of the Holy Spirit (*Spiritus Sancti consortium*).

The Roman Catholic Church sees pneumatology as the safeguard of the life of tradition. It is the task of the Third Person of the Trinity to make sure that even when people are scattered across time and place, they are able to come to and share the unique form of truth, and therefore life, that is found in the gospel.[68] This is because the Spirit is the omnipresence of God that is not bound by time and location, and therefore, the Spirit can be universal while being particular and interior. Because he is the Spirit of Christ, what the Spirit does is always about realizing and infusing the personality of Christ—the same Christ who keeps watch and intercedes at the right hand of the Father—to the life of the people through the saving truth found in the good news of Christ contained in the Scriptures.[69] Through the work of the Spirit, what is eternal and perpetual becomes present and active. This has been the principle that is held by the teachers of the church in the way that they understood the word of God and defended its truth when faced with false teachings that arise in the church.[70] The Spirit has animated the community of believers since the day of Pentecost and is always working to ensure the unity of the fellowship of diverse communities and persons throughout history.[71]

Critical Engagement with the Roman Catholic Understanding

While acknowledging that there are many differences Pentecostals have with Roman Catholics—not least for the main topic of this discussion is their practice of closed communion—in this subsection, I want to present three key takeaways from the Roman Catholic tradition: First, their understanding that the living tradition is part of a continuous community of faith from past to present and the future. As we have seen from Congar's quote of Thurman, tradition is a pneumatologically thrusted, universal, and ecumenical reading of Scripture by the church. I use the word "thrust" intentionally as a true, universal, and ecumenical reading can happen only because of the work of the Holy Spirit. As we have

---

68. Congar, *Meaning of Tradition*, 53.
69. Congar, *Meaning of Tradition*, 54.
70. Congar, *Meaning of Tradition*, 56.
71. Congar, *Meaning of Tradition*, 58.

seen above, this is similar to Pentecostals, at least in Yong's view, who see community as the whole of the human community and see the purpose of interpreting Scripture as gaining a greater understanding of how the church should relate to the world.[72]

Second, as Archer has argued, Pentecostals favor the narrative critical approach because it provides a connection for the community to be taken and shaped by the transforming stories of Scripture.[73] Roman Catholics' allegorical reading that seeks to retell the salvific story in connection with the use of modern critical tools—one of them would be the narrative critical approach—could add richness to how Pentecostals encounter the mystery of Christ and of the church as a community. The Roman Catholic understanding of spiritual meaning as the meaning of Scripture for the church would also help prevent an individualized spiritualization reading of the text that sometimes happens in the Pentecostal tradition.

Finally, Thomas has shown that a text-community-Spirit hermeneutic will trust that the Holy Spirit is always working to ensure the unity of the fellowship of diverse communities and persons throughout history and know that his role is to create a context to interpret Scripture that will guide the life of these diverse communities.[74] This is in line with the Roman Catholic Church, which sees the Holy Spirit safeguarding the life of tradition that is universal while particular and interior, and at the same time, infusing the personality of Christ in the members of the community. All this is to say that the horizon of Roman Catholic reading, through a pneumatological imagination, can be fused to the horizon of Pentecostals, resulting in the amalgamation that enriches the Pentecostal reading of the text. I proceed now to talk about how that would work.

GADAMER'S FUSION OF HORIZONS

As I mentioned earlier above, a "pneumatological imagination" opens an opportunity for what Hans-Georg Gadamer calls the "fusion of horizons." In this section, I aim to give an account of Gadamer's hermeneutical philosophy for the interpretation of Scripture, found in his magnum opus *Truth and Method* (originally published in German as *Wahrheit*

---

72. Yong, *Spirit, Word, Community*, 297.

73. Archer, *Pentecostal Hermeneutic*, 168.

74. Thomas, "Reading the Bible," 119.

und Methode), specifically in the chapter entitled "Element of a Theory of Hermeneutic Experience." For Gadamer, to understand is to interpret. In considering that, what he seeks to do is to address "how hermeneutics, once freed from the ontological obstructions of the scientific concept of objectivity, can do justice to the historicity of understanding."[75] In Gadamer's view, hermeneutics is not so much about the methodology of understanding, in which the primary way to try to understand a text is by subjecting it to a scientific inquiry so that one gains verifiable knowledge; instead, it is more about seeking "the experience of truth" through an investigation of the phenomenon of understanding.[76] However, even as he acknowledges that hermeneutics is not about method per se, he also admits that "meanings cannot be understood in an arbitrary way," hence, there must still be some sort of method that is involved in trying to understand a text.[77] This method is unlike those used by the Enlightenment project that assumes the possibility of coming to a position of objective neutrality by treating the text as an object to be dissected and scrutinized, so to speak, under a microscope. What Gadamer offers to the discipline of biblical hermeneutics is significant. It once again puts the text of the Bible in the position of the subject, and to understand the biblical text, the reader must put themselves in an open posture so that they can accept and receive the truth that the text wants to communicate to the reader.[78] The text has rights, and in a sense, the text "reads" the reader.

In order to see the significance of his contribution, we first need to go back and see the hermeneutical project of the modern Enlightenment, which directs its critique primarily at Christianity and the Bible.[79] The modern Enlightenment movement claims that the only way to understand correctly is through reason. They believe authority propagates "superstition," "prejudices," and "overhastiness," all of which, in their view, prohibit rational understanding.[80] Hence, the only way to be freed from such biases is to reject the dogmatic interpretation of the Bible and make

---

75. Gadamer, *Truth and Method*, 278.
76. Gadamer, *Truth and Method*, xx–xxi.
77. Gadamer, *Truth and Method*, 281.
78. Gadamer, *Truth and Method*, 305.
79. Gadamer, *Truth and Method*, 284.
80. Gadamer, *Truth and Method*, 284, 289.

tradition and authority subject to reason.[81] Gadamer believes the modern Enlightenment project is mistaken.

Gadamer maintains that it was not until the Enlightenment that the idea of prejudice gained a negative connotation, one that still lasts even until today. He defines prejudice as "a judgment that is rendered before all the elements that determine a situation have been finally examined."[82] In the German legal language, it is understood to be a provisional verdict before the final judgment is given. That interim verdict may be adverse, but that negative sense is "only derivative" and does not necessarily mean it is wrong or false.[83] Gadamer argues that in its attempt to be "objective" by elevating reason above everything else, the modern Enlightenment movement has committed prejudice themselves. He explains that "there is one prejudice of the Enlightenment that defines its essence: the fundamental prejudice of the Enlightenment is the prejudice against prejudice itself, which denies tradition its power."[84] That is, their supposed "objectivism" is none other than the Enlightenment sticking mindlessly to their own fore-meaning and thus failing "to understand the meaning of another."[85]

Gadamer shows that the Cartesian *cogito ergo sum* manifesto of the Enlightenment is insufficient for understanding because human beings will not come to any understanding, even an understanding of themselves, apart from the relationships they have. He points this out by saying, "Long before we understand ourselves through the process of self-examination, we understand ourselves in a self-evident way in family, society, and state in which we live."[86] Gadamer, therefore, suggests that there are "prejudices" that are entirely legitimate; in fact, these legitimate prejudices are the only way we can take full account of a person's "historical mode of being."[87] However, he is quick to acknowledge that even when we accept the idea of legitimate prejudices, they are not to be held too rigidly; rather, they are a way to situate ourselves within our context and the context of the other. We will know and understand a person or

---

81. Gadamer, *Truth and Method*, 286.
82. Gadamer, *Truth and Method*, 283.
83. Gadamer, *Truth and Method*, 283.
84. Gadamer, *Truth and Method*, 283.
85. Gadamer, *Truth and Method*, 281.
86. Gadamer, *Truth and Method*, 289.
87. Gadamer, *Truth and Method*, 289.

a text if we open ourselves up to our legitimate prejudices and to those from which the other person or the text is coming.[88] This is a significant turn in hermeneutics because, for quite some time before Gadamer, the biblical text was treated as if it were an object in the laboratory of reason, to be cut apart and dissected in order to get to what is believed to be verifiable truth.

At this point, I would like to discuss the philosophical hermeneutic that Gadamer proposes. Gadamer begins by asserting that to approach something—whether that something is a person or a text—one must begin by opening oneself to the otherness of the person or text and be sensitive to their uniqueness. The person seeking a "hermeneutical consciousness" must come with the posture that is ready to receive; that is, they understand that the other person or the text has something to give or tell them.[89] Gadamer would later develop this into what is known as the hermeneutic of trust, although he never used the term himself; for example, in his response to Jacques Derrida, Gadamer says, "One does not go about identifying the weaknesses of what another person says in order to prove that one is always right, but one seeks instead as far as possible to strengthen the other's viewpoint so that what the other person has to say becomes illuminating."[90] Gadamer says this posture "involves neither 'neutrality' with respect to content nor the extinction of one's self, but the foregrounding and appropriation of one's own fore-meanings and prejudices."[91] What this posture requires is an awareness of one's own prejudices and that these will come directly face to face with the otherness of the person or text.[92] The posture then should develop into a connection or bond between the person seeking to understand and the subject matter, which, according to Gadamer, is what gives hermeneutics its real thrust.[93] After developing a sense of bond to the text, the next step is to keep being aware of the distance one has with the subject, which Gadamer calls "a polarity of familiarity and strangeness," and these two are to be held together in tension, putting hermeneutics in a place of "in-between." Gadamer elaborates on this in-between place as "the play

---

88. Gadamer, *Truth and Method*, 281.
89. Gadamer, *Truth and Method*, 282.
90. Gadamer, "In Response," 55.
91. Gadamer, *Truth and Method*, 282.
92. Gadamer, *Truth and Method*, 282.
93. Gadamer, *Truth and Method*, 306; cf. 283.

between the traditionary text's strangeness and familiarity to us, between being a historically intended, distanced object and belonging to a tradition."[94]

Having established this in-between place, the interpreter can then begin to enter into the world of the text in an oscillating movement that moves continuously from the whole to the part and back again to the whole. This movement aims "to expand the unity of the understood meaning centrifugally" by coming to a sense of harmony between the whole and the small details as the benchmark of right understanding.[95] Gadamer is adamant that it is impossible to come to a correct understanding without coming to this sense of harmony, as without it, the hermeneutical process has actually failed. According to Gadamer, the way an interpreter can come to this sense of harmony is "to try to transpose ourselves into the perspective within which [the author] has formed his view" for the purpose of understanding that what the author is saying is correct and to reinforce the author's argument.[96] Having done so, the task of hermeneutics can then be completed because agreement concerning the subject matter can be accomplished, rectifying the disturbance of meaning and understanding that existed prior to the investigation. This understanding of coming to a sense of harmony does not negate dissonance, because rectifying disturbance requires the reader to think and rethink their conclusion in a provisional sense that continues to acknowledge their method as tentative.

The means to transpose ourselves into the perspective within which the view takes its shape is what Gadamer understands to be *tradition*, as that is where the tension between the text and our present context is experienced.[97] This experience of tension is necessary and should not be concealed; rather, because of the otherness of the text, this tension should be fully acknowledged and brought to the fore. Earlier, Gadamer says, "The effect of a living tradition and the effect of historical study must constitute a unity of effect, the analysis of which would reveal only a texture of reciprocal effects."[98] Through tradition, one can "clarify this

---

94. Gadamer, *Truth and Method*, 306.
95. Gadamer, *Truth and Method*, 302.
96. Gadamer, *Truth and Method*, 303.
97. Gadamer, *Truth and Method*, 317.
98. Gadamer, *Truth and Method*, 294.

miracle of understanding" because it is there that the sharing of the common meaning that Gadamer mentions takes place.[99]

To be sure, the outcome of the hermeneutical process is not to come to a perfect understanding but to an understanding that is most fully realized.[100] Understanding, therefore, is accepting the invitation to participate in a tradition or event from the past.[101] This understanding is neither static nor formal in nature, but, as Gadamer says, it is the interplay of the movement of tradition and the movement of the interpreter. Gadamer elucidates further, saying, "The anticipation of meaning that governs our understanding of a text is not an act of subjectivity but proceeds from the commonality that binds us to the tradition. Tradition is not simply a permanent precondition; rather, we produce it ourselves inasmuch as we understand, participate in the evolution of tradition, and hence further determine it ourselves."[102]

Earlier, I mentioned that hermeneutic consciousness involves a posture that is ready to receive. This posture is worked out in a way in which we are to approach the text by assuming its completeness and to do so until we find it to be intelligible, when only then can we be suspicious of the text and begin to find ways to remedy this intelligibility. Gadamer explains this by saying, "The fore-conception of completeness that guides all our understanding is, then, always determined by the specific content. Not only does the reader assume an immanent unity of meaning, but his understanding is likewise guided by the constant, transcendent expectations of meaning that proceed from the relation to the truth of what is being said."[103] Gadamer uses the example of a person who receives a letter and reads it with the understanding that what she is reading is an account of what the writer experienced and accepts it as truth without suspecting whether the writer has an agenda or not; so too, the person who receives "traditionary texts" accepts the possibility that the writer of the text is much more informed than he and is actually telling him the truth.[104] Gadamer calls this the posture of acceptance, in which the text is acknowledged as conveying both meaning and truth as "the prejudice of

---

99. Gadamer, *Truth and Method*, 303.
100. Gadamer, *Truth and Method*, 304.
101. Gadamer, *Truth and Method*, 302.
102. Gadamer, *Truth and Method*, 305.
103. Gadamer, *Truth and Method*, 305.
104. Gadamer, *Truth and Method*, 305.

completeness."¹⁰⁵ This type of prejudice allows the person who is seeking to understand to be bonded to the subject matter, allowing for an expansion of horizon.

I now proceed to try to put all of this into the practice of interpreting the biblical text and to see why Gadamer's philosophical hermeneutic is very significant in understanding the Bible again as Scripture. In interpreting the biblical text as Scripture, Gadamer dictates that we should begin by looking into the big picture. The interpreter is to analyze the text's central motifs as a whole and begin to notice the things that spark interest and curiosity in the text. This process is where the bond to the subject matter takes place, and as readers, we can then begin to describe and articulate this bond.¹⁰⁶ While doing so, at the same time, we will need to be aware of our particularities, horizons, and worldviews that may form our prejudices. In consultation with biblical commentaries, we can then describe our projections and enter into the historical horizon of the text, noticing the alterity of that horizon as compared to our present horizon. The one thing that should immediately be noticeable to us is the tension between both horizons, something that needs to be accentuated rather than concealed.¹⁰⁷ Because we are not the only interpreters, we must also take into account how the text has been interpreted throughout history. We are one among many in the tradition of interpreters, and seeing how different interpretative traditions understand the text will yield a fuller understanding of the text. This process is what Gadamer describes as the principle of history of effect or *Wirkungsgeschichte*, a process that is not necessarily required but helps us to determine "what seems to us worth inquiring about and what will appear as an object of investigation."¹⁰⁸ From this point, our task is to articulate the meaning of the text both in its own words and in our words and to recognize that the philological, legal, and theological hermeneutics belong together and are integral in shaping understanding. Gadamer points out that "a law does not exist in order to be understood historically, but to be concretized in its legal validity by being interpreted. Similarly, the *gospel* does not exist in order

---

105. Gadamer, *Truth and Method*, 305.
106. Gadamer, *Truth and Method*, 306.
107. Gadamer, *Truth and Method*, 317.
108. Gadamer, *Truth and Method*, 311.

to be understood as a mere historical document, but to be taken in such a way that it *exercises its saving effect.*"[109]

After having done all of that, at this point, we are then ready to see which sacred realm is being revealed by the text. Gadamer says our goal in coming to an understanding is to establish an agreement with the text. Here, our task is to describe at which point we have come to an agreement, where, in these places of agreement, our intention is to make the argument of the text even stronger.[110] At this point, we can begin to fuse the horizons of the text and ours by allowing the text to address our present situation. This is done in two ways. First, we project ourselves into the world of the text, trying to see ourselves as being located within the world of the text. Second, we then go back to our world and see how the text addresses us in our own world. This oscillation happens simultaneously and continuously so that "our understanding will always retain the consciousness that we too belong to that world, and correlatively, that the work also belongs to our world."[111] The method set out by Gadamer to interpret the text of the Bible will help us to see the Bible as Scripture that becomes what it was meant to be as passed down through generations, the teaching of the apostles to which we can devote ourselves to eucharistically (Acts 2:42).

FUSION OF HORIZONS AT WORK

In this section, my goal is to show how this fusion of horizons—one that takes place between the text, the reading of other traditions, and ours—can take shape. The basic idea is that in the fusion of horizons, there is an expansion of our horizon so as to take into account the differences between the two and enrich our perspective. The intention is to come to that place of agreement Gadamer mentions in order to make the argument of the text stronger.[112] We will do that by establishing an in-between place where, through a pneumatological imagination contained in the text-community-Spirit principle that I discussed above, we can enter into the world of the text through another lens of interpretation, thus enabling us to arrive at the point of understanding that is both a reproductive and

---

109. Gadamer, *Truth and Method*, 319; emphasis added.
110. Gadamer, *Truth and Method*, 303.
111. Gadamer, *Truth and Method*, 301.
112. Gadamer, *Truth and Method*, 303.

productive activity.[113] This essentially means that we accept understanding as dialectical, meaning it is participating in a dialogical process of question and answer with the text so that, as a reader, we come to a fuller understanding of the message. Here, both the self and the other are called forward to a new understanding as we participate in the genuine dialogue. In this unfolding process, as readers, we get to experience something that has not been experienced before. As I proposed earlier, the fusion of horizons will move us to an ecumenical awareness in which horizons of reading communities are fused, creating a more extensive and expanded sense of community, allowing us to embrace the way other Christian traditions interpret the text.

That in-between place we can use to enter the world of the text is in the fact that for the church fathers, rather than being *sui generis*, the Bible is, in its own way, a tradition that came from the community of faith, created to serve an anamnetic purpose.[114] The remembering that comes from this way of looking at the text is, as we have seen earlier, more than just a linear remembrance to recall events in the past. Instead, because the remembrance is pneumatological in nature, the community of faith is also enabled to relive salvific events of the past in a way that brings its fulfillment, which the church fathers understood to be what interpretation is all about.[115] The events of Christ, beginning with his incarnation, ministry, crucifixion, ascension, and the outpouring of his Spirit, are relived and actualized in the Eucharist and, at the same time, experienced as a life-giving message that is received by the church as a community and by those individuals who welcome it with faith. Because the process of remembering is safeguarded by the activity of the Third Person of the Trinity, each community of faith, including the Pentecostal community, can become what Lubac calls a "tradition-minded" community that *lives* the tradition in their present context, being made aware of their connection to the past and future communities of faith.[116] The Holy Spirit works beyond denominational, even geographical boundaries, to ensure that believers can come to and share the unique truth that is found in the gospel tradition and live it.[117]

113. Gadamer, *Truth and Method*, 302.
114. Breck, *Scripture in Tradition*, 3.
115. Breck, *Scripture in Tradition*, 12.
116. Lubac, *Splendor of the Church*, 15.
117. Congar, *Meaning of Tradition*, 53.

Therefore, theologically speaking, the reproductive and productive activity that fuses different horizons has always been the work of the Holy Spirit, who works through the relationship of faith communities. Having and being in a relationship is, as we have seen earlier, precisely what Gadamer proposes in order for anyone to come to an understanding that is beyond what the Cartesian *cogito ergo sum* manifesto of the Enlightenment can ever achieve. This, then, allows Pentecostals to be in an embodied posture of openness towards other communities in order to accomplish a productive activity that could inform their way of looking into the Eucharist. The Holy Spirit allows Pentecostals to be hospitable to both the Roman Catholic and Eastern Orthodox Churches even though those churches are not in communion with Pentecostals. A relationship with other communities through the way they read the text about the Eucharist, guided by a pneumatological imagination, could present an opportunity to probe the interpretation of these different traditions, paying attention to their unique vernacular, in order to compare, and therefore construct, an understanding that will correlate with the SET process of Pentecostal spirituality, creating the fusion of horizons. This is precisely what participating in the ever-widening *koinōnia* of the Trinity that marks a pneumatic hermeneutic looks like; understanding is always, as Cartledge points out, an "appeal to the wider ecumenical Christian discussion and ask how different contemporary communities, presumably with differing reading traditions, approach particular issues of interpretation."[118] Because this process is always anamnetic in nature, it is then, in its own right, an SET process. With all these in mind, we are now ready to experiment with widening our understanding of community through our *koinōnia* with other reading traditions.

REREADING THE BIBLICAL TEXT

In this section, we will look at biblical texts in light of their role as Scripture being the norming norm of and in the celebration of the Eucharist (see Cartledge, that Scripture "functions normatively within the community of faith").[119] We do that by a dialectic process, which is part of the SET model. We project ourselves into the world of the text, trying to see ourselves as being located within the world of the text, and then go back

---

118. Cartledge, "Pneumatic Hermeneutic," 186–87.
119. Cartledge, "Text-Community-Spirit," 134.

to our world and see how the text addresses us in our own world. The texts that will be looked at are 1 Cor 10:14–22, 11:17–34; Matt 14:13–21, 26:26–30; Mark 14:12–26; Luke 22:14–20, 24:13–35; and John 6:11–14, 51–58. The reading strategy for this section will be to read together 1 Cor 10:14–22 and 11:17–34; and then also read together the synoptic accounts of the Lord's Supper (Matt 26:20–30, Mark 14:1–26, Luke 22:14–20); and then read together one of the miraculous feedings of the Synoptics, namely Matt 14:13–21, and the Johannine account in John 6:11–14, 51–58; and finally read the road to Emmaus account of Luke 24:13–35. As I have shown in the exposition of various Pentecostal hermeneutical methods above, Pentecostals see the biblical text as the source of guidance and teaching to live in the world. One area that has not been explored much by Pentecostals is how the text of Scripture guides the worship life of the Pentecostal community in a eucharistic way. This is where the possibility of listening to how other traditions have heard and used the text normatively to guide the worship life of the church would be beneficial to the development of the Pentecostal theology of the Eucharist—in itself, a process of SET.

As we have seen above, the Eastern Orthodox Church considers the purpose of the biblical text primarily as informing their liturgical life. For the Eastern Orthodox Church, Scripture and tradition are inseparable because Scripture *is* tradition in the sense that it was birthed in and came out of the community of believers and became the norming norm. It is in this norming norm sense that Scripture becomes the living word as it is alive in the liturgical worship of the church. For example, the eucharistic prayer of St. Basil, which is still used by the Orthodox Church during the Great Lent, is a prayer that is filled with numerous direct quotations and allusions to the text of Scripture.[120] A plausible reason for this, which I will show below, is because the entire New Testament is by nature closely related to the Eucharist, and its origin is eucharistic, to begin with. When Basil and other church fathers wrote their prayers, they were not in a sense prooftexting the Scriptures; rather, they were recomposing the eucharistic materials in which they were steeped to make new ones. As Orthodox scholar Dennis Farkasfalvy maintains, "Historians and scripture scholars have repeatedly recognized the texts in which the New Testament consists have been both historically and logically preceded by, prepared for,

---

120. Lash, "Prayers of the Liturgy."

and based upon the Eucharist."[121] In what follows, the reading of the New Testament text I will provide does not follow the more standard methods that will be limited to an analysis of the Synoptic Gospels and First Corinthians words of institution, followed by an examination of the bread of life discourse, and the resurrection account in Luke and John, and so on. Instead, what I will attempt to do in looking at these texts is to project ourselves into the world of the text and to see ourselves being located within the world of the text (see Gadamer), a world that shows that the origin of the New Testament is organically birthed out of a eucharistic practice.

Reading Paul in First Corinthians 10:14–22, 11:17–34

The earliest of the letters of Paul that we have in the New Testament were written as early as twenty to twenty-five years after Jesus's death and resurrection, and they were written with diverse purposes and on diverse occasions. Nearly all scholars agree that First Corinthians is one of Paul's seven letters that are considered authentic.[122] In this subsection, we will look at 1 Cor 10:14–22 and 11:17–34 together rather than separately, as my purpose in discussing the text here is to show the plausibility that First Corinthians, like the rest of the New Testament, has a eucharistic origin. One of the ways this is plausible is seen directly in 11:1–16, the text between 10:14–22 and 11:17–34, that Raymond Brown argues, which, I agree, provides the Corinthian community with some kind of guidance for their "liturgical behavior."[123] With the existence of other liturgical elements, whether in the form of blessings in these two sections of First Corinthians or other forms such as greetings, prayers, and fragments of hymns, which are found in other parts of the letter, it is plausible to deduce that these things are signs that this letter (and other Pauline letters as well) were supposed to be read in the gathering of the communities related to the celebration of the Eucharist. Farkasfalvy argues that reading Paul's letters in the context of the Eucharist is warranted.[124] We begin now by looking into 10:14–22:

---

121. Farkasfalvy, "Eucharistic Provenance," 28.
122. Johnson, *Writings of the New Testament*, 271.
123. Brown, *Introduction to the New Testament*, 522.
124. Farkasfalvy, "Eucharistic Provenance," 28.

14 Therefore, my dear friends, flee from the worship of idols. 15 I speak as to sensible people; judge for yourselves what I say. 16 The cup of blessing that we bless, is it not a sharing in the blood of Christ? The bread that we break, is it not a sharing in the body of Christ? 17 Because there is one bread, we who are many are one body, for we all partake of the one bread. 18 Consider the people of Israel; are not those who eat the sacrifices partners in the altar? 19 What do I imply then? That food sacrificed to idols is anything, or that an idol is anything? 20 No, I imply that what pagans sacrifice, they sacrifice to demons and not to God. I do not want you to be partners with demons. 21 You cannot drink the cup of the Lord and the cup of demons. You cannot partake of the table of the Lord and the table of demons. 22 Or are we provoking the Lord to jealousy? Are we stronger than he?

In 10:14–22 Paul continues his reflection on the Exodus experience of Israel, which is very much on his mind since 10:2. Paul argues that baptism and the eucharistic cup of blessing are a sharing (*koinōnia*) in the blood of Christ, while the breaking of bread is a sharing (*koinōnia*) in the body of Christ (10:16). What Paul wrote can be said to have furnished the church with insights into the subsequent understanding of sacramental theology, as it is evident that Paul demonstrates to them God's deliverance through baptism and sustenance through the Eucharist, although at the same time makes clear that these things neither inoculate from sin those who participate and receive nor exempt them from divine judgment. Because the partakers, who are many, are, at the same time, one body, participation in the Eucharist cannot exist alongside involvement in pagan sacrifices being offered to demons, which make them partner with demons. A person belonging to Christ cannot participate in the table of the Lord and still participate in the table of demons. It is crucial to notice that the cup-bread sequence here is different from the bread-cup sequence we see later in 11:23–26. The cup-bread sequence in 10:16 is also found in the Didache 9:2–4, whose language and motif of blessing, breaking the bread, and the unity of the community are also similar to our text.[125] The eucharistic cup is an *anamnēsis* of the cup that Jesus himself drank, the cup that Paul proclaims, "For as often as you . . . drink the cup, you proclaim the Lord's death until he comes" (11:25–26; cf. Matt 26:27, Mark 14:23, Luke 22:17, 20), and it is a cup in which the community receives and experiences God's blessing. As for the breaking

---

125. Milavec, *Didache*, 23.

of the bread ritual, the early Christian practice retains the Jewish ritual of breaking bread, in which the male house leader will say a blessing, break the bread, and distribute it to those at the table who receive it as a "symbolic mediation of the blessing."[126] We will go back to the significance of the *anamnēsis* again in my discussion of 11:17–34 below.

> 17 Now in the following instructions I do not commend you, because when you come together it is not for the better but for the worse. 18 For, to begin with, when you come together as a church, I hear that there are divisions among you; and to some extent I believe it. 19 Indeed, there have to be factions among you, for only so will it become clear who among you are genuine. 20 When you come together, it is not really to eat the Lord's supper. 21 For when the time comes to eat, each of you goes ahead with your own supper, and one goes hungry and another becomes drunk. 22 What! Do you not have homes to eat and drink in? Or do you show contempt for the church of God and humiliate those who have nothing? What should I say to you? Should I commend you? In this matter I do not commend you! 23 For I received from the Lord what I also handed on to you, that the Lord Jesus on the night when he was betrayed took a loaf of bread, 24 and when he had given thanks, he broke it and said, "This is my body that is for you. Do this in remembrance of me." 25 In the same way he took the cup also, after supper, saying, "This cup is the new covenant in my blood. Do this, as often as you drink it, in remembrance of me." 26 For as often as you eat this bread and drink the cup, you proclaim the Lord's death until he comes. 27 Whoever, therefore, eats the bread or drinks the cup of the Lord in an unworthy manner will be answerable for the body and blood of the Lord. 28 Examine yourselves, and only then eat of the bread and drink of the cup. 29 For all who eat and drink without discerning the body, eat and drink judgment against themselves. 30 For this reason many of you are weak and ill, and some have died. 31 But if we judged ourselves, we would not be judged. 32 But when we are judged by the Lord, we are disciplined so that we may not be condemned along with the world. 33 So then, my brothers and sisters, when you come together to eat, wait for one another. 34 If you are hungry, eat at home, so that when you come together, it will not be for your condemnation. About the other things I will give instructions when I come.

---

126. Collins, *First Corinthians*, 376.

In 11:17-34, immediately following the liturgical guidelines he gives in 11:1-16, Paul goes back to the topic of the Eucharist and the love meal (cf. Jude 12) in which it was set. Paul expresses his disapproval of the Corinthian behavior because those divisions that we see in chs. 1-4 are being carried over to "the Lord's Supper" (κυριακὸν δεῖπνον). When the Corinthians meet together as a church (11:18) to reenact a remembrance (*anamnēsis*) of what Jesus did and said on the night he was given over (11:20, 23-26), there are those, presumably the wealthy members, who have a meal that precedes the eucharistic celebration. In contrast, "those who have nothing" (v. 22) are excluded and go without food. This situation may perhaps have come as a result of the church gathering requiring a large space that could take place only in the home of a wealthy person. While all Christians, including the poor and slaves, are accepted for the Eucharist into the hospitality area of the house, it is plausible that the owner was inviting only his well-off friends of status to enjoy the first meal at his table. Collins points out that these wealthy guests,

> presumably those served by slaves, could join the host in the triclinium (the dining room proper). Latecomers would be relegated to the hall (*atrium*) or the courtyard (*peristylum*). The physical location of the latecomers attested to their social location within the community and underscored the social division that rent the community at Corinth.[127]

Certainly, this is not what Paul had in mind when he was talking about the church of God (11:22; cf. Gal. 3:28); all should be welcome to come and eat the meal together. If not, they should eat first in their own homes (11:33-34). The purpose of the celebration of the breaking of bread in the Lord's Supper is *koinōnia* (10:16), not to turn it into another divisive issue in the community.

Paul cites an early Christian tradition, an account that predates his letter, and reminds them of what he had previously shared with them (11:23-26), emphasized by using the postpositive *gar* to explain what he means by the Lord's Supper and why what the Corinthians are doing is not the Lord's Supper (11:20). It is important to note that this tradition informing Paul, especially concerning the proclamation of the Lord's death until he comes, echoes an exclamation found in the eucharistic liturgy: *Maranatha!*[128] His purpose is not to teach them something new; in-

---

127. Collins, *First Corinthians*, 418-19.
128. Wainwright, *Eucharist and Eschatology*, 75.

stead, he recalls them to a eucharistic tradition that he has already taught them but that has lost its significance in the Corinthian community, as demonstrated by their behavior.[129] The *anamnēsis* or remembrance came from Jewish roots, that in the Jewish remembering, "prior salvific events [become] foundational for salvation in the present and enables [sic] those who participate in a cultic activity to share in the effects of the salvific events that are remembered."[130]

Paul's letters were set in a Greco-Roman culture that appreciates and has already developed a robust art of writing letters. One of the primary purposes of First Corinthians was pastoral, in a sense in which, through this letter, Paul is intent on correcting their problematic behaviors, including their practice of the Eucharist, while the letter is being read in their eucharistic gathering.[131] Reading the text in such a way will enable us to see that the church is not just a community of believers with their "variety of states of minds and self-expressions"; instead, the church is a eucharistic community that expresses their faith in the Lord through a sacramental act of coming to him while always in the posture of waiting for his return.[132] Hence, reading the text eucharistically will always bring the church into an eschatological dimension.

The Gospels

The reading strategy for this section will be to read together the synoptic accounts of the Lord's Supper (Matt 26:20–30, Mark 14:1–26, Luke 22:14–20), and then to read together one of the miraculous feedings of the Synoptics, namely Matt 14:13–21, and the Johannine account in John 6:11–14, 51–58. Finally, the post-resurrection account on the road to Emmaus in Luke 24:13–35 will also be discussed. I reiterate that I do this because the purpose of this reading is to accentuate the eucharistic hints we get in these texts. The gospels were written and redacted to fulfill a specific purpose within a particular situation that arose in the communities of the early church.[133] As I mentioned earlier, one of those purposes

---

129. Collins, *First Corinthians*, 426.
130. Collins, *First Corinthians*, 428.
131. Johnson, *Writings of the New Testament*, 268.
132. Farkasfalvy, "Eucharistic Provenance," 45.
133. Moloney, "John 6," 244.

was liturgical, specifically in relation to the community's celebration of the Eucharist.

The Lord's Supper in the Synoptics

Matthew 26:20–30

20 When it was evening, he took his place with the twelve; 21 and while they were eating, he said, "Truly I tell you, one of you will betray me." 22 And they became greatly distressed and began to say to him one after another, "Surely not I, Lord?" 23 He answered, "The one who has dipped his hand into the bowl with me will betray me. 24 The Son of Man goes as it is written of him, but woe to that one by whom the Son of Man is betrayed! It would have been better for that one not to have been born." 25 Judas, who betrayed him, said, "Surely not I, Rabbi?" He replied, "You have said so."

26 While they were eating, Jesus took a loaf of bread, and after blessing it he broke it, gave it to the disciples, and said, "Take, eat; this is my body." 27 Then he took a cup, and after giving thanks he gave it to them, saying, "Drink from it, all of you; 28 for this is my blood of the covenant, which is poured out for many for the forgiveness of sins. 29 I tell you, I will never again drink of this fruit of the vine until that day when I drink it new with you in my Father's kingdom." 30 When they had sung the hymn, they went out to the Mount of Olives.

Mark 14:17–26

17 When it was evening, he came with the twelve. 18 And when they had taken their places and were eating, Jesus said, "Truly I tell you, one of you will betray me, one who is eating with me." 19 They began to be distressed and to say to him one after another, "Surely, not I?" 20 He said to them, "It is one of the twelve, one who is dipping bread into the bowl with me. 21 For the Son of Man goes as it is written of him, but woe to that one by whom the Son of Man is betrayed! It would have been better for that one not to have been born." 22 While they were eating, he took a loaf of bread, and after blessing it he broke it, gave it to them, and said, "Take; this is my body." 23 Then he took a cup, and after giving thanks he gave it to them, and all of them drank from it. 24 He said to them, "This is my blood of the covenant, which is poured out for many. 25 Truly I tell you, I will never

again drink of the fruit of the vine until that day when I drink it new in the kingdom of God." 26 When they had sung the hymn, they went out to the Mount of Olives.

Luke 22:14–20

14 When the hour came, he took his place at the table, and the apostles with him. 15 He said to them, "I have eagerly desired to eat this Passover with you before I suffer; 16 for I tell you, I will not eat it until it is fulfilled in the kingdom of God." 17 Then he took a cup, and after giving thanks he said, "Take this and divide it among yourselves; 18 for I tell you that from now on I will not drink of the fruit of the vine until the kingdom of God comes." 19 Then he took a loaf of bread, and when he had given thanks, he broke it and gave it to them, saying, "This is my body, which is given for you. Do this in remembrance of me." 20 And he did the same with the cup after supper, saying, "This cup that is poured out for you is the new covenant in my blood. 21 But see, the one who betrays me is with me, and his hand is on the table. 22 For the Son of Man is going as it has been determined, but woe to that one by whom he is betrayed!" 23 Then they began to ask one another which one of them it could be who would do this.

What we have here are the three synoptic accounts of the Last Supper of Matthew, Mark, and Luke. The focus of my discussion in looking at these texts is not to do a verse-by-verse exegesis, as that process does not serve the purpose of this discussion. Instead, the focus of looking at these texts will be to point out the theological presentation contained in them. Such a reading, I contend, will reinforce locating the Pentecostal understanding of the Eucharist within an SET framework. Eastern Orthodox New Testament scholar Theodore G. Stylianopoulus argues that biblical hermeneutics contains three differentiated yet interconnected levels, namely, exegetical, interpretive/evaluative, and transformative.[134] According to Stylianopoulus, the transformative level is "the level of the direct experience of God . . . is most profound [and where] . . . the actualization of [the] deepest value of Scripture" takes place.[135] In this discussion, it is the transformative level, a level that shows the possibility

---

134. Stylianopoulus, *Scripture, Tradition, Hermeneutics*, 188.
135. Stylianopoulus, *Scripture, Tradition, Hermeneutics*, 216–17.

of a person encountering the living Word himself and, as a result, being changed by that encounter, with which I am most concerned.

Through the words of institution found in these texts, the gospel writers seek to present a theological overture connecting the meal with the passion, making it eucharistic.[136] In the Last Supper narrative of the Synoptics, Jesus gives the disciples a command to take the bread as "my body," at the same time instituting the Eucharist. Just as Paul's letters have a eucharistic origin, as already discussed above, the tradition behind the Synoptics also came from a "eucharistic cradle" of early Christian worship practice where, through the liturgical practices, the experience the disciples had with Jesus is being reenacted and relived.[137] Jesus's act of institution, therefore, is the culmination of all eucharistic overtones found throughout the gospel narrative in the way the gospel writers redacted the flow of the narrative.[138] As we will see shortly in the next section, this is especially spelled out in the miraculous feeding narratives. For now, I want to point out that these miraculous feeding narratives found in the Synoptics and John that present Jesus looking up to heaven, giving thanks, breaking the bread, and distributing them can only be explained as eucharistic.[139] The institution, connecting the meal Jesus shares with his disciples to the passion, functions as a reiteration that Jesus is the new Moses, whose body is the bread of life that is able, unlike manna during Moses's time, to give eternal life to those who receive it in faith.[140] In Jesus, the Passover takes on a new meaning as disciples are marked by the blood of the new covenant. In the institution, whose words are repeated by those who preside—which in my view is irrespective of church tradition—Jesus makes himself sacrificially present in and through the Spirit, not to repeat the once and for all sacrifice but to draw disciples, making them participants in his suffering and, ultimately, his victory. As O'Connor puts it,

> The Last Supper and Calvary and the Mass are all the same sacrifice, not because the historical acts of the past are repeated or

---

136. Farkasfalvy, "Eucharistic Provenance," 29.
137. Farkasfalvy, "Eucharistic Provenance," 34–35.
138. Farkasfalvy, "Eucharistic Provenance," 35.
139. Farkasfalvy, "Eucharistic Provenance," 30–31.
140. Morse, "Presence of Christ," 136.

re-presented but because of the intrinsic unity that all these actions, past and present, possess in the one Priest and Victim.[141]

That is what the early church did from the beginning, as they liturgically repeated the stories of Jesus in their assemblies after Pentecost. It is in the repeating of the words of institution in their eucharistic gathering that the early church encountered the Lord, who institutes the meal himself. Read in this way, the value of the written word is actualized in the deepest and most profound sense. The community becomes receptive to the work of the Holy Spirit, who makes the written word have that transformative power where two or three gather in the name of Jesus; he is present in the life of the community, bringing them into the eschatological reality of the Eucharist. We now proceed to look into the gospel accounts of the feeding miracle.

The Feeding Miracle of Matthew 14:13–21 and John 6:11–14, 51–58

Matthew 14:13–21

> 13 Now when Jesus heard this, he withdrew from there in a boat to a deserted place by himself. But when the crowds heard it, they followed him on foot from the towns. 14 When he went ashore, he saw a great crowd; and he had compassion for them and cured their sick. 15 When it was evening, the disciples came to him and said, "This is a deserted place, and the hour is now late; send the crowds away so that they may go into the villages and buy food for themselves." 16 Jesus said to them, "They need not go away; you give them something to eat." 17 They replied, "We have nothing here but five loaves and two fish." 18 And he said, "Bring them here to me." 19 Then he ordered the crowds to sit down on the grass. Taking the five loaves and the two fish, he looked up to heaven, and blessed and broke the loaves, and gave them to the disciples, and the disciples gave them to the crowds. 20 And all ate and were filled; and they took up what was left over of the broken pieces, twelve baskets full. 21 And those who ate were about five thousand men, besides women and children.

John 6:11–14, 51–58

> After this Jesus went to the other side of the Sea of Galilee, also called the Sea of Tiberias. 2 A large crowd kept

---

141. O'Connor, *Hidden Manna*, 309.

following him, because they saw the signs that he was doing for the sick. 3 Jesus went up the mountain and sat down there with his disciples. 4 Now the Passover, the festival of the Jews, was near. 5 When he looked up and saw a large crowd coming toward him, Jesus said to Philip, "Where are we to buy bread for these people to eat?" 6 He said this to test him, for he himself knew what he was going to do. 7 Philip answered him, "Six months' wages would not buy enough bread for each of them to get a little." 8 One of his disciples, Andrew, Simon Peter's brother, said to him, 9 "There is a boy here who has five barley loaves and two fish. But what are they among so many people?" 10 Jesus said, "Make the people sit down." Now there was a great deal of grass in the place; so they sat down, about five thousand in all. 11 Then Jesus took the loaves, and when he had given thanks, he distributed them to those who were seated; so also the fish, as much as they wanted. 12 When they were satisfied, he told his disciples, "Gather up the fragments left over, so that nothing may be lost." 13 So they gathered them up, and from the fragments of the five barley loaves, left by those who had eaten, they filled twelve baskets. 14 When the people saw the sign that he had done, they began to say, "This is indeed the prophet who is to come into the world."

51 I am the living bread that came down from heaven. Whoever eats of this bread will live forever; and the bread that I will give for the life of the world is my flesh." 52 The Jews then disputed among themselves, saying, "How can this man give us his flesh to eat?" 53 So Jesus said to them, "Very truly, I tell you, unless you eat the flesh of the Son of Man and drink his blood, you have no life in you. 54 Those who eat my flesh and drink my blood have eternal life, and I will raise them up on the last day; 55 for my flesh is true food and my blood is true drink. 56 Those who eat my flesh and drink my blood abide in me, and I in them. 57 Just as the living Father sent me, and I live because of the Father, so whoever eats me will live because of me. 58 This is the bread that came down from heaven, not like that which your ancestors ate, and they died. But the one who eats this bread will live forever."

The feeding miracle is the only miracle in the ministry of Jesus that appears in all four canonical gospels. In his commentary on the Gospel of Matthew, Reformed New Testament scholar Frederick Dale Bruner argues that the reason for this is to show that Jesus is the answer to all human needs, physical as well as spiritual; thus, he is not "impotent before the great social problem hunger."¹⁴² Jesus cares for the hungry by doing something tangible about it: he feeds the hungry. Not going as far as saying that the text is eucharistic in provenance, Bruner does admit that the text echoes the Eucharist and concludes that the gospel writers want to point out to the readers that the Eucharist is the primary way Jesus feeds his church to prepare her for the work of feeding the world.¹⁴³

The Matthean text we have here immediately follows the narrative of John the Baptist's beheading, which took place also around a meal. That meal was held in Herod's palace, attended by his cronies. This meal took place in a deserted place attended by a hungry crowd. Although not explicitly spelled out in the Matthean text, the feeding here not only satisfies the hunger of the crowd but also anticipates the spiritual nourishment that Jesus himself provides as the bread of life through his sacrifice on the cross—a notion more pronounced in John 6 and the Lord's Supper accounts. The miraculous feeding in Matthew points to and anticipates the Lord's Supper, which is the first time the Eucharist is instituted (by Christ himself) and celebrated, a culminating act of Jesus feeding the disciples that will be celebrated continually in order for Jesus to nourish believers across space and time.¹⁴⁴

It is important to reiterate what I have previously stated above: that the gospel narratives were constructed and organized eucharistically in order for the assemblies gathered to be able to relive and reenact their experience with the risen Christ.¹⁴⁵ One of the ways in which the gospel writers or redactors shaped and formed the narratives was to follow the traditional style of midrashic preaching. This is what we see in the feeding narratives. In the case of the Synoptics, which altogether tell the story six times, Farkasfalvy argues that the stories where Jesus is presented to be looking up to heaven, giving thanks, breaking the bread, and distributing them can only be explained as eucharistic because they contain "christological and ecclesiological reality which constitutes the core of the Christian faith."¹⁴⁶ In the case of John 6, Moloney argues that the way the narrative is constructed follows the tradition known as homiletic midrash, in which a sermon is formed by quoting an Old Testament

---

142. Bruner, *Churchbook*, 66.
143. Bruner, *Churchbook*, 70.
144. Lewis, "Feeding of the Multitudes," 11–12.
145. Farkasfalvy, "Eucharistic Provenance," 34–35.
146. Farkasfalvy, "Eucharistic Provenance," 30–31.

text, which afterward gets paraphrased and retold to make a point, often done with bringing other texts to help with making the point.[147] For Moloney, the proof of a eucharistic celebration in the Johannine community is found in the feeding miracle of the Johannine text. Although John is not primarily concerned about spelling out the presence of Jesus in the Eucharist because that notion is already taken for granted, the midrashic context in which the text came about is immediately brought in relation to the eucharistic celebration.[148] The whole point of doing so, for John, is to construct a theology of salvation by means of liturgically recalling and commemorating the event of the crucifixion.[149] For John, salvation and eternal life come from believing in Jesus, and the Eucharist functions to emphasize to the community "that you may believe that Jesus is the Christ, the Son of God, and that believing you may have life in his name."[150]

The Road to Emmaus of Luke 24:13–35

Luke 24:13–35

13 Now on that same day two of them were going to a village called Emmaus, about seven miles from Jerusalem, 14 and talking with each other about all these things that had happened. 15 While they were talking and discussing, Jesus himself came near and went with them, 16 but their eyes were kept from recognizing him. 17 And he said to them, "What are you discussing with each other while you walk along?" They stood still, looking sad. 18 Then one of them, whose name was Cleopas, answered him, "Are you the only stranger in Jerusalem who does not know the things that have taken place there in these days?" 19 He asked them, "What things?" They replied, "The things about Jesus of Nazareth, who was a prophet mighty in deed and word before God and all the people, 20 and how our chief priests and leaders handed him over to be condemned to death and crucified him. 21 But we had hoped that he was the one to redeem Israel. Yes, and besides all this, it is now the third day since these things took place. 22 Moreover, some women of our group astounded us. They were at the tomb early this morning, 23 and when they

---

147. Moloney, "John 6," 244–45.
148. Moloney, "John 6," 249.
149. Moloney, "John 6," 249–50.
150. Moloney, "John 6," 251.

did not find his body there, they came back and told us that they had indeed seen a vision of angels who said that he was alive. 24 Some of those who were with us went to the tomb and found it just as the women had said; but they did not see him." 25 Then he said to them, "Oh, how foolish you are, and how slow of heart to believe all that the prophets have declared! 26 Was it not necessary that the Messiah should suffer these things and then enter into his glory?" 27 Then beginning with Moses and all the prophets, he interpreted to them the things about himself in all the scriptures. 28 As they came near the village to which they were going, he walked ahead as if he were going on. 29 But they urged him strongly, saying, "Stay with us, because it is almost evening and the day is now nearly over." So he went in to stay with them. 30 When he was at the table with them, he took bread, blessed and broke it, and gave it to them. 31 Then their eyes were opened, and they recognized him; and he vanished from their sight. 32 They said to each other, "Were not our hearts burning within us while he was talking to us on the road, while he was opening the scriptures to us?" 33 That same hour they got up and returned to Jerusalem; and they found the eleven and their companions gathered together. 34 They were saying, "The Lord has risen indeed, and he has appeared to Simon!" 35 Then they told what had happened on the road, and how he had been made known to them in the breaking of the bread.

Continuing the previous understanding that the gospels are shaped and formed within the eucharistic tradition of the early church, I will attempt to provide a reading of this text with the understanding that the narrative informs the early church's eucharistic celebration. This way of approaching the text is due to the fact that the gospels demand a "deeply subjective" understanding that requires intimacy with the subject at hand (that is, Jesus) as opposed to an understanding that is detached and distant.[151]

What we have in the above text is one of the best-known stories of the gospel—a story that begins with the disciples downcast and ends with them not only having their hearts burning after listening to Jesus open the Scriptures to them but also recognizing Jesus, who is the subject of the Scriptures. The story shows the disciples moving from a knowledge that is objective and distant to subjective and intimate and a trajectory that has become a model for the readers of the text. It is this sort of

---

151. Johnson, "Eucharist and the Identity," 230.

knowledge that makes the possibility of learning from the text limitless. Johnson puts it correctly by saying,

> The faithful reading of the Gospel does not ask, "What really happened?" but asks instead, "Who is this who speaks and acts now in my life? How can I learn from him in my present from this witness and interpretation of his past as read by those who first experienced him also as present to them after his death?"[152]

The focus of this reading, therefore, is in v. 31, where Jesus is recognized, because it is in recognizing Jesus that our limitless learning takes place. The verb that Luke uses, ἐπιγινώσκω, literally means "to come to a recognition," and we can, therefore, understand this story as a story about learning to recognize the risen Jesus. Johnson argues that the way Jesus is recognized in this story is when the disciples, who were participants in the events of Jesus's passion, through divine action coupled with the physical act of breaking, blessing, and sharing of the bread, come to remember (*anamnēsis*) him.[153] Taking our cues from Luke, Johnson argues that we also remember Jesus in a way that we come to a recognition of Jesus through the physical gestures of sharing his table. The Eucharist becomes, for us, just like for the disciples, a place in which we remember Jesus, an act in which he reveals his identity to the church.[154] In the Eucharist, the identity that Jesus himself explains to the disciples on his journey with them to Emmaus, the same identity contained in the early hymn that Paul incorporates into his exhortation to the Philippians (2:5–11), is recognized not just by our mind, which is the location of the exegetical and the interpretive level, but by our heart, the location of the transformative level, resulting in inner reception (their eyes were opened, they recognized him, and their hearts burning [vv. 31–32]), which leads to action (proclamation of the risen Lord [vv. 34–35]).

CONCLUSION

Pentecostals are known to be people whose passion is to become a Spirit-filled community like the one we see shaped by the coming of the Holy Spirit on the day of Pentecost described in Acts 2. This is with good reason. John Stott comments that through the narrative we see in Acts 2,

152. Johnson, "Eucharist and the Identity," 230.
153. Johnson, "Eucharist and the Identity," 231.
154. Johnson, "Eucharist and the Identity," 234.

"Luke goes on to show us the effects of Pentecost by giving us a beautiful little cameo of the Spirit-filled church."[155] I want to conclude this chapter by briefly looking at what Luke describes in what Stott calls "cameo." The purpose is to reiterate the possibility of, and the importance of, looking at the text of Scripture eucharistically for Pentecostals because therein is a process of search and encounter that will bring about transformation in the community.

If we pay close attention to the text, the Spirit-filled community Luke describes here, especially in v. 42, is said to be devoted to four specific things, namely and literally, *the* teaching of the apostles, *the* fellowship, *the* breaking of bread, and *the* prayers. Together these four things are none other than a process of search and encounter taking place, and the result is a community experiencing transformation. Let us look at how a process of SET is taking place in the community Luke describes.

The word translated "devoted" (προσκαρτερέω) contains in it an idea of devotion that is embodied rather than abstract. According to BDAG, the word contains nuances of sticking by, being close at hand, being attached to, waiting on someone faithfully like a soldier to his commander, and persisting by busying oneself with the object of one's devotion.[156] In the text, all of these four things to which the disciples devoted themselves are preceded by a definitive article, suggesting that they are a specific and particular kind of Spirit-animated devotion. This is relatively easy to pick up in the case of *the* teaching; it is specifically *the* apostles' teaching in which they persist by busying themselves with it. Regarding the fellowship, the definite article suggests that it is not just any fellowship, but most importantly, it is *the* fellowship (*koinōnia*) that is Trinitarian in experience.[157] The Holy Spirit who was poured out at Pentecost is the embodiment of the fellowship of the Father and the Son, and the Holy Spirit brings the disciples into that *koinōnia* ("We declare to you what we have seen and heard so that you also may have fellowship with us; and truly our fellowship is with the Father and with his Son Jesus Christ" [1 John 1:3]). The breaking of bread and the prayers is not to suggest that it is just a gathering in which the disciples share a meal together and offer Spirit-led prayers for their needs. Instead, the definite article indicates that the breaking of bread is specific. Namely, they are sticking together

---

155. Stott, *Message of Acts*, 81.
156. BADG 881.
157. Stott, *Message of Acts*, 83.

by busying themselves celebrating *the* Eucharist, and the prayers are that which have been used liturgically by the disciples, namely *the* Psalms, but now understood in a new way that is made possible by the Spirit of truth.[158] We are then shown the fruit of a devoted Spirit-filled community that has eucharistically encountered the risen Jesus through their search for him in their devotions.

Luke tells his readers that a transformation took place. There were miracles (signs and wonders) in the community. These miracles were deeds of Jesus that Luke tells in his gospel, deeds that include reconciliation, healing, and freeing people from captivity. All these miracles brought awe (*phobos*), which is appropriately understood as the fear of the Lord (v. 43). The fellowship they have in and with the Triune God enables the disciples to practice social justice by having "all things in common [*koinós*]" (v. 44). Eating together is a show of unconditional acceptance in many cultures, especially in the Middle East.[159] There is acceptance and inclusivity exhibited by this community as they eat together with "glad and generous hearts" (v. 46). Finally, the outcome of this Spirit-filled community is the work of evangelism where "day by day the Lord added to their number those who were being saved" (v. 47).

In this chapter, I have argued that the "pneumatological imagination" that comes from the freedom afforded by the Third Person of the Trinity (2 Cor 3:17) allows me to arrive at the point of understanding that, according to Gadamer, is a *productive* and *reproductive* activity.[160] I have also shown that inherent in the Pentecostal text-community-Spirit hermeneutical principle is a certain "fluidity" in the definition of the community of interpreters that provides enough elasticity to allow the accommodation of other reading traditions. This accommodation, I argued, is not a compromise to the Pentecostal spirit or principle. Instead, as I have pointed out, it is precisely what participation in the ever-widening *koinōnia* of the Trinity that marks a pneumatic hermeneutic looks like.[161] The result of this *koinōnia* is a fusion of horizons with other reading traditions. We saw in these reading traditions an understanding of tradition that makes the Scripture embodied, as the text is not *sui generis* but something that is materialized from the worshipping community and

---

158. Stott, *Message of Acts*, 85.

159. See the commentary on the story of Zacchaeus encountering Jesus (Bailey, *Jesus through Middle Eastern Eyes*, 180).

160. Gadamer, *Truth and Method*, 307.

161. Cartledge, "Pneumatic Hermeneutic," 186–87.

becomes the revelatory norming norm for the life of the community. The reason for this, as I have presented, is because tradition is understood to be living in the sense that it is the life of the Holy Spirit working in the community of believers, which is the church. It makes sense then for Pentecostals to consider how other traditions have understood the eucharistic provenance of text and to read it eucharistically as well because the purpose of the text and the act of reading it—a process of "search"—is remembrance or *anamnēsis*, which is a process of "encounter." Having presented that, we are now ready to proceed to the next chapter to talk about what exactly are the transformations brought about by the Eucharist that can really strengthen Pentecostals in their passion for becoming a Spirit-filled community. I now proceed to present my main proposal in the next chapter, which is to construct a renewal theology of the Eucharist.

5

A Renewal Theology of the Eucharist

I remain convinced that it is possible to revision and reform the Pentecostal worship around the Eucharist event in such a way that the believing community becomes more and more apt for Christ's transformative presence in the Spirit. —Chris E. W. Green[1]

If there is a sense in which the Spirit is especially present in the eucharist, could it not become the focal point of Pentecostal worship? —Simon Chan[2]

INTRODUCTION

This chapter presents the main task I wish to accomplish, namely, to develop a *renewal theology of the Eucharist*. What makes this theology "renewal" is the pneumatological lens within an implicit Trinitarian framework that I will use to construct the theology. By implicit, what I mean is that I will not go into an exposition of Trinitarian theology in constructing my argument. However, I believe that throughout my presentation, the readers will notice enough "signposts" showing the pneumatological hand of the Trinity is at work complementing the christological hand. Through a pneumatological lens, I maintain that there is an internal logic

---

1. Green, *Toward a Pentecostal Theology*, 317.
2. Chan, *Pentecostal Theology*, 108.

of SET in the Eucharist that informs the spirituality of Pentecostalism in a way that mediates the *via salutis*. This renewal theology is essentially *a* Pentecostal theology for the reason that I am a Pentecostal theologian, even if what I am developing here does not necessarily represent what other Pentecostals see as Pentecostal theology or what they see in the Eucharist. That should not be an issue, especially considering its many different expressions, such that the Pentecostal tradition has never been known as monolithic but instead as pluralistic.[3] Therefore, this theology seeks to make a distinct theological contribution to the ongoing conversation, with the intention that Pentecostals will continue to develop a greater appreciation for the meal Jesus gave to his church. Although this contribution will have some continuity with classic Pentecostal theology, it will, in many places, present findings that will be in discontinuity with it, as my goal is to push the boundary line of knowledge.

The proverbial saying "You are what you eat" suggests the notion that to be fit and healthy, a person needs to eat good and nutritious food. In the same way, the church, as the body of Christ, can be healthy and fit only when she feeds on him, the Bread of Life, who promises that those who come to him will never go hungry but be satisfied (John 6:35). In the previous chapter, by looking at the cameo given by Luke in Acts 2 of what the Spirit-filled church looks like, specifically v. 42, we saw that the mark of this Spirit-filled church consists of devotion to four specific things, namely, *the* teaching of the apostles, *the* fellowship, *the* breaking of bread, and *the* prayers.[4] In that chapter, I argued that these four things together are a process of search and encounter taking place, resulting in a community experiencing transformation. As a result, the Spirit's presence and work are manifested in the community through the communal life of the church, which points to the awaited eschatological reality, in which the event of Pentecost is an event that inaugurates the church as Christ's image and body in the world.[5] As the image and body of Christ, the church then becomes what Maximus the Confessor says, "the representation and image of God[,] because she possesses the same activity as his according to imitation and representation."[6] The Spirit-filled church is to represent the activity of God in the world, bringing justice, liberation, healing, and

---

3. As suggested by Anderson, it is better to define this tradition using the plural form, that is *Pentecostalism/s* ("Varieties, Taxonomies, and Definitions," 13).

4. Stott, *Message of Acts*, 81.

5. Augustine, *Pentecost, Hospitality, and Transfiguration*, 29.

6. Maximus the Confessor, *On the Ecclesiastical Mystagogy*, 51.

freedom from oppression just like her Lord during his earthly ministry (Luke 4:18-19). The idea is that the coming of the Spirit made the church ontologically able to participate in the life-giving death and resurrection of Jesus. At the same time, that ontological ability can be shown only if the church lives out that participation. Thus, living out that participation is a requirement that makes the church *the church*. This participation, made possible by the Spirit, which will inevitably include suffering and persecution, is indicative of the fellowship the church has with the Father and the Son (1 John 1:3). As Daniela Augustine puts it,

> Therefore, through the Christoforming work of the Spirit, the Church becomes also an extension of the *koinōnia* of the Trinity in-fleshed in the redeemed human community. As the teleological creation of the Triune God, the Church exhibits the synergistic work of Christ (the eternal, incarnated Word) and the Spirit according to the will of the Father. Therefore, the work (*leitourgia*) of the Body of Christ is the work of God on earth.[7]

Enlivened by the Holy Spirit, the *one, holy, catholic,* and *apostolic* church, in her mystical union with her Lord, becomes the body of Christ, the embodied agent of God's welcome of all cosmos into his Triune *koinōnia* and love.[8] Yet the church has some ways to go before she will be an answer to the Lord's prayer that they may be one. The meal that Christ himself has given to the church as a gift to feed her with himself has, throughout history, been the issue by which the church has been divided. In constructing this renewal theology of the Eucharist, readers may sometimes suspect that I have left Pentecostalism entirely. My response to that is an emphatic *no* because if Pentecostal theology is first and foremost about an encounter with the Triune God whom we see in Jesus Christ and is mediated by the Holy Spirit, then some classical Pentecostal understanding may undoubtedly be challenged or even overturned without harming the Pentecostal faith.[9] This is precisely the pneumatological imagination afforded by the Holy Spirit that we saw in the last chapter. In this chapter, the pneumatological imagination will guide my conversation with sources from different Christian traditions and help me construct several explicit descriptions of the meaning contained in the Eucharist that is seen, at least implicitly, in the cameo Luke gave

---

7. Augustine, *Pentecost, Hospitality, and Transfiguration*, 16-17.
8. McIntosh, *Mystical Theology*, 156.
9. Warrington, *Pentecostal Theology*, 20.

of the Spirit-filled church in Acts 2. This will allow me to deduce seven ways to understand the Eucharist as a result of the disciples' devotion, namely solidarity, justice, the satisfaction of hunger, healing, a missional impulse, eschatological anticipation, and a preview of the restoration of all things (*apokatastasis*) in the wedding supper of the Lamb. Therefore in this chapter, I will explicitly construct a way to look at the Eucharist as a meal of solidarity, the Eucharist as a celebration that demands justice and right-relatedness (righteousness), the Eucharist as a gift to the church for managing the world's hunger, the Eucharist as healing, the Eucharist in which the church would find her missional impulse, the Eucharist as a meal enacting the eschatological heavenly assembly, and the Eucharist as a preview of the restoration of all things (*apokatastasis*). It is through these meanings that, following Lubac, I maintain that "the Eucharist makes the church," meaning that the Eucharist makes the church participants of Christ's sacramental reality as the church anticipates Christ's glorious presence fully revealed in the eschaton.[10] In each of these themes, I will show where we can notice the SET paradigm is carried out.

Explaining SET

Before proceeding, it will be helpful to briefly restate and reiterate what a SET paradigm is once again, even though I have touched on this subject in the previous chapters. The model that Cartledge constructed will be understood in this way: people will undergo a process of transformation only through a dynamic and intentional encounter they have with the other. This transformation happens every day as we go about our lives. We are never the same person after an encounter with another person. In our spiritual life, we understand that our spiritual transformation comes through our encounter with "the other," who, in this case, is the Lord who calls us to himself in our quest. Through this encounter, fundamental transformation can be explained as coming "out of one's self and into the truth of one's mission in life, out of provisionality and into the adventure of the incarnation."[11] Spirituality intersects with theology in that both are a search process directed at discoveries that bring new ways for a person to approach and discern their reality, grounded in an encounter

---

10. Lubac, *Corpus Mysticum*, 88.
11. McIntosh, *Mystical Theology*, 6.

with God.¹² If spirituality is the experience one has in the transformative encounter with God, theology is the process of understanding and articulating that transformative encounter. In both, the primary agent enabling the mechanism is God himself. With that in mind, I will now begin to articulate this renewal theology of the Eucharist.

RENEWAL THEOLOGY OF THE EUCHARIST

To construct a renewal theology of the Eucharist, I must begin by stressing two critical points. First, to construct a theology, what we are looking for is the transformation of the whole people of God, that is, the body of Christ. In the theology I am developing, the main "people of God" I have in mind is the church to which I belong and am ordained as a minister. Second, the constructed theology must not, and cannot, be abstract; instead, the transformation of the people of God requires an embodied theology. It is worth pondering whether constructing an abstract theology of the Eucharist is even possible, but that is a pitfall into which one can easily fall. In arguing that the Eucharist is a liturgy that counters the liturgy of torture practiced by the state, which is a kind of "liturgy" that is designed to strike fear in people, William T. Cavanaugh makes an excellent point in saying that when the Eucharist is given "meaning," often it becomes what he calls "gnostic internalization" that completely misses the formative aspect of the Eucharist as liturgy.¹³ Such gnostic internalization, which is to be understood as merely a cognitive or intellectual way of understanding the Eucharist, can also result in alienation of those partaking and indifference to the point that they become powerless and unable to answer the questions that come out of the everyday human condition, which includes suffering and injustice. Liturgy is always about the whole community of believers becoming more than the sum of all the members together (just as Cavanaugh shows that in the liturgy of torture, the community together becomes a fearful community).¹⁴

To end up making a theology of the Eucharist that is "gnostic" is undoubtedly not a trap into which I want to fall when discussing the

---

12. McIntosh, *Mystical Theology*, 6.

13. Cavanaugh, *Torture and Eucharist*, 12.

14. Cf. Schmemann, who defines liturgy as "an action by which a group of people becoming something corporately which they had not been as a mere collection of individuals" (*For the Life of the World*, 25).

Eucharist concerning *solidarity, justice/righteousness, hunger management, healing, mission, eschatology,* and a preview of *apokatastasis.* Therefore, it is essential to call our attention to the significance of the pneumatologically charged event of *anamnēsis,* or remembrance, in the Eucharist. Through a pneumatological act of remembering, the participants remember and simultaneously re-declare their allegiance and self-identification to Christ and his purposes and commit to acting on it. Therefore, it is only in the remembering that is empowered by the Holy Spirit that the meanings I will discuss will remain embodied and not be gnostic. In a pneumatologically charged remembering, the *kerygma* of the church can become concrete in the lived action of the community rather than abstract. The story of salvation is manifested in the transformed lives and actions of the people who have experienced an encounter with God.[15] The latter, that is, the abstract, according to Lubac, seems to be the pitfall into which the scholastics have walked.[16] Lubac argued that Christ's real presence in the Eucharist is not about objectified meaning; instead, it is a dynamic presence that is a link between Christ's sacramental presence and his passion and sacrifice on Calvary, which should bring about transformation in the life of the church.[17] To remember Christ anamnetically is to bring the reality of Christ in the Eucharist to edify and re-member the church as his body. Hence, Lubac says, "The Eucharist corresponds to the Church as a cause to effect, as a means to an end, as a sign to reality."[18] When we remember Christ, we are re-membered (as in reincorporated) as Christ's body. When we remember Christ and his solidarity with us, we are re-membered as the body of Christ who lives in solidarity with and toward others. When we remember Christ, whose justice has made us righteous, we are re-membered as the body of Christ, who works toward justice and righteousness. When we remember that our hunger is satisfied by Christ, we are re-membered as his body tasked to relieve the hunger of others in the world. The same goes for the other items to be discussed in this chapter. The *anamnēsis* brings the past into the present, pneumatologically enacting the salvation narrative in the affective, charging the edified church into action in anticipation of the meal hosted by God himself, when "people will come from east and west, from

---

15. Vondey, *Pentecostal Theology,* 25.
16. Lubac, *Corpus Mysticum,* 223–30.
17. Lubac, *Corpus Mysticum,* 83.
18. Lubac, *Corpus Mysticum,* 13.

north and south, and will eat in the kingdom of God" (Luke 13:29). With that in mind, I now proceed to the first discussion of the Eucharist, which is concerning solidarity.

Eucharist as Solidarity

The Eucharist is a meal of proclamation, in which the church proclaims her allegiance, self-identification, and commitment to the cause of Jesus Christ, her Lord. In the SET paradigm, this is the beginning of the transformation of the individual and the community of believers as a whole. That transformation, however, happens only after an encounter takes place. As I begin this renewal theology of the Eucharist with the discussion of solidarity, the transformative encounter with Christ, the one who stands in solidarity with us, will be the first focus of this discussion. The encounter happens when, in the celebration of the Eucharist, we remember Christ in his generous solidarity with us, "the others" for whose sake he willingly became poor so that we may become rich in him (2 Cor 8:9). Through the incarnation, God shows himself to be one with human flesh by Christ's act of self-emptying solidarity or *kenosis*. As Eugene F. Rogers Jr. puts it, "What the Word assumes is a human nature," and because of that, broken humanity "was elevated to be with God."[19] The event of Pentecost reminds us that as disciples of Jesus, we are also empowered by the Holy Spirit to self-empty ourselves for the sake of others. The Spirit breathes on the disciples of Jesus, making them *imago Spiritus* who function as *imago Christi*, who live a life of self-giving and surrender, making them the true embodiment of the *imago Dei*.[20] In other words, as we remember Jesus's generous kenotic solidarity in the Eucharist, we, too, are called to be in solidarity with "the others" who are in our midst. When Christ's solidarity is remembered in the power of the Holy Spirit, a transformation can and should take place in the person and in the community of persons.

The solidarity of Jesus is best exemplified in the letter to the Hebrews that showed its readers the priesthood of Christ being demonstrated not as separation from things unclean as demanded by the Levitical law; instead, it was exhibited precisely in the place of utter uncleanness "outside the camp" (Heb 13:13). This demonstration is a display of holiness that

---

19. Rogers Jr., *After the Spirit*, 126.
20. Vondey, *Pentecostal Theology*, 192.

is in a "disturbing discontinuity and dislocation" with the holiness code of the Jewish tradition.[21] As explained by Barton in his very helpful essay "Dislocating and Relocating Holiness,"

> For the author of Hebrews, the holiness of God revealed in the death of the Son of God is a holiness offered, ironically and paradoxically, through the profanity and defilement of a corpse. Now, that which sanctifies is precisely the dead corpse outside the camp.... Holiness as separation—of life and death, male and female, priest and lay, Jew and Gentile, purity and impurity—is displaced by *holiness as solidarity:* the solidarity of Jesus the great high priest in sharing human nature as flesh and blood and, above all, in accepting the defilement of death (cf. Heb. 2.14–15, 17).[22]

Barton also maintains that through this displacement, Jesus has reinterpreted the Jewish holiness tradition in terms of solidarity, not just with humanity but with all creation.[23] This fact then demands his followers to express the call to "be holy, because I am holy," also in terms of solidarity with fellow human beings and the whole created order.

This astonishing idea of Christ's solidarity outside the camp, the location in which he displaces life and death, male and female, priest and lay, Jew and gentile, pure and impure, is what must be anamnetically experienced by those who partake of the Eucharist as an encounter with the risen Christ. The reason is, in this remembrance, every person's deep hunger for creative love is being satisfied. In her positive view of humanity, Roman Catholic theologian Monika J. Hellwig points out that every human has an inherent hunger for creative love. Like physical hunger, this hunger is powerful because, for Hellwig, this "very demanding and exigent force" is tied intrinsically to the personhood of every human being.[24] Hellwig argues that when a person feels unaccomplished, this feeling is caused by a deep hunger for creative love. Often, this unfulfilled hunger manifests itself in people, mostly in more affluent societies, indicated by their behavior of accumulating, hoarding, and, after that, quickly disposing of what they have amassed.[25] (This might have been seen in the

---

21. Barton, "Dislocating and Relocating Holiness," 205. I was introduced to this work in Green, *Sanctifying Interpretation*, 96.

22. Barton, "Dislocating and Relocating Holiness," 206; emphasis in original.

23. Barton, "Dislocating and Relocating Holiness," 208.

24. Hellwig, *Eucharist and the Hunger*, 11.

25. Hellwig, *Eucharist and the Hunger*, 10.

toilet paper shortage happening in affluent countries worldwide at the beginning of the COVID-19 pandemic.)

This hunger for creative love is satisfied by allowing a person to feel that something is being demanded of them. According to Hellwig, a person feels loved not only when they are appreciated, respected, and feel that they are the recipient of affection but also when responsibilities are demanded of that person, because the demand put on them "expresses confidence and respect for what [they] can become."[26] Hellwig maintains that this demand is an expression of true love "because it calls into being what is not yet."[27] In fulfilling the demand to become truly human, which in the Christian understanding is found in the person of Jesus Christ, a person would find their personal worth and have their hunger for creative love satisfied. Again, Hellwig explains:

> A true foundation of personal worth, in a person who is fully mature, needs to be such as to offer the possibility of authentically altruistic action. In other words, it must have grown to a point of being no longer dependent on praise or blame, transcending the need for approval and affirmation.[28]

Hellwig further argues that unmasking this deep hunger for creative love, one that will prompt a sense of altruism when satisfied, is one of the most significant tasks of the church. This is the antidote to the selfish, frantic hoarding that often happens in societies that already have a disproportionate share of material things, which is really a sense of insecurity on the part of that society.[29] The posture to be willing to take altruistic actions is the most significant transformation that needs to occur in not just individuals but the whole society, especially the church.

Through its anamnetic and epicletic nature, the Eucharist has been understood to be a Pentecost event happening each time it is celebrated.[30] It is plausible then to conclude that in the Eucharist, there lies an opportunity for the participants to experience what Daniela Augustine earlier calls "the Christoforming work of the Spirit."[31] This is an experi-

---

26. Hellwig, *Eucharist and the Hunger*, 11.
27. Hellwig, *Eucharist and the Hunger*, 9.
28. Hellwig, *Eucharist and the Hunger*, 12–13.
29. Hellwig, *Eucharist and the Hunger*, 13–14.
30. For example, Zizioulas explains the four ways that the Eucharist reveals truth (*Being as Communion*, 114–16).
31. Augustine, *Pentecost, Hospitality, and Transfiguration*, 16.

ence in which the church first experiences the gracious invitation into the perichoretic *koinōnia* of the Triune God, transforming them to become the extension of that fellowship to the world. The extension of that fellowship is carried out in the pattern of Jesus Christ, the incarnate Second Person in the mutually indwelling fellowship of the Trinity, who, in his solidarity with the world, suffered outside the gate and demanded his followers also to follow suit and go outside the camp (Heb 13:11–13) through their work of solidarity (*leitourgia*).[32] This demand is actually a call to become the new person his followers are called to be, a renewed human being whose vision is given by the crucified and risen Christ himself, a demand that will ultimately satisfy a person's hunger for creative love and at the same time propel them to participate in Christ's work of breaking the "self-maintaining cycle of hungers and oppressions."[33] Therefore, whenever the church gathers to celebrate and receive the Eucharist (and to remember and relive the salvific story of Christ through the whole procession of liturgical worship), it is essential for the gathered to take a posture of receptivity so that the Spirit who is called upon may empower them to remember "Christ, the alienated and crucified one whose alienation is, in fact, his solidarity with us in our forsakenness" and be ready to do the same, that is to stand in solidarity with the suffering world, as he satisfies their hunger.[34] Every Eucharist that begins with a process of searching for a divine encounter becomes an event by which the church is transformed (SET), enabled to declare the mighty deeds of God (Acts 2:11) and exclaim a continuous amen to the fulfilling of the promises of Christ's incarnation given in the song of his mother, the Magnificat (Luke 1:45–55). Nourished by Christ, the host of the meal, the church becomes a Spirit-filled community of justice and mercy, ready and willing "to bear the burdens and sufferings of others in loving solidarity."[35]

Eucharist as Justice

In this section, the focus of the discussion is a pneumatologically charged remembrance of the Eucharist as justice. How can the Eucharist address injustice in the Pentecostal church? At the time of writing this section,

---

32. Augustine, *Pentecost, Hospitality, and Transfiguration*, 16–17.
33. Hellwig, *Eucharist and the Hunger*, 13.
34. Green, *Sanctifying Interpretation*, 97.
35. Macchia, *Jesus the Spirit Baptizer*, 129.

I was in anguish, shocked at witnessing the modern-day lynching of George Floyd, the horrendous blatant supremacist act committed by Amy Cooper, and the video that surfaced about the vigilante killing of Ahmaud Arbery happening within one month. Granted, it all took place geographically distant from where I am, but the United States has always been emotionally near to me since spending part of my childhood there. Injustice, taking the form of racism, systemic or otherwise, is terrible. What happened in the United States serves as a catalyst for the discussion in this section. Although it takes a hideous form in America, the injustice of white privilege is not just an American problem. It is, and has been, a global problem, even in a place like Indonesia. To some extent, we Indonesians, like many of our Asian neighbors, are guilty of allowing this sort of injustice to be perpetuated.

Through my roughly fifteen years of experience working in various corporate settings before going into the ministry, I noticed that some companies in Indonesia, including those for which I worked, like to hire Caucasians to the executive board. The hiring is not necessarily because of better qualifications, but because hiring a white man (as the majority appointed to these positions will be males, which brings up the issue of sexism as well) will look good cosmetically, resulting in an increase in the company's market valuation. In her sobering book, sociologist Patricia A. Banks argues that whiteness is an essential component of "brand aesthetics" and that this value affects the way many companies are hiring.[36] Companies in China even go as far as renting white people as "models" to be put into their company profile as window dressing.[37] This "brand aesthetics" rationality has unfortunately also seeped into some international churches in Indonesia, especially of Pentecostal denominations, where there is a held perception that an international church in Indonesia has to be led by a white man in order to be successful. This is quite ironic because the biggest international churches in Indonesia are comprised of 75 to 80 percent Indonesians. This perception brings with it an attitude of entitlement not unlike those found in corporations. How does understanding the Eucharist as justice address this?

Vietnamese American Roman Catholic theologian Peter Phan maintains that the most urgent task for Asian churches is to become the church that is "*in* Asia [and] *of* Asia," which will be "a transparent

---

36. Banks, *Race, Ethnicity, and Consumption*, 83.

37. Farrar, "Chinese Companies 'Rent' White Foreigners"; Yan, "White People Wanted."

sign of and effective instrument for the saving presence of the reign of God, the reign of justice, peace, and love." Phan also argues that what is needed in a pluralistic and multireligious region is no longer a "geographical and institutional expansion of the Church."[38] I agree with Phan that a Pentecostal church expansion that is focused on growth or territory, which breeds a Western-style individualistic version of the faith, can become counterproductive. At the same time, I also maintain that to be a church *in* and *of* Asia that is an instrument of justice, peace, and love, the Pentecostal church in Asia should first look to the Eucharist as a resource because the Eucharist requires justice and reconciliation (Matt 5:23–24). The 1982 WCC "Baptism, Eucharist and Ministry" document, also known as the "Lima Text," is explicit in this matter.[39] It says, "The eucharistic celebration demands reconciliation and sharing among all those regarded as brothers and sisters in the one family of God and is a constant challenge in the search for appropriate relations in social, economic, and political life (Matt 5:23–24, 1 Cor 10:16–17; 11:20–22; Gal 3:28). All kinds of injustice, racism, separation, and lack of freedom are radically challenged when we share in the body and blood of Christ."[40] The *anamnēsis* of the Eucharist must bring us to remember that, in the words of liberation theologian Gustavo Gutiérrez, "to be the cause of fracture of fellowship disqualifies one from participation in that worship which celebrates the action of the Lord which establishes a profound community among persons."[41]

What does it look like for the Eucharist to be a resource to counter injustice? What does it look like for Pentecostals in Indonesia to have a pneumatologically charged remembrance of the Eucharist as justice that follows an SET pattern? When Christians come to search for Christ in the eucharistic worship experience, the outcome should be a pneumatic encounter with Christ in the Eucharist that entails recognizing Christ in

---

38. Phan, *In Our Own Tongues*, 14; emphasis in original.

39. This may look like an odd document to cite in a Pentecostal work, but it is a far better document to cite compared to one written by another Christian tradition. Although the Indonesian Assemblies of God is not a member of the World Council of Churches (WCC), it has been a member of the ecumenical body the Communion of Indonesian Churches (Persekutuan Gereja-Gereja di Indonesia or PGI), which is like the Indonesian wing of the WCC. This is unlike the Assemblies of God USA, which has no affiliation with either the US National Council of Churches or the WCC. See PGI, "Sinode Gereja Anggota PGI"; and Assemblies of God, "Affiliations."

40. Faith and Order Commission, "Baptism, Eucharist and Ministry," 2.20.

41. Gutiérrez, *Theology of Liberation*, 149.

the others because they are also those for whom Christ died. At the same time, this encounter also calls us to repentance for not recognizing Christ in the others. As Gregory Walter helpfully puts it,

> The Eucharist . . . demands that Christians take responsibility for their misconception of others. Every Christian community needs to recognize its own shortcomings and failures in its own way, its own locale, and its own history. The specific failure to respect religious freedoms, its lack of courage to learn from others or even to simply live indifferently among other religious communities, all this is exposed in the Eucharist.[42]

As I mentioned above, Indonesians are also culpable in perpetuating injustice that includes white privilege. The following is a plausible reason. In the colonial days, the Dutch East India Company (in Dutch, the Vereenigde Oostindische Compagnie, abbreviated as the VOC) implemented a divide-and-conquer policy known as *devide et impera*. Through this policy, the VOC would take advantage of an already-existing tension among the sultanates in Java, escalating it to turn them into war against each other.[43] This policy continued to be used when colonization was nationalized into the Dutch East Indies by the Netherlands. After gaining independence, however, this divide-and-conquer policy was again utilized by the New Order Regime (*Rezim Orde Baru*), led by then-President Soeharto, to maintain control over different factions in the country, including the church.[44] Though there are certainly exceptions, among other things, the long-term implication of this policy ranges from an attitude of indifference, at best, and a growing sentiment of distrust, at worst, toward fellow Indonesians that also allows for the perpetuation of white superiority—the misconception of others that Walter mentions above. The hiring of Caucasians in a white-savior-complex fashion falls within the spectrum of the implications. For that, Christians in Indonesia must take responsibility, recognizing our failures and history, as Walter suggests. The Eucharist, through a pneumatically driven remembering, is a resource to take responsibility and understand that the church "may be the victims of their own misperception" that resulted in the act of

---

42. Walter, *Being Promised*, 93–94.

43. For a good discussion on how this divide and conquer plays out, see Ricklefs, *History of Modern Indonesia*, 143–54.

44. Aritonang and Steenbrink, *Christianity in Indonesia*, 257–58.

injustice.⁴⁵ The Christ encounter in the Eucharist, made possible by the Spirit, forces the church to confront its shortcomings as they are sent out into their mission. This is precisely the transformation taking place. This pneumatologically driven transformation would include the willingness to discard accepted paradigms perpetuating injustice by being involved in "the process of discussion, exchange, and learning from one another."⁴⁶

Although taking place in a different setting, we see this sort of transformation concretely in the creative work of Aldrin Peñamora. Peñamora is an evangelical theologian from the Philippines who has focused on extensive peace-building work with the Muslim-majority Bangsa Moro in an attempt to make the church be their true neighbor.⁴⁷ He does this by employing at least two different approaches, both intended to seek justice for the Moros. Peñamora constructed a Christian ethic of responsibility using the Filipino concept of *kapwa* (neighbor) and used the Eucharist as a resource for Christian justice and peacemaking ethics. The Muslim-Christian relationship in the Philippines, familiarly known as the Moro problem, "is really about the Christians being the problem of the Moros."⁴⁸ Through their history, the Moros have been the recipient of injustice through systematic marginalization in their own homeland, Mindanao. Spaniards first committed the systematic marginalization, followed by the United States, and then the Western Christian–oriented government of the Philippines, and it came in the form of "economic destitution, political marginalization, religious intolerance, and threats to Moro identity."⁴⁹

According to Peñamora, a Filipino Christology and the theology of struggle that is related to it can be helpful to deal with the Moro situation because such theology is "primarily . . . *in* and *of* struggle that is generated through solidarity with the struggling Filipino people."⁵⁰ The resource to practice this theology can be found in the Eucharist, which Peñamora maintains as "a crucial resource for a Christian justice and peacemaking ethic."⁵¹ Peñamora points out that the Eucharist is paradigmatic for

---

45. Walter, *Being Promised*, 94.
46. Walter, *Being Promised*, 94.
47. Peñamora, "Ethics of Responsibility," 107.
48. Peñamora, "Eucharistic Justice," 33.
49. Peñamora, "Ethics of Responsibility," 101.
50. Peñamora, "Ethics of Responsibility," 99; emphasis in original.
51. Peñamora, "Eucharistic Justice," 31–32.

"equitable economic distribution" and "revolutionary" in propelling the church to follow Jesus in his ministry of Jubilee, which includes canceling debts and redistribution of property (Luke 4:18–20).[52] He also stresses that the Eucharist could alleviate affective and spiritual poverty, which is more intense physical poverty, and maintains that the Eucharist addresses a hunger more significant than physical, which is the hunger for "creative love."[53] The idea of spiritual poverty that Peñamora describes came from his engagement with Hellwig, whose work does some engagement with liberation theology.[54] It is worth explaining what it means. According to Gutiérrez, spiritual poverty is the only kind of poverty that one can have voluntarily and, when addressed, has a redemptive value. The cause of *material* poverty, a scandalous idea in Scripture, is human exploitation and alienation, both the result of human selfishness; *spiritual* poverty, on the other hand, is driven by the love of neighbor.[55] Thus, only by rejecting exploitation that causes material poverty and being in solidarity with the poor can the church address its lack of spiritual poverty.[56] Remembering the Eucharist as justice allows the church to be "an active and concrete way to be the sacrament of the salvation of the world."[57]

Peñamora's "eucharistic justice" proposal is not about inviting the Moro neighbors to celebrate the breaking of bread in a religious context. Instead, Peñamora is proposing that when celebrating the Eucharist, Christians ought, first of all, to lament because of the injustice suffered by their neighbors and, second, to respond to the "call for [Christians] to act justly toward our Muslim neighbors."[58] Christians are reminded that the celebration is "paradigmatic for the preferential for the poor."[59] Here, Peñamora came to that conclusion not from liberation theology but from Anabaptist theologian John Howard Yoder's *Body Politics*.[60] However, if that were the case, it is something I could affirm because poverty and exploitation of the poor according to Scripture are scandalous (Deut 24:17–22; Lev 19:9–10, 23:22). The transformation in remembering that

52. Peñamora, "Eucharistic Justice," 36–37.
53. Penamora, "Eucharistic Justice," 38.
54. Hellwig, *Eucharist and Hunger*, 15–20.
55. Gutiérrez, *Theology of Liberation*, 172.
56. Gutiérrez, *Theology of Liberation*, 173.
57. Gutiérrez, *Theology of Liberation*, 148.
58. Peñamora, "Eucharistic Justice," 40.
59. Peñamora, "Eucharistic Justice," 37.
60. Peñamora, "Eucharistic Justice," 38.

when one celebrates the Eucharist one has to be in solidarity with the poor comes in the form of regarding Christ not from a worldly (as in worldly power) point of view any longer (2 Cor 5:16). Instead, they can take on the mind of Christ that understands both greatness and power are expressed fully by being the servant and slave to all (Phil 2:1–11, Matt 20:26–27) and respond to the call given to them as ministers of reconciliation.

It is worth investigating what Peñamora's experiment would look like in an Indonesian context. Although the result remains to be seen, I maintain that a similar eucharistic justice, if made by Indonesian Christians who are part of the religious minority, would, at the very least, be an opportunity to really witness Christ's hospitality.[61] The implication is far reaching. Connecting the Eucharist with hospitality and justice demands that we focus our understanding of salvation in terms of the righting (or in Pentecostal language, the healing) of the relationship that humanity has with God, the created order, and one another. Righteousness is precisely the righting of relationship that the Spirit of Christ is working out in people. A meal that is preferential for the poor, whether economically or spiritually, offers a religious minority, who are already rich in Christ, the ability to not demand hospitality from the other. Instead, they are empowered to kenotically offer themselves to others, participating in the one who is rich, yet became poor for the sake of all, so that by his poverty, and the poverty that Indonesian Christians may experience because of injustice, all may become rich (2 Cor 8:9). Here we see the Eucharist becomes an SET event. The celebration that begins with a search turns into a divine encounter as the meal mediates the Spirit's work, making Christ real. This results in a transformation: Indonesian Christians are empowered to empty themselves for the sake of others, bringing God's shalom in the form of the healing of relationships with the other.

Eucharist as Hunger Management

This section seeks to present the Eucharist as a means to alleviate the hunger of the world. Jesus made eating to be the central act of worship of the church. This shows us, not least, the pivotal nature of people being fed, hence displaying the social justice implication of the Eucharist. Far from being a human agenda, however, social justice finds its source in

---

61. I have discussed this at length in Simatupang, "Christian Hospitality," 233–35.

the God that Jesus reveals. Paul echoes this in his critique of the Corinthian church (1 Cor 10:16-17, 11:20-22). I would argue that, if examined through an SET paradigm, participating in an unworthy manner happens precisely when the community eats the bread and drinks the cup of the Lord in a way that does not result in transformative actions (1 Cor 11:27).

In his homily on Acts 2:42 (the verse I maintain above as presenting us with the mark of a Spirit-filled church), Pope Emeritus Benedict XVI points out that the text tells us that "the Church subsists as *Liturgy* and in Liturgy" so that the Eucharist reflects "the way to go and the manner of going in human life."[62] This means that the church's eucharistic liturgy explains the core understanding of the church's calling in her priestly task of being sent to the world and offering it back to God in thanksgiving.[63] In essence, this is the heart of transubstantiation beyond the teaching of the bread and wine becoming the body and blood of Christ. In presenting his case for *nouvelle théologie*, also known as the *ressourcement* movement, being a helpful resource for rediscovering evangelical sacramentality, Hans Boersma shows that transubstantiation having transformation as its telos is found in the writing of Augustine of Hippo. Boersma states,

> When we talk about transubstantiation, we think of the teaching that the bread becomes the Body of Christ. Augustine [in Sermon 227] says something different: *You* become the Body of Christ; *you* become what you eat. We could perhaps say—somewhat anachronistically—that, for Augustine, transubstantiation meant that the Spirit changed *our* substance into the Body of Christ. . . . As Augustine would put it, we become what we have received.[64]

Boersma maintains that Augustine's sermon is not to doubt the real presence of Christ in the elements or the doctrine of transubstantiation but to emphasize the unity of the eucharistic body and the ecclesial body.[65] Although the primary purpose of Boersma's discussion is to argue how the thinking of the *ressourcement* movement is the antidote to neo-Thomistic Roman Catholicism's loss of sacramental ontology, he is also pointing out that for Augustine in the fourth century, all the way to medieval Roman Catholicism, the telos of transubstantiation is always

---

62. Ratzinger, *God Is Near Us*, 122; emphasis in original.
63. Ratzinger, *God Is Near Us*, 123.
64. Boersma, *Heavenly Participation*, 114; emphasis in original.
65. Boersma, *Heavenly Participation*, 109.

about the transformation of the people of God.⁶⁶ Hence, Henri de Lubac, who is one of the chief *ressourcement* theologians, points out, "From the affirmation of bodily reception, we are led by implication, the affirmation for a bodily presence [so that the] Church of Christ . . . is the Body of Christ on earth."⁶⁷ Cavanaugh points out that for Lubac, the correct way to indicate a "eucharistic realism" is through an "ecclesial realism" that sees the purpose of Christ's real presence in the elements as the church edified to do the work of Christ.⁶⁸

Thus, for our discussion purposes, I maintain that as Jesus feeds us with himself in the Eucharist, an act we find narrated in the gospel stories, in which we see him distributing bread as having echoes of the Eucharist, he is preparing us to be willing participants in his work of feeding the world. That is precisely the transformation, the telos, of the Eucharist taking place. My discussion on the Eucharist as solidarity above, in a way, has implied how the Eucharist also manages the hunger of the world, that is, when the church, whose hunger has been satisfied by the one who stands in solidarity with her, has the willingness to be in solidarity with others. In the following, I will argue that the Eucharist calls people to action in hunger management in a reversal of an ever-expanding consumption of goods.

As an antidote to excessive consumerism, the Eucharist calls participants to understand that when they consume in a manner that prioritizes themselves over others so that others are left out and deprived, they end up depriving themselves as well, thereby experiencing deep dissatisfaction and ultimately death. Daniela Augustine maintains that the celebration of the Eucharist "deconstructs the logic of free-market consumerism" for the fact that when a person receives the Eucharist, beyond taking Christ into themselves, they are being taken up *into* Christ.⁶⁹ As a member of the body of Christ, excessive individualism, excessive consumerism, and hoarding are acts that sever oneself from the body. When a person has been taken up into Christ, they anamnetically remember they are part of the body of Christ, and at the same are re-membered as members of the body who have been called into joining Christ in feeding a broken and hungry world. Thus Augustine continues,

---

66. Boersma, *Heavenly Participation*, 110–11.

67. Lubac, *Corpus Mysticum*, 155–56.

68. Cavanaugh, *Torture and Eucharist*, 213.

69. Augustine, *Pentecost, Hospitality, and Transfiguration*, 103.

The Eucharist detoxifies us from the dehumanizing poisons of consumerism and helps us to build immunity towards its seductive lure. It cultivates the community of faith as a dissident force of resistance against the commodification of market logic and forms it as an incarnated critique of the utilitarian objectification of God's creation.[70]

The transformation of persons, in my view, is the key to how this works. In the Gospel of John, we see Jesus saying to his disciples, "I am the bread of life. Whoever comes to me will never be hungry, and whoever believes in me will never be thirsty" (John 6:35). In the Eucharist, we come to encounter Jesus through the physical act of receiving. This physical act of coming to Jesus, responding to his invitation to feed on him, is, most importantly, an embodied act of receiving Christ, who is Wisdom in the flesh. Commenting on the John 6 narrative, James T. O'Connor, who asserts that the text has "a sapiential theme," maintains that coming to Jesus is responding to "an invitation to faith in Wisdom incarnate and to the understanding and life that such a faith will give."[71] The Christian faith never understood wisdom as abstract but always as embodied in the person of Jesus Christ. For example, when Paul commends the church in the city of Philippi to think of things that are true, honorable, just, pure, pleasing, commendable, excellent, and worthy of praise, he is ultimately commending them to think of Christ (Phil 4:8). Hence, with the understanding that one becomes what one eats, the church grows wise in eating, "and in that eating there is a manifestation of the harmony that God has established between the human race's fall and its restoration."[72] The church gains wisdom, is re-membered into the body of her self-giving Lord, and is made ready to give herself to the world to be eaten as its consequence in order to alleviate the world's hunger.

As the Pentecostal community comes to search and encounter Christ at the table and is fed by the Lord at his table, they are given a foretaste of the uninterrupted eschatological feast of the kingdom of God. In this eschatological feast, no one goes hungry because all will be fed by the Lord himself, who dwells among his people. As the Spirit gives the Spirit-filled community a foretaste of this reality, the Spirit's Christoforming work transforms them to be God's agents in the world in providing the

---

70. Augustine, *Pentecost, Hospitality, and Transfiguration*, 104.

71. O'Connor, *Hidden Manna*, 304.

72. O'Connor, *Hidden Manna*, 304.

world a foretaste of the abundance that is to come. The work of feeding the world becomes part of the *leitourgia* of the body of Christ, joining the work of God on earth, which is offered in thanksgiving.[73] This brings us full circle to what Pope Benedict XVI already said above: that the church exists as liturgy and in the liturgy, which in our language would be a process of SET.

Eucharist as Healing

I begin my discussion on the Eucharist as healing by quoting Ignatius of Antioch, who, in his epistle to the Ephesians, says that it is "the medicine of immortality, the antidote against death, and everlasting life in Jesus Christ."[74] For Pentecostals, to have a discussion on the Eucharist as healing is critical and necessary. More than just a source of nourishment that has the potential to alleviate the world's hunger, as I have discussed in the above section, the church throughout history has always understood the Eucharist as *pharmakon*.[75] In chapter 2, I have maintained that because healing is near and dear to the Pentecostal framework, rediscovering the Eucharist as medicine, affirming the healing that is offered in the celebration, is a way to emphasize its Pentecostal-ness. Pentecostals have always connected healing to their understanding of the atonement, and the Eucharist has a role in it, and, at the same time, expresses the understanding of it. It is not uncommon for Isa 53:5, "By his stripes we are healed," to be cited when Pentecostals celebrate the Eucharist.[76] This declaration would be the process of search in the SET paradigm, and it is in line with our notion of empowerment given by the Holy Spirit. In celebrating the Eucharist, the calling upon the Holy Spirit in the *epiclēsis* prayer in Pentecostal services is not so much about the consecration of the eucharistic elements; instead, it is about "invoking the Spirit's intervention in healing and restoration."[77] This event is where the encounter with the divine takes place, is experienced, and manifested in a transformation of the community. The transformative manifestation of the Holy Spirit has never been understood as limited to the spectacular signs and wonders but

---

73. Augustine, *Pentecost, Hospitality, and Transfiguration*, 16–17.
74. Ign. *Eph.* 20:2, in Harmer, *Apostolic Fathers*.
75. Yong, *Spirit Poured Out*, 163.
76. Cartledge, *Testimony in the Spirit*, 51.
77. Cartledge, *Mediation of the Spirit*, 69.

extends to the "patterned and routine aspects of Church life," which includes the Eucharist, where the routine and the spectacular complete one another, as they are "the same eschatological and soteriological reality."[78] Pentecostals then understand the Eucharist as one of the pneumatological processes of receiving salvation and conversion, by which a believer is incorporated and transformed into the body, making it one of a few "communal matri[ces] for the reception of salvation."[79]

In what follows, I will approach the theme of the Eucharist as healing from three angles, namely, as a place that heals (that is, make whole) the Pentecostal experience of Spirit baptism, a place for personal healing, and a place for the hope of cosmic healing. As I have shown above, in explaining that the Eucharist reveals truth in four ways, Eastern Orthodox theologian John D. Zizioulas maintains that the Eucharist, through its anamnetic and epicletic nature, has been understood to be a charismatic event, so that each time it is celebrated, it replicates Pentecost.[80] For Pentecostals, one of the most, if not *the* most, essential aspects of the event of Pentecost is Spirit baptism. We know that historically, this experience has been understood chiefly concerning "initial evidence" and "the enduement of power for life and service, the bestowment of the gifts and their uses in the work of the ministry," which are held to be "non-negotiable tenets."[81] More recently, however, this way of looking at Spirit baptism has been understood to be too narrow of a construal. Frank Macchia, for example, suggests that for the New Testament, "the boundaries of possible meanings for the metaphor [of Spirit baptism]" are much broader than how Pentecostals have classically understood it.[82] A narrowly construed understanding of Spirit baptism has created a "spiritual fatigue" in Pentecostal churches so that we begin to have difficulties in passing down this distinctiveness that we have.[83] It has been argued that understanding Spirit baptism in a sacramentally robust way would alleviate this spiritual fatigue, just as the suggestion that Pentecostals need to put sacramentality front and center again is much more common these days.[84]

78. Cartledge, *Mediation of the Spirit*, 102.
79. Cartledge, *Mediation of the Spirit*, 162.
80. Zizioulas, *Being as Communion*, 114–16.
81. Assemblies of God, "Assemblies of God," points 7 and 8.
82. Macchia, *Baptized in the Spirit*, 257.
83. Chan, *Pentecostal Theology*, 8.
84. Vondey and Green, "Between This and That."

How should we understand Spirit baptism sacramentally, that is, that the experience really becomes an event that mediates grace? I am helped by the definition Chris Green gives regarding Spirit baptism. He maintains that being baptized in the Spirit "means we are empowered for a life of self-emptying intercession, a life of bearing others in their sin, suffering with and for them, so they are borne along toward forgiveness, restoration, and healing."[85]

It is a known fact that Pentecostals often use Spirit baptism as an elitist *shibboleth* test determining who is in and who is out, and perhaps this way of seeing Spirit baptism contributes to the spiritual fatigue as well.[86] I maintain that the experience of Spirit baptism through the Eucharist is the sacramental way to heal the illness of being unable to pass down our distinctiveness caused by the spiritual fatigue plaguing the Pentecostal church. This is because the showiness and fanfare of the typical Pentecostal "altar call" often demanded to be replicated, creating that spiritual fatigue, can be reduced to a more mundane yet healthy contemplative experience. The reason is that in the Spirit baptism through the Eucharist model, the meal once again becomes the center of the altar experience. Through the baptism of the Spirit, Pentecostals, being people who are steeped in Scripture, can anamnetically remember that the narrative given in the four gospels relates Jesus's activity of feeding the multitude with healing so that the act is, in fact, "the dispensation of divine mercy not only through the service of teaching but also by restoring the sick to health."[87] I will continue my discussion on Spirit baptism before proceeding to the subject of personal healing shortly.

In the previous chapter, regarding the Spirit-filled community Luke describes in Acts 2:42, I have pointed out the fact that the community was devoted to four specific things, namely and literally, *the* teaching of the apostles, *the* fellowship, *the* breaking of bread, and *the* prayers. I have maintained that, together, these four things are a process of search and encounter taking place, resulting in a community experiencing transformation (SET). Here, I will maintain that the three specific devotions, the apostles' teaching, the breaking of bread, and the prayer, which together are a celebration of the Eucharist, open the disciples up to experience

---

85. Green, *Sanctifying Interpretation*, 90.

86. For example, in a similar way, Castelo also maintains that Pentecostals are not known for being contemplative and tend to be prideful regarding Spirit baptism (*Pentecostalism as a Christian Mystical Tradition*, 129).

87. Farkasfalvy, "Eucharistic Provenance," 31.

Spirit baptism, which is none other than the *koinōnia* in and with the Triune God through the Spirit. Regarding this *koinōnia*, Macchia explains,

> The structure of Spirit baptism is thus Trinitarian, in which the divine lordship or monarchy of the Godhead is mediated through the Trinitarian relations. . . . Christ as Spirit Baptizer is essential to his role. The Spirit who mediated the love between the Father and the Son is now poured out so as to draw humanity into the *koinōnia* of God and to gift and empower the Church to participate in the mission of God in the world.[88]

In my view, by the work of the Spirit, the *koinōnia* of women and men being taught the word of God, breaking bread, and being in prayer becomes their *koinōnia* with God mediated by the Spirit and experienced through a baptism of the Holy Spirit. Here we see the process of SET taking place in the early church. Hence, the apostle John writes: "We declare to you what we have seen and heard so that you also may have *koinōnia* with us; and truly our *koinōnia* is with the Father and with his Son Jesus Christ" (1 John 1:3 AT, based on NRSV). With Macchia, I also agree that the most important outcome of this *koinōnia* is the outpouring of divine love.[89] This outpouring of love given by the Spirit of love resulted in the community reciprocating that love back to God through all the signs and wonders Luke mentioned happening within the community (1 John 4:19, Acts 2:43–47). Thus, the eucharistic celebration opens up the Pentecostal community to be baptized by the Spirit, resulting in signs and wonders while, at the same time, healing us from a showy understanding of Spirit baptism.[90] We now proceed to the topic of the Eucharist as a place for personal healing, focusing on all aspects of healing related to persons.

The church has always seen the Eucharist as *pharmakon*, as offering healing not only to our physical and spiritual dimensions but also to the relationships in the community, and Pentecostals are included in this. For example, Amos Yong points out that when believers receive the Eucharist with discernment, the event becomes a place in which God manifests his healing grace. This is because healing is part and parcel of the Pentecostal understanding of atonement so that as Pentecostals participate, they "internalize the body and blood of Christ [and] release its healing virtues for

---

88. Macchia, *Baptized in the Spirit*, 258.

89. Macchia, *Baptized in the Spirit*, 261.

90. Green notes that in the Lord Supper we encounter Jesus "as the one who sanctifies us by healing and baptizing us in the Spirit in and through the Eucharist-event" (*Toward a Pentecostal Theology*, 275).

broken bodies."[91] As I mentioned earlier, it is not uncommon for Isa 53:5 to be referenced in a Pentecostal celebration of the Eucharist. Cartledge saw and documented this in Hockley Pentecostal Church, an Assemblies of God church in Birmingham, United Kingdom. This Isaiah text and others, for example, 1 Pet 2:24, which quotes Isa 53:5 and Jas 5:13–16, not only connect the work of Christ on the cross to forgiveness of sins but also to divine healing.[92] This should not be surprising because Pentecostals' dominant metaphor for salvation is healing, which is "the objective and holistic nature" of Christ's sacrifice on the cross.[93] For another, one of the core beliefs of Pentecostals is in the fact that concrete matters and actions, for example, handkerchiefs and the laying on of the hands, mediate and communicate gifts of the Holy Spirit, including healing. Pace Yong, however, who would see this strictly from a pneumatological perspective, I suggest a pneumatological reconsideration of the understanding of transubstantiation.[94]

In my discussion on the doctrine of transubstantiation of Roman Catholicism in chapter 3, I argued that this doctrine could potentially provide a greater understanding of the embodiedness of our faith, especially in terms of being *pharmakon* for our holistic healing. In that chapter, I have pointed out that the idea of the elements becoming the body and blood of Christ goes back much earlier than St. Thomas Aquinas. Dealing with the issues of his days, Aquinas, using Aristotelian concepts and terminology, is the first to seek to describe the process (as opposed to explain the process).[95] Roman Catholic theologian James T. O'Connor maintains that in Aquinas's mind, because Christ, who is fully divine, is fully human, his flesh has become the "conjoined instrument" of God's work of salvation, and through that exact human nature, God continues to reveal the reality and effect of his salvific work in and through human flesh. What is essential to our discussion is, for Aquinas, the salvific work of Christ is a spiritual reality that operates through grace, and the response in faith to it takes place in person-to-person, body-to-body contact.[96] Christ heals and saves because he is *really* present to his people. Without

---

91. Yong, *Spirit Poured Out*, 163.
92. Cartledge, *Testimony in the Spirit*, 50.
93. Cartledge, *Testimony in the Spirit*, 51.
94. Yong, *Spirit Poured Out*, 163–64.
95. O'Connor, *Hidden Manna*, 280.
96. O'Connor, *Hidden Manna*, 277–78.

going to Aristotelian metaphysics, Eugene F. Rogers Jr. helps us. He said, "At the Annunciation, the Spirit bids the Father to receive a body from the Spirit so that those with bodies can receive the Spirit from the Son. The Spirit invokes Mary for the Son to become incarnate, so that a priest may invoke the Spirit for the bread and wine to become the Son."[97] As the people receive the elements, they experience a life-giving touch of Christ that absorbs the broken bodies of the recipients into his own body.[98] If the nearness of the kingdom brought by Jesus in his earthly ministry is still present post-resurrection, then it is the contact with his flesh in the Eucharist (cf. John 1:14) that manifests that nearness. Therefore, the doctrine of transubstantiation could present an opportunity for Pentecostals to reshape and reconfigure their doctrine of healing in a more corporate way.[99] When touched physically by the risen Jesus in the eucharistic elements, the community of believers is transformed into a healed community. Healed from physical, emotional, spiritual, and relational ailments, they are transformed into a healing community, conjoined instruments who are Christ-bearers, declaring the shalom and transformative power he is bringing and completing. Wolfgang Vondey presents this idea well, saying, "Salvation aims at the healing (rather than curing or restoring) of humankind in relationship to God, creation, and one another. The human *imago Spiritus* functions, therefore, in the same manner as the human *imago Christi* is the embodiment of the *imago Dei* through self-giving and surrender."[100] This is worked out by Kimberly Alexander, who points out that social justice is as much part of Jesus's "saving-healing" work as physical healing. She maintains that if the oppression of the weak, the exploitation of the poor, and the divisions caused by race and gender are not included in the Pentecostal understanding of healing, then Pentecostals, in fact, have lost their understanding of their fundamental identity as the people of God.[101] Being Spirit filled, which in my view is a genuine eucharistic experience, Pentecostals are called to proclaim the healing that Christ has ushered in to every area of life, especially areas made sick by structural sin.

---

97. Rogers Jr., *After the Spirit*, 208–9.
98. O'Connor, *Hidden Manna*, 278–79.
99. Green, *Toward a Pentecostal Theology*, 275.
100. Vondey, *Pentecostal Theology*, 192.
101. Alexander, "Pentecostal Healing Community," 203–4.

This brings us to discuss the Eucharist as a place for the hope of cosmic healing. Another way to emphasize the Pentecostal-*ness* of the Eucharist is to highlight the healing that offers healing not only to our physical, emotional, spiritual, and relational aspects but cosmic healing as well. This holistic healing is, in fact, what is contained in the theme of *Christus Victor*, and it reminds the church that the transformative work of the Spirit always relates cosmically to our existence in our material-ness.[102] However, we need to remember that *Christus Victor*'s benefits are not yet fully realized and are experienced only as a foretaste in the Eucharist. Thus, the Eucharist prevents an over-realized eschatology, maintaining the already-not-yet tension. At the same time, we also are demanded to examine ourselves (1 Cor 11:28) as a community in which our posture is in relation to the radical hospitality and healing that God extends throughout the cosmos, and our concern is whether we are trying to monopolize these gifts or be their heralds as we are called to be.[103] This is a reality that is expressed by Peter paradigmatically in Acts 11:17, "If then God gave them the same gift that he gave us, . . . who was I that I could hinder God?" In the Eucharist, an event of transfigured created things, the community is transformed into agents of a holistic mission by the Spirit to do his work.[104] The healing that is anticipated is cosmic in scale, something that Pope Francis puts forward in his encyclical letter *Laudato Si'*, summarized in his sentence "In the Christian understanding of the world, the destiny of all creation is bound up with the mystery of Christ."[105] With this anamnetic and epicletic understanding of healing that we can receive from the Eucharist, Pentecostals are then ready to embark on their mission.

Eucharist as Mission

We come now to the theme of the Eucharist as mission. I maintain that this is a critical discussion to have for Pentecostals because of the movement's missionary impulse.[106] From its beginning until now, the Pente-

---

102. Chan, *Grassroots Asian Theology*, 109.

103. Hellwig, *Eucharist and Hunger*, 20.

104. Chan, *Grassroots Asian Theology*, 109.

105. Francis, "*Laudato Si'*," §99; see §§96–100.

106. On this missionary impulse see especially the chapter on "Mission and Evangelism" in Anderson, *Introduction to Pentecostalism*, 198–221.

costal movement has been about mission, and it is vital that Pentecostals get their missionary momentum not from a mission conference but from the Eucharist, the missionary meal of the church. Chris Green even goes as far as maintaining that the Eucharist is so essential to Pentecostal spirituality that "it belongs to every domain of Pentecostal thought and practice."[107] Historically, however, in how they carried out their missions, Pentecostals, especially Western Pentecostal missionaries, often fell into the trap of seeing the other as merely those who needed conversion, a view often accompanied by a superiority attitude.[108] The missional impulse that comes from the Eucharist brings about, not least, community discernment that is otherwise impossible (I will discuss this as one of the implications of seeing the Eucharist as mission).[109]

As I mentioned in the first chapter, Orthodox theologian John D. Zizioulas maintains that the coming of the Spirit in the Eucharist, invoked in the prayer of *epiclēsis*, makes the act of remembrance, or *anamnēsis*, nonlinear and multidimensional.[110] Through this remembering, each time the Eucharist is celebrated, it becomes a Pentecost event. This is helpful for Pentecostals. We also see the outpouring of the Holy Spirit on the day of Pentecost not as a one-time event but a "repeatable celebration that is essential *to the mission* of the Church."[111] Therefore, I am convinced that understanding the Eucharist as creating a local Pentecost event would prove to be helpful if Pentecostals are to live out their calling to mission as the people of God.

Drawing his conclusion directly from the narrative of Jesus and the account of the Last Supper given to us in the gospels, Peter Phan points out that "the Eucharist is . . . the sacrament of mission par excellence."[112] The gospels present to us the person of Jesus whose being is inseparable from his Father, whose identity is determined by his relationship with his Father, and who is solely about what his Father assigns him to do. Phan, therefore, points out that the Last Supper, the farewell dinner Jesus had with his disciples, was, like all farewell dinners, an event of the passing of

---

107. Green, *Toward a Pentecostal Theology*, 307.
108. Tupamahu, "American Missionaries," 235–39.
109. Vondey, "Pentecostal Ecclesiology," 45.
110. Zizioulas, *Being as Communion*, 115–16.
111. Vondey, "Pentecostal Sacramentality," 94; emphasis added.
112. Phan, *In Our Own Tongues*, 51.

the torch. Jesus knew his mission, the very thing that was most important to him, was not yet finished. Thus, Phan says,

> So when he commanded his disciples to eat his body and drink his blood, he was effectively saying to his disciples: *You who are my followers, take over my mission and complete it for me, since I am prevented from completing it. By eating my body and drinking my blood, you are taking on my mission for the kingdom of God.*[113]

One does not have to agree with the way Phan paraphrases the event. Taken out of context, it can be mistakenly read as Jesus's complete handing over of his mission to his disciples, which will, at least, beg the question of how that fits with Jesus's own understanding of what he says, "I am with you always" (Matt 28:20), within a Trinitarian framework. We can, however, agree with the emphasis that Phan is making on the fact that the Eucharist *is* a missionary meal.[114] Clearly, Jesus's complete handing over his mission to his disciples is not the understanding Phan intends. He later maintains that, following the official Roman Catholic teaching, the Eucharist is "the *culmen et fons* (summit and font) of the Church's life." The Eucharist as summit and font is a blueprint of the structurally Trinitarian "liturgy of life" by which people come to experience "God's gracious self-communication, available to all human beings, in the midst of life and in all concrete situations."[115]

What I want to deal with now is to try to answer, "In what way is the Eucharist missional?" I maintain that the Eucharist is missional in at least three ways, namely, discernment in seeing the other; sending Christians to their mission (John 6); and finally, the sign of the great eschatological feast. I will begin with discernment, and Wolfgang Vondey is helpful in this matter. Proposing a "eucharistic discernment," he points out that the meal is

---

113. Phan, *In Our Own Tongues*, 51; emphasis in original.

114. The Eucharist being a missionary meal is affirmed by many traditions, including the Roman Catholic and the Anglicans. The closing prayers of the Eucharist Rite 2 of the Episcopal Church say, "You have fed us with spiritual food in the Sacrament of his Body and Blood. Send us now into the world in peace" or "We thank you for feeding us with the spiritual food of the most precious Body and Blood of your Son our Savior Jesus Christ.... And now, Father, send us out to do the work you have given us to do" (Episcopal Church USA, *Book of Common Prayer*, 365–66).

115. Phan, *In Our Own Tongues*, 89.

an exercise that seeks to recognize the presence of Christ in the other and thereby acknowledges the other as a member of the one body. This exercise is a fundamental ecumenical endeavor. It is as much a theological undertaking as it is an emotional, psychological, ethical, and social responsibility.[116]

In his view, the others include those who were part of the community but are now estranged. Pace Vondey, I maintain that the other would extend beyond, to those who are outside of the community as well. Through the anamnetic remembering of the Eucharist, believers are enabled to discern God's preferential for the other as well. This is clearly shown on the day of Pentecost by the many tongues, as Daniela Augustine also puts it, "the language of the other stands at the center of the Pentecost event as an expression of the prioritization of the other in the Kingdom of the new humanity."[117] Through a Pentecost event in the Eucharist, the Pentecostal church, people who have experienced divine embrace and hospitality, discern themselves as being invited to participate in God, embracing the world, offering and extending God's hospitality to others. In the *anamnēsis* Pentecostals remember that while we were God's enemies, Christ reconciled us to God (Rom 5:10). The Eucharist as mission enables Christians to discern the call Christ has given them, that is, to be ministers of reconciliation precisely towards the others who perhaps were considered enemies before.

The second aspect of the Eucharist being missional is the very plain fact that it is a missional meal. Before he went to the cross, Jesus set a meal in his church as the central act of worship, a meal that reminds the disciples of the connection Jesus made about the manna that comes from heaven and points to himself as the bread of life. Thus, when the people anamnetically remember the Eucharist as mission, the people are brought into the very act by which Jesus feeds his people with himself for the "spiritual nourishment" to go on their mission in the world.[118] This idea of nourishment has been held by the faithful since the church's beginning, and the martyrs of the early church actually understood the Eucharist as crucial for preparing and sustaining them in what awaited them.[119] In this meal, the community is reminded of Jesus's self-giving for

---

116. Vondey, "Pentecostal Ecclesiology," 49.
117. Augustine, *Pentecost, Hospitality, and Transfiguration*, 4.
118. Archer, "Nourishment for Our Journey," 82.
119. Cavanaugh, *Torture and Eucharist*, 225.

his church, which propels them into a life of self-giving and ministry as well. It is in this act of self-giving that the church experiences the fullness of life Jesus promised to them as a messianic community.

Finally, the Eucharist is missional because it points to the great banquet that God will provide in the final kingdom. The missionary significance of the meal comes in the fact that it is a foretaste of the "universal triumph of his saving will and purpose."[120] Scripture testifies that there will be a heavenly banquet prepared for God's people who come "from east and west, from north and south, will come and sit down at the feast in the kingdom of God" (Luke 13:29; cf. Matt 8:11). As Geoffrey Wainwright puts it,

> To his feast in the final kingdom, God is inviting all people, for he has willed to have mercy on all (Rom. 11:32); and the invitation to the sacramental meal which is the sign of that final feast is therefore likewise universal. The universality of the invitation makes of every celebration of the eucharist a missionary event.[121]

In the life of the Pentecostal church, this is worked out in what Vondey calls "the ecclesio-missiological framework of Pentecostals" that calls us to experience salvation, sanctification, Spirit baptism, and healing from the perspective of eschatology.[122] From this eschatological perspective, salvation is an experience of coming into the "training program" of a fellowship of missionaries; sanctification is an experience of radical personal transformation from a life of the flesh to life in the Spirit; Spirit baptism is an experience of being equipped for Christian witness; healing is an experience of encounter with the coming Christ in this present reality.[123] This ecclesio-missiological framework is precisely the experience of the Eucharist as mission in an SET paradigm. However, pace Wainwright, who sees that some will reject the offer of salvation, I maintain that the transforming presence of Christ continues to restore all humanity to fulfill the promise "that God may be all in all" (1 Cor 15:28). I will begin to elaborate on this point in the next section, but more explicitly in the last section entitled "Eucharist as *Apokatastasis*" below.

---

120. Wainwright, *Eucharist and Eschatology*, 159.
121. Wainwright, *Eucharist and Eschatology*, 161.
122. Vondey, *Pentecostal Theology*, 136.
123. Vondey, *Pentecostal Theology*, 136–37.

Eucharist as Eschatology

Eschatology has become a very significant doctrinal issue for Pentecostals, so much so that according to Frank Macchia, it has become one of the reasons that Spirit baptism has been displaced as a Pentecostal theological distinctive.[124] Hence, the inclusion of a discussion on an anamnetic remembrance of the Eucharist as eschatology is pertinent for our purpose. I will approach the subject of this discussion in two ways. First, I will argue that a greater appreciation of the Eucharist as eschatology can offer Pentecostals a way to look into eschatology that is more hopeful, having greater confidence in the gospel of Jesus Christ. Second, because of the greater confidence in the gospel, Pentecostals can then work towards the hopeful eschatological unity of the body of Christ by celebrating a meal that is open and available.

When it comes to understanding eschatology, Pentecostalism has been seen to be committing either an abandonment of history or an overly friendly embrace of millenarian hopes, which is, in my view, quite faulty if compared to a hopeful biblical eschatology.[125] A few clarifications need to be made to explain where I am coming from. First, with mainstream Christian orthodoxy, I affirm the expectation of the personal, visible return of the Lord Jesus Christ.[126] Second, realizing that there is no one perfect model when it comes to the millennial view, from the onset, I also need to say that I hold to an amillennialist view of the book of Revelation.[127] This view has not been the typical Pentecostal view. This view is certainly not the official view of the Indonesian Assemblies of God, which happens to follow a modified version of the eleven points of the World Assemblies of God Fellowship statement of faith as opposed to the sixteen fundamental truths of the US Assemblies of God.[128] There have been, however, a growing minority of Pentecostals holding to an

---

124. Macchia, *Baptized in the Spirit*, 26–28.

125. Chan, *Pentecostal Theology*, 110.

126. For a brief explanation of the different views concerning the return of Christ see Bloesch, *Last Things*, 33–34.

127. For an explanation of the purpose of the millennium of the book of Revelation see Bauckham, *Theology of Revelation*, 106–8.

128. It is a modified version because in GSJA, "Pengakuan Iman GSJA," they do not specifically mention "speaking in tongues as the initial evidence," as found in World AG Fellowship, "Statement of Faith"; cf. Assemblies of God, "Assemblies of God."

amillennialist perspective more recently.¹²⁹ I include myself in this growing minority even though I do not stand on Jakarta's street corner, waving a banner declaring my view.

Simon Chan suggested that Pentecostals should appropriate the pneumatological richness one can find in Eastern Orthodoxy, especially its eucharistic theology.¹³⁰ In my opinion, he is correct in his suggestion because, as *arrabōn*, the Spirit is who guarantees what is to come (2 Cor 1:11) by giving a foretaste of what is waiting for us in the kingdom of God. Yet, simultaneously, the Spirit also grounds us in our present reality, reminding us of the "not yet." Chan points out that Pentecostals have understood this foretaste as "signs and wonders." Chan also suggests that when experiencing that foretaste, Pentecostals, who often fall into an over-realized eschatology, must carefully maintain "the tension between the 'has come' and the 'not yet.'"¹³¹

In his closing remark to the church in Philippi (4:1–9), Paul gives his readers several exhortations. He specifically urges his readers in v. 6 to not be anxious; instead, present to God their prayer and supplication with thanksgiving. Gordon Fee points out that thanksgiving is the basic posture for petitioning God, which is a posture of acknowledging our creaturely dependence on him in recognition that all we have in life is a gift.¹³² I have argued in chapter 4 that the New Testament is constructed out of a eucharistic provenance. In light of that, I think Fee does not go far enough with his understanding of thanksgiving as a posture. Here I argue that this posture of thanksgiving is found entirely and expressed with the highest intensity in the Eucharist. The reason for this is the indicative phrase, which grounds all the exhortations Paul gives, in the text "the Lord is near" (v. 5b). The nearness of the Lord that brings with it his peace, which Paul mentions in the text, is a foretaste of the eschaton that is given by the Holy Spirit and experienced most intensely by the community in the Eucharist. This is what is implied in the liturgical celebration of the Eastern Orthodox Church, as Alexander Schmemann puts it:

> Orthodox ecclesiology is indeed a eucharistic ecclesiology. For in the Eucharist the Church accomplishes the passage from this world into the world to come, into the eschaton; participates in

---

129. Warrington, *Pentecostal Theology*, 311.
130. Chan, *Pentecostal Theology*, 108.
131. Chan, *Pentecostal Theology*, 110.
132. Fee, *Paul's Letter to Philippians*, 409.

the ascension of its Lord and in his messianic banquet; tastes of the joy and peace of the kingdom.[133]

The Eucharist is *that* passage for the church to experience the Lord's eschatological nearness, not in the form of an over-realized eschatology, but in an experience of peace that transcends all understanding that precisely maintains the tension of "already" and "not yet." This, I argue, is how Pentecostals can ultimately appreciate the hope found in the gospel of Christ that I mentioned earlier. The peace that comes from the nearness of God given in the Eucharist, in Geoffrey Wainwright's words, is our ultimate destination "glimpsed by the eyes of faith but [that] has not yet [fully] permeated and transformed opaque and recalcitrant humanity."[134] At the same time, in the Eucharist, the Holy Spirit gives the church the vision of Christ through his character, which Paul describes as true, honorable, just, pure, pleasing, commendable, excellent, and worthy of praise (v. 8). This vision, in an SET paradigm, is precisely the encounter that transforms the celebrating community to be able to take on the character of Christ as well. Through the Spirit's power, the anamnetic remembering in the Eucharist is not just a remembering of the past but also a future remembering of his eschatological act that is the second coming.[135] Having this eschatological confidence in the gospel through the Eucharist, Pentecostals can then participate more intensely in working towards the hopeful eschatological unity of the body of Christ, which is the next subject of our discussion.

Before Jesus went to the cross, he prayed to his Father for his disciples, "that they may all be one" (John 17:21a). The Eucharist, the meal that is supposedly the mark of the church being one in Christ, has yet to be a celebration that makes us one. In proposing a theological possibility that promotes visible unity, I find George Hunsinger to be very helpful in this regard. He maintains that the task of such an ecumenical theology is threefold: first, the respect of Nicaea and Chalcedon; second, the willingness to embrace both "academic liberal theology" on the left and what he calls "enclave theology" on the right, which he defines as "a theology based narrowly in a single tradition that seeks not to learn from other traditions"; finally, that ecumenical theology is, in essence, ecclesial

---

133. Schmemann, "Missionary Imperative," 198.
134. Wainwright, *Eucharist and Eschatology*, 73.
135. Gavrilyuk, "Eschatological Dimension," 176.

theology, a reflection grounded in the life of the church.[136] I contend that it is that last task to which Pentecostals can offer our contribution. As Green points out, it is time for Pentecostals to join the party. Pentecostals are in the habit of joyful, exuberant, "explosive praise" in anticipation of the great eschatological hope.[137] Pentecostals would contribute generously to the unity of the church if, in the celebration of the Eucharist, they would be enacting the kingdom of God, in which eating and drinking are more than just about physical sustenance but more about having our hunger for righteousness, peace, and joy being satisfied in the Holy Spirit by Jesus, who is the host of the meal (Rom 14:17; cf. Matt 5:3–9).

Eastern Orthodox scholar Paul Gavrilyuk argues that as an eschatological sign, the Eucharist possesses the possibility "to relativize all forms of existing human alienation," including those that we see in the church, because regardless of "how deeply entrenched, these divisions are dissolved as a result of incorporation into Christ."[138] If the eschatological implication of the Eucharist is taken seriously, then intercommunion is not an impossibility—although currently, it is highly unlikely. There are three reasons for this, according to Gavrilyuk. First, the Eucharist is about celebrating the new humanity that the incarnation brought into being, which is lived out in continuity through the church and will be finally consummated in the kingdom to come.[139] Second, regardless of the different understanding of sacramental theology held by different church traditions, from an eschatological perspective, it is possible for other people belonging to different ecclesial communions to have the same eucharistic experience, hence experiencing the same communion.[140] What Gavrilyuk means by this is that the primary eucharistic experience for most people does not depend on expert knowledge, for example, the understanding of the metaphysical mechanism of the Eucharist. Instead, what is more important and sufficient is the partial knowledge that comes from noncognitive factors, which is where the realm of faith is primarily located.[141] Third, in the kingdom that is to come, there can and will be no confessional division. The Eucharist must then be remembered as a

---

136. Hunsinger, *Eucharist and Ecumenism*, 1–9.
137. Green, *Toward a Pentecostal Theology*, 259.
138. Gavrilyuk, "Eschatological Dimension," 176–77.
139. Gavrilyuk, "Eschatological Dimension," 180.
140. Gavrilyuk, "Eschatological Dimension," 181.
141. Gavrilyuk, "Eschatological Dimension," 179–80.

foretaste of that unity in which Christ breaks the boundaries between the community of believers, including those created by confessional divisions.[142] Gavrilyuk argues, following John D. Zizioulas, that this breaking down of barriers is possible, especially in light of the view of apostolic succession that sees it not only finding its authority in the risen Christ but also, more importantly, having its final destiny in him too.[143] Gavrilyuk, however, is not comfortable with open communion. That is, he still maintains that to receive communion, one has to follow the proper initiation sequence, meaning one has to be baptized first as the "first medication" before one can experience the benefit of the "second medication" that is the Eucharist.[144] This is where I part ways with him because I do not see him as going far enough in seeing the eschatological dimension of the Eucharist.

I maintain that in proposing an open Eucharist Pentecostals have an excellent opportunity to enact the foretaste of the eschatological righteousness, peace, and joy that will be made complete by the Holy Spirit. I do not for once recommend that Pentecostals should stop upholding the standard of self-examination for anyone participating in the Eucharist, making it a free-for-all event, hence nullifying its meaning. However, Pentecostals have shown the Eucharist can be an altar-call experience, in which people respond to the call of God and encounter him.[145] Therefore, in terms of relating it to baptism and the idea of medication or medicine (*pharmakon*) contained in both sacraments, Pentecostals do not necessarily have to see it as one medicine needing to follow the other in an *ordo salutis* understanding. Rather, Pentecostals should see baptism and the Eucharist as complementing one another in *via salutis* understanding, that even when they are not done in order, one medicine would not be complete without the other. Practiced in this complementary way, the Eucharist then truly becomes a meal that is a foretaste of the messianic banquet and a sacrament of communion with Christ, with people joining and taking their places from "east and west and north and south" (Luke 13:29).

I maintain that this does not betray the understanding of the Pentecostal *via salutis*. Kenneth J. Archer defines the Pentecostal *via salutis* as

142. Gavrilyuk, "Eschatological Dimension," 182.
143. Gavrilyuk, "Eschatological Dimension," 178.
144. Gavrilyuk, "Eschatological Dimension," 181.
145. Tomberlin, *Pentecostal Sacraments*, 190.

a "faith journey" in which the sacraments are acts done by the Pentecostal community and serve as means of grace for their shaping their identity while on that journey.[146] I do not for once suggest that the sacraments are to be defined differently. Baptism is still initiation; the Eucharist is still nourishment; foot washing, as a sacrament carried out by some, is still sanctification.[147] However, in my view, they are what happens in the journey instead of what makes it. What makes the journey is that our faith is strengthened in Jesus Christ, the one who leads the journey. To see the Eucharist fitting into a *via salutis* pattern, as opposed to insisting it follow the *ordo salutis*, fits the way Christ, who is the host of every table celebrated by his church, performs his salvific work in Cornelius, whose story is found in Acts 10. We see in Cornelius a process of the sanctification work of the Holy Spirit, followed by an experience of Spirit baptism, and only then is Cornelius baptized in water by Peter. Hence Peter's enthusiastic exclamation in Acts 11:17, "If then God gave them the same gift that he gave us, . . . who was I that I could hinder God?" This would allow Pentecostals to put spirituality and doctrine in a both/and relationship as opposed to an either/or, resulting in the ability to see that "spirituality has something to say about doctrine, doctrine also has something to say about spirituality."[148] Our Spirit-filled preaching, like Peter's, should be what calls people to an unexamined participation. As Gregory Walter puts it, "Acting after Jesus, continuing on his place, the obligation of the community, those charged to declare it, is to simply communicate it to others," and in serving the meal, the church must continue to make it a meal "that is itinerant, iterable, and open."[149] In making the adjustments to the Eucharist, making it available and open, the Pentecostal church could also make allowance for careful modifications and changes to be made in the spiritual life of the church. The spiritual life of the Pentecostal church then becomes a search that opens itself to the transformative encounter with Christ in anticipation of the eschatological kingdom where all will be restored anew. This restoration of all things is the subject of our next section.

---

146. Archer, "Nourishment for Our Journey," 79.
147. Archer, "Nourishment for Our Journey," 95.
148. Stephenson, *Types of Pentecostal Theology*, 116.
149. Walter, *Being Promised*, 91.

Eucharist as *Apokatastasis*

The purpose of this section is to discuss the Eucharist as a preview of *apokatastasis*, or the restoration of all things, the phrase mentioned by Peter in the book of Acts 3:21 when he declares that Jesus "must remain in heaven until the time of universal restoration [*apokatastaseōs pantōn*] that God announced long ago through his holy prophets." I will discuss below how the church understood the universal restoration idea that Peter exclaims. I will begin, however, by stating the obvious: since the early church until now, the topic of *apokatastasis* is not without controversy, not least because now the word is almost explicitly understood in relation to the doctrine of universal salvation set forth by Origen, the second-century Alexandrian theologian who is, unfortunately, not without controversy.[150] To discuss this in relation to the Eucharist in a Pentecostal proposal will, no doubt, add to that. Therefore, before I explain my understanding of how the Eucharist gives us a preview of the restoration of all things, which I am convinced is being worked out by the Triune God, what Monika Hellwig says helps my discussion provide an anchor. Hellwig maintains that

> every Eucharist we celebrate demands that we ask ourselves individually and collectively where we stand in relation to God's hospitality in the world—whether we are acting as fellow hosts of God's hospitality in the world or trying to corner a monopoly on it.[151]

Thus, the trajectory of this discussion of the Eucharist as *apokatastasis* is to stay as far as possible from the likelihood of cornering a monopoly on God's radical transformative and endless hospitality towards his creation.

It is not the purpose of this section to discuss the doctrine of *apokatastasis* thoroughly. For example, that task has been undertaken very carefully by classics and early Christianity scholar Ilaria Ramelli. I will, however, review the doctrine sufficiently enough to give context to our discussion. The Christian use of the word *apokatastasis* is varied. Although Origen acknowledges receiving the word from a Greek philosophical tradition with a wide range of meanings, his use of the word is always connected to his understanding of universal salvation

---

150. Ludlow, *Universal Salvation*, 38.
151. Hellwig, *Eucharist and the Hunger*, 20.

and restoration.¹⁵² On the other hand, aside from universal salvation, Gregory of Nyssa also considers the meaning of the word as a person's return to health and a sinner's return to the church.¹⁵³ Modern scholars have different opinions regarding the understanding of how the word is used in Acts 3:21. Ramelli maintains that in Acts 3:21, the word already contains the understanding of the eschatological restoration of all things, although patristic scholar Morwenna Ludlow tends to be more careful in affirming whether such understanding can already be implied in the text or whether Peter is simply talking about the end time.¹⁵⁴ Ramelli maintains that the doctrine is grounded in Christ and Scripture, making it "authentically Christian."¹⁵⁵ Ludlow also takes this position, although she considers the doctrine to be a minority tradition in the early church.¹⁵⁶ The doctrine of *apokatastasis* as an authentic Christian doctrine is the position I take in this discussion. In essence, this doctrine says that because God is the supreme Good, and based on Christ's incarnation, death, and resurrection, God will grant mercy to all humans, who will be saved "and reach the knowledge of Truth."¹⁵⁷ This doctrine sees that the *imago Dei* in every human being can be broken by sin but can never be canceled, and it is the restoration of this brokenness that continues to be worked out by God.¹⁵⁸ This doctrine insists that because of God's salvific will and Christ's redemptive power, salvation cannot but be absolutely universal.¹⁵⁹ The *apokatastasis* doctrine maintains that God's omniscience, omnipotence, and universal benevolence are incompatible with an understanding of the eternal damnation of those who do not receive Christ.¹⁶⁰ Finally, this doctrine also sees that in light of what Paul says in 1 Cor 15:28 that God will be all in all, the telos of all will include the annihilation of the power of evil and death and the submission (voluntarily, for Origen) of all God's enemies.¹⁶¹ This brings us to the question of how

152. Ramelli, *Christian Doctrine of Apokatastasis*, 3–4.

153. Ludlow, *Universal Salvation*, 42.

154. Ramelli, *Christian Doctrine of Apokatastasis*, 4; Ludlow, *Universal Salvation*, 41.

155. Ramelli, *Christian Doctrine of Apokatastasis*, 817, 819.

156. Ludlow, Review of *Christian Doctrine*.

157. Ramelli, *Christian Doctrine of Apokatastasis*, 817.

158. Ramelli, *Christian Doctrine of Apokatastasis*, 820.

159. Ramelli, *Christian Doctrine of Apokatastasis*, 821.

160. Ramelli, *Christian Doctrine of Apokatastasis*, 822.

161. Ramelli, *Christian Doctrine of Apokatastasis*, 817.

to reconcile the problematic biblical passages that seem to suggest eternal punishment for the damned.

It is also not the primary purpose of this subsection to discuss at length the problematic passage that seems to suggest eternal punishment for the damned, like what is found in Matt 25:41. David Bentley Hart, in the concluding postscript of his New Testament translation, points out that when it comes to rendering the *aiōnios* in the New Testament, "there is a genuine ambiguity in the term in Greek that is impossible to render directly in an English equivalent."[162] Hart goes on to say,

> In the early centuries of the Church, especially in the Greek and Syrian East, the lexical plasticity of the noun and the adjective was fully appreciated—and often exploited—by a number of Christian theologians and exegetes. . . . Late in the fourth century, for instance, Basil the Great, bishop of Caesarea, reported that the vast majority of his fellow Christians (at least, in the Greek-speaking East with which he was familiar) assumed that "hell" is not an eternal condition, and that the "*aiōnios* punishment" of the age to come would end when the soul had been purified of its sins and thus prepared for union with God.[163]

This ambiguity is attested by others as well. Three scholars with different views of universal salvation, Michael McClymond (who is against it), Ludlow, and Ramelli concur that the word *aiōnios* was not necessarily understood as eternal in ancient and patristic sources.[164] The standard Greek lexicon BDAG gives "pertaining to a long period of time" as its first definition of *aiōnios* and only then followed by "pertaining to a period of time without beginning or end" and "pertaining to a period of unending duration," as its second and third definitions, which at the very least gives room for the argument of ambiguity.[165] Bishop Kallistos Ware, although not explicitly holding to the understanding of the rendering of *aiōnios* as eternal that Hart and others maintain (Ware asks, "How can a God of love accept that even a single one of his creatures whom he has made should remain for ever in hell?"), or to Hart's universalism, for that matter, points out that because of God's great love, hell is not a

---

162. Hart, *New Testament*, 444.

163. Hart, *New Testament*, 445–46.

164. McClymond, "*Origenes Vindicatus*," 824; Ludlow, *Universal Salvation*, 34; Ramelli, *Christian Doctrine of Apokatastasis*, 28, 55; Ramelli, "Reply," 832.

165. BDAG 33.

place absent of God's presence.[166] It is plausible to connect Ware's with the thought of second-century church father Clement of Alexandria, who, in his doctrine of punishment, sees hell as "medicinal and pedagogical" as opposed to vindictive, which is alien to the character of God.[167] This presence is, of course, accomplished by Christ's descent to hell, his ultimate act of self-emptying, which another Eastern Orthodox writer points out has always been celebrated in the Eastern liturgy to be "the starting point of humanity's ascent toward deification (*theōsis*)."[168]

I will point out, however, that the idea of a restoration of all things should not surprise Christians, as it is hinted at in many places, even in the Hebrew Scriptures. Through the prophet Ezekiel, the Lord speaks of the restoration of Eden after the day of cleansing of iniquities that he brings forth (36:33–38). Through the prophet Isaiah (65:17–25), the Lord speaks a promise to a group of unfaithful people about a new heaven and new earth, a place where none of the former things will again be remembered. The theme of the promise that God speaks through Isaiah includes joy, life, liberty, and justice, the very things for which the old creation is waiting. The very same theme is found in the last two chapters of the book of Revelation. In my view, the hope for the restoration of all things given by Scripture must be the lens through which we read difficult texts such as Matt 25:41 above. Another example of a difficult text in the New Testament is Luke 14:24, in which the disheartened king, after being stood up by the original group of people he had invited to attend his banquet, says, "For I tell you, none of those who were invited will taste my dinner." Along with reading it through the lens of restoration given by Scripture, in particular, we must also read this one in light of the parables given by Jesus that we find in the next chapter. In Luke 15, we encounter the act of relentless searching done by the shepherd for his lost sheep and the woman for her lost coin, followed by the constant waiting of the father for his younger son who went to the faraway land, and the act of humbling himself when he went out to find the older son—representing the church folks—who threw a tantrum and rejected participating in the banquet thrown by his father (Luke 15:1–32).

As I have shown in the previous section, at least for the Eastern Orthodox Church, there is already contained in the Eucharist the idea of

---

166. Ware, *Orthodox Way*, 135–36.
167. Ludlow, *Universal Salvation*, 32.
168. Alfeyev, *Christ the Conqueror*, 217.

the celebration as the church's passage from this world into the world to come, by which the church is given a foretaste of the joy and peace of the kingdom.[169] I maintain that this is precisely where the Eucharist provides the church with a preview of *apokatastasis*. Geoffrey Wainwright seems to begin to go in that direction when he says,

> To his feast in the final kingdom God is inviting all people, for he has willed to have *mercy on all* (Rom. 11:32); and the invitation to the sacramental meal which is the sign of that final feast is therefore likewise universal.[170]

From here on, however, I part ways with Wainwright. He maintains that the meal offers salvation "to all who will accept; and on the shadow side, those who will not yet, or who will no longer, accept the invitation are choosing death rather than life, are excluding themselves from salvation."[171] In my view, it is difficult to exclude oneself from the offer of salvation even if one were to throw a tantrum, leave the church, and reject the hospitality banquet thrown by the Father, like what we have seen with the older son, or if one were first to choose the way of hell to get to the banquet like the younger son. It is on the grounds that Christ is present even in hell that the younger son is able to "come to himself" (Luke 15:17). In the place of judgment, as the image of his father, he realizes how far he has drifted from his father's likeness. This image and likeness, which are genuinely found in Christ, are revealed to him by the Holy Spirit and are impossible to reject ontologically. We are made in God's image and likeness, and one can turn away from that ontological reality only so far that, at one point, there is nowhere else to go but to return. Even at that far place, Christ is present through the Holy Spirit, and as Sergius Bulgakov puts it, "It is impossible to appear before Christ and to see Him without loving Him."[172]

The Father is always inviting his children to the banquet he is hosting to celebrate them in his kingdom. Hence, the Eastern Orthodox Church has always called the Eucharist the sacrament of the kingdom, a meal through which the church enters the kingdom, which they celebrate by exclaiming in their liturgy, "Blessed is the Kingdom of the Father, and

---

169. Schmemann, "Missionary Imperative," 198.
170. Wainwright, *Eucharist and Eschatology*, 161; emphasis added.
171. Wainwright, *Eucharist and Eschatology*, 161.
172. Bulgakov, *Bride of the Lamb*, 459.

the Son and the Holy Spirit, now and ever and unto ages of ages."[173] For this reason, I maintain that the Eucharist is a sign of the restoration of all things, a sign that points to the kingdom that is all about justice, righteousness, peace, and joy, which continues to be wrought by the Holy Spirit, who is the leaves of the tree of life healing the nations until no one accursed is found (Rom 14:17, Rev 22:2–3).

The implication of seeing the Eucharist as a preview of *apokatastasis* for Pentecostals is far reaching. For this section, I will limit myself to looking at it only from our SET paradigm. The transformation that is sought after and begins to take place at the altar in the church's encounter with her risen and living Lord will need to be seen holistically. First, transformation *is* restoration. It is not just about the transformation of the people as a community but also the whole cosmos that is created through and for and held together by Christ, who is before all things (Col 1:15–17). Viewed in this way, in celebrating the Eucharist, the participants are genuinely transformed into their priestly vocation, offering the whole of creation with thanksgiving to God, who will restore all things.

Second, transformation cannot *but* be restoration, because there is nothing transformative about annihilation and eternal damnation. In the Eucharist, we anamnetically remember that the Christian faith is built on the hope of a love that never ends nor fails (1 Cor 13:8, 13). As Chris Green puts it, "The mark of perfect love is perfected in the ineluctable desire to see to the good of the beloved. Love is perfected not in the one loving but in the one loved."[174] The Pentecostal church is reminded, therefore, that every time they celebrate the Eucharist, we subject ourselves to this love that will see to it that "God will be all in all" (1 Cor 15:28). We are sent into the world to live a holy life that is holistic, which Green says is "lived sanctifyingly—offered up, eucharistically, for the sake of the neighbor and the neighbor's world. [It is exemplified in] the love that we see in God's gospel-hospitality for us."[175] Because in the end, all humanity, joined by the whole of creation, will become part of the intimate Trinitarian mutual indwelling, "being wholly taken up into the circle of love that exists within God."[176]

These are the two implications directly related to the SET paradigm. I will discuss other implications relating to this proposal for a renewal

173. Schmemann, *Eucharist*, 40.
174. Green, *Sanctifying Interpretation*, 86.
175. Green, *Sanctifying Interpretation*, 86.
176. Ware, *Orthodox Way*, 28.

theology of the Eucharist as a whole, which will also include the implications for ecclesial practices in the concluding chapter that comes next.

CONCLUSION

In this chapter, I have constructed a *renewal theology of the Eucharist* using a pneumatological lens within an implicit Trinitarian framework. Through the lens of pneumatology, I maintain that there is an internal logic of SET in the Eucharist that informs the spirituality of Pentecostalism in a way that mediates the *via salutis*. The renewal theology I constructed attempts to offer a revision to the Pentecostal sacramental theology and practice. As I have said earlier, what has been developed here does not necessarily represent what other Pentecostals see as Pentecostal theology or what they see in the Eucharist. That is why it needs to be grounded in pneumatology. It is the Holy Spirit, in the freedom that he affords, who makes it possible for a Pentecostal theologian to think constructively (2 Cor 3:17) and make a distinct theological contribution to the ongoing conversation with the intention that Pentecostals will continue to develop a greater appreciation for this meal that Jesus gave to his church.

In this chapter, I have proposed to look at the Eucharist as a meal of solidarity, the Eucharist as a celebration that demands justice and right-relatedness (righteousness), the Eucharist as a gift to the church for managing the world's hunger, the Eucharist as healing, the Eucharist in which the church would find her missional impulse, the Eucharist as a meal enacting the eschatological heavenly assembly, and the Eucharist as a preview of the restoration of all things (*apokatastasis*). By doing so, I maintain that Pentecostals will be the eschatological people they really are in a hopeful sense as the Eucharist makes them into the church, the bride of Christ they are called to be.

6

Conclusions and Implications for Ecclesial Practices

THE CONTRIBUTION OF THIS BOOK

IN THIS BOOK, I argue that the Eucharist can be examined theologically through a Pentecostal spirituality framework known as SET. As I pointed out in the previous chapters, the SET paradigm is a model for understanding Pentecostal spirituality that Mark J. Cartledge constructed. The model is a way to see the spiritual transformation process that people experience through a dynamic and intentional encounter with God as people respond in their search for the divine. I contend that looking at the Eucharist using a SET paradigm will inform Pentecostalism's theology and spirituality in such a way as to broaden the Pentecostal understanding of *via salutis*. The findings of my research have presented several contributions to renewal/Pentecostal theology in general and the sacramental theology of renewal/Pentecostal scholarship in particular. A deeper understanding of sacramentality is the right vehicle with which to make sense of our experience of a life-transforming participatory encounter with God. Non-Western Pentecostals may perhaps be the ones leading the recovery of sacramental ontology in the future, as, in contrast to the West, their world is essentially sacramental.[1] As the primary outcome of this research, I hope that the Pentecostal church will consider celebrating the Eucharist every time they gather to worship. In what follows, I will summarize these contributions in the order they appear in this research.

First, I began by presenting an analysis of the eucharistic theology of major Pentecostal denominations. I showed that although Pentecostalism is inherently sacramental, this sacramentality has yet to come out explicitly in the language of the systematic theology volumes that can be considered de facto official systematic theology of the denomination. With the systematic theology put out by the US Assemblies of God, it was quite evident that these volumes do not even attempt to be creative. Instead, they seem to be focusing merely on expounding on the AG sixteen fundamentals, meaning that they are more concerned with defending their doctrinal position. This results in a deficient theological language to explain the inherently Pentecostal sacramental praxis. The same goes for the Cleveland school; known to be theologically more creative in general, it is not yet reflected in the Church of God's systematic theologies. Even as the importance of the experiences of encounters with the divine is pointed out, how this encounter takes place, whether metaphysically, mystically, or pneumatologically, was never explained. With regard to the systematic theologies of Foursquare, they do not attempt to be constructive; instead, they provide scriptural proof texts to demonstrate the church's beliefs and understanding of the Lord's Supper. It was quite surprising that the discussion on remembrance was a genuinely eucharistic *anamnēsis*, a discussion missing from the other systematic theology volume. From all the denominations' systematic theology volumes, the key finding is that there is too little evidence of the pneumatology at play in their theological construction and a lack of material to map the Eucharist into a celebration that is a SET process.

Following the denominations' systematic theologies, I presented the most current contributions regarding the theology of the Eucharist from a Pentecostal perspective written as journal articles, monographs, or books that contain a discussion on the Eucharist. In looking at these works, I specifically tried to map their way of looking at the Eucharist into a SET process. In contrast to the eucharistic theology of major Pentecostal denominations, these theological contributions showed a more positive progression of Pentecostal thinking, embracing its inherent

---

1. Chan, *Pentecostal Ecclesiology*, 116.

sacramentality. I showed that Kenneth Archer's embrace of metaphorical language could help move Pentecostals from the strictly cognitive way of understanding the Eucharist to a more affective way that would enrich Pentecostal's narrative-praxis reflection as they go through the experience of *via salutis*. For Simon Chan, even if the historic position that he adopts could be an obstacle to Pentecostals, it is important to note his insistence that total transformation comes from the Trinitarian "encounter" that is both pneumatologically Christocentric and christologically pneumatic. For Chris Green, a search that begins in the proclamation of the word becomes a eucharistic encounter through the pneumatic operation of the Spirit in the meal, meaning believers have their eyes opened in the breaking of bread, resulting in the "transformation" of the believer's lives. For Christopher Stephenson, an encounter with the Spirit in the Eucharist, while remembering the physical absence of Jesus—although Jesus is never absent—should bring awareness in the church that they need to respond by concrete actions to address the brokenness around them. The "search" in Dan Tomberlin comes in "active-representation," remembering that gives believers an "encounter" and offers full participation in the ongoing divine drama of salvation, resulting in "transformation" in the lives of the believers. Wolfgang Vondey reads the Pentecostal story in a sacramental way marked by four movements: the creation of a sacramental environment, a call to divine-human encounter, a response to the encounter, and the transformative effects. What can be deduced from the most current writers is all the theologians discussed issue a call to the Pentecostal church to take the celebration of the Eucharist more seriously and to incorporate it more fully into the life of the church. What they propose in their reading of the Eucharist fits well within the SET paradigm and is distinctively Pentecostal, yet not without any commonality with the eucharistic theology of other church traditions.

In chapter 3, I began by exploring the pneumatology found in the eucharistic theology of John D. Zizioulas as a representative of Eastern Orthodoxy. In doing so, my goal was to show that for Eastern Orthodoxy, it is clear that the *epiclēsis* makes the Eucharist; that is, it is because of the work of the Holy Spirit that the *anamnēsis* or "remembering" becomes a multidimensional charismatic event that reenacts the event of Pentecost. The day of Pentecost is what propels the disciples to become the church, and in the reenacting of this day, a process of SET can be traced. Following that, I investigated the role of the Holy Spirit in Roman Catholic eucharistic theology. This was accomplished by piecing together some of

CONCLUSIONS AND IMPLICATIONS FOR ECCLESIAL PRACTICES   185

what has been written by Roman Catholic thinkers on the subject matter, namely, Bouyer, Congar, Lubac, Dulles, and O'Connor. Here, I pointed out that the *epiclēsis* takes a slightly different role in the Roman Catholic Church. Up until the Second Vatican Council, the Holy Spirit was somehow overshadowed by the pope, the Virgin Mary, and the practice of eucharistic adoration.[2] Having said that, the Roman Catholic Church sees the Holy Spirit himself, who is working in the background, sanctifying the gifts on the altar and being responsible for the transubstantiation of the elements. The process of SET in the Roman Catholic Church is more visible as embedded in the liturgical language of the Eucharist. Subsequently, I explored the role of pneumatology in the eucharistic theology of three main Protestant Reformers, namely, Zwingli, Luther, and Calvin, and how their view of the Eucharist is quite different. Regardless of the differences, it is pneumatology that offers a way for Protestants to be "eucharistic people" because a pneumatological lens is what enables the Protestant church to create a sympathetic historical and theological climate, which is required in order for the Eucharist to be central in the worship life of the Protestant church. I also contend that because the Holy Spirit is responsible for making "eucharistic people," then pneumatology is the driving force of the SET process. Finally, as the goal was to continue the ongoing dialogue the Pentecostal tradition has with those who are outside as its way to participate with the Holy Spirit in the work of bringing unity in the church, I concluded by showing key takeaways available for Pentecostal eucharistic theology, or the contribution that Pentecostal theology could offer, both in light of the SET paradigm.

In the fourth chapter, I demonstrated that the Pentecostal text-community-Spirit hermeneutic allows an amalgamation of how other Christian traditions read the eucharistic text into Pentecostal reading to construct, expand, and precisely locate the Pentecostal understanding of the Eucharist within an SET framework. Using a "pneumatological imagination" inherent in text-community-Spirit, I demonstrated the possibility of coming to a reading of the text that possesses an ecumenical awareness, which, in essence, is an understanding of the "community" of interpreters that has been expanded and enlarged, allowing incorporation of how other traditions interpret the "text." I showed that the Eastern Orthodox use of Scripture as primarily to be experienced in the context of liturgical worship is similar to, and therefore may inform,

---

2. Congar, *I Believe*, 1:160.

how Pentecostals see Scripture as normative as a source of guide and teaching to live in the world. I also showed that it is possible to see the Roman Catholic understanding of "living tradition" as having similarity to, and therefore possibly informing, the understanding of "community" in text-community-Spirit. This enlarged understanding of community is precisely how the Pentecostal text-community-Spirit hermeneutical principle allows for a certain "fluidity" in the definition of the community of interpreters. That is, the idea of community is elastic enough to accommodate other reading traditions into "our community," compelling Pentecostals to be open to other traditions as having insights into God's truth that could be incorporated into our understanding.

I also looked into the Pentecostal hermeneutical principles that have been presented by several Pentecostal scholars, namely John Christopher Thomas, Kenneth J. Archer, and Amos Yong. The purpose of this was to show that the work of interpretation does not take place in a vacuum but within the community's contextual horizon, which I argued always necessitates, even requires, the interaction with the reading of other communities as well. This interaction is what participating in the ever-widening *koinōnia* of the Trinity that marks a pneumatic hermeneutic is all about. Looking into the hermeneutical principles of these Pentecostal theologians confirms the elasticity of the idea of community that allows the accommodation of other reading traditions into ours. This was followed by showing how Gadamer's fusion of horizons—one that takes place between the text, the reading of different traditions, and ours—can take shape. I showed that in the fusion of horizons, there is an expansion of our horizon so as to take into account the differences of the other and enrich our perspective. I argued that if explained theologically, the reproductive and productive activity that fuses different horizons has always been the Holy Spirit's work, which works through faith communities' relationships. To be in relationship is the way to understand, which is beyond what the Enlightenment's Cartesian *cogito ergo sum* manifesto can ever achieve. The result allows Pentecostals to be in an embodied posture of openness towards other communities in order to accomplish a productive activity that could inform their way of looking into the Eucharist. The Holy Spirit allows Pentecostals to be hospitable to both the Roman Catholic and Eastern Orthodox Churches through the way they read the text about the Eucharist. The process is guided by a pneumatological imagination that presents an opportunity to probe the interpretation of these different traditions in order to compare and, therefore, construct an

CONCLUSIONS AND IMPLICATIONS FOR ECCLESIAL PRACTICES   187

understanding that correlates with the SET process of Pentecostal spirituality, creating the fusion of horizons.

I then proceeded to demonstrate that the entire New Testament is by nature closely related to the Eucharist and that its origin is eucharistic. We saw this when Basil and other church fathers wrote their prayers. They were not prooftexting the Scriptures but recomposing the eucharistic materials in which they were steeped to make new ones. The redaction process of the New Testament has been both historically and logically preceded by, prepared for, and based upon the Eucharist. I argued that it makes sense for Pentecostals to consider how other traditions have understood the eucharistic provenance of text and to read it eucharistically as well, because the purpose of the text and the act of reading it, a process of "search," is remembrance or *anamnēsis*, which is a process of "encounter." Reading the text that way is the prerequisite of the sought transformation. I then presented a reading of Luke's cameo in Acts 2 of what the Spirit-filled church looks like, specifically v. 42. Through that text, I maintained that we are given the mark of this Spirit-filled church, which consists of devotion to four specific things: *the* teaching of the apostles, *the* fellowship, *the* breaking of bread, and *the* prayers. These four things together are a search and encounter process, which result in a community experiencing transformation. As a result, the Spirit's presence and work are manifested in the community through the church's communal life that points to the awaited eschatological reality, where the event of Pentecost is an event that inaugurates the church as Christ's image and body in the world.

Moving to this study's main constructive presentation, in chapter 5, I developed a *renewal theology of the Eucharist*, which is a theology constructed using a pneumatological lens within an implicit Trinitarian framework. Using a pneumatological imagination to guide my conversation with sources from different Christian traditions helped me construct several explicit descriptions of the meaning contained in the Eucharist. I maintained that it is plausible to deduce seven ways to understand the Eucharist. These seven things are the Eucharist as a meal of solidarity, the Eucharist as a meal that demands justice and right-relatedness (righteousness), the Eucharist as a gift to the church for managing the world's hunger, the Eucharist as healing, the Eucharist in which the church would find her missional impulse, the Eucharist as a meal enacting the eschatological heavenly assembly, and the Eucharist as a preview of the restoration of all things (*apokatastasis*). This is all made possible by the *anamnēsis*. That is, when believers in the power of the Holy Spirit remember Christ, we are re-membered (as in reincorporated) as Christ's body. We will review them one at a time.

In my discussion of the Eucharist as a meal of solidarity, I maintained that it is a meal that provides a transformative encounter with Christ, the one who stands in solidarity with us. By the power of the Holy Spirit, the meal enables us to self-empty ourselves for the sake of others. When Christ's solidarity is remembered in the power of the Holy Spirit, a transformation can and should take place in the person and the community of persons. The meal gives the church firsthand experience of the gracious invitation into the Triune God's perichoretic *koinōnia*, transforming them to become the extension of that fellowship to the world.

In the next part, I focussed on the Eucharist as a meal that demands justice and right-relatedness (righteousness) through a pneumatologically charged remembrance of the Eucharist as justice. First, the Christ encounter in the Eucharist, made possible by the Spirit, forces the church to confront their shortcoming as they are sent out into their mission. This is precisely the transformation taking place. I argue that this pneumatologically driven transformation includes the willingness to discard accepted paradigms that perpetuated injustice. I then specifically looked into my Indonesian context and maintained that a eucharistic justice made by Indonesian Christians who are part of the religious minority would be an opportunity to witness Christ's hospitality. The implication of connecting the Eucharist with hospitality and justice demands that we focus our understanding of salvation in terms of the righting (or in Pentecostal language, the healing) of the relationship that humanity has with God, the created order, and one another.

I then followed with a presentation of the Eucharist as a means to alleviate the hunger of the world. Because Jesus made eating the central act of worship of the church, this shows us the pivotal nature of people being fed, displaying the Eucharist's social justice implication. I maintained that social justice finds its source from the God that Jesus reveals. In that section, I also argued that, if examined through a SET paradigm, participating in an unworthy manner happens precisely when the community eats the bread and drinks the cup of the Lord in a way that does not result in transformative actions. Therefore, as Jesus feeds us with himself in the Eucharist, he is preparing us to be willing participants in his work of feeding the world. That is precisely where the transformation brought by the Eucharist takes place.

The next discussion was my attempt to rediscover the Eucharist as medicine, affirming the healing that is offered in the celebration, which, in my view, is a way to emphasize its Pentecostal-ness. The approach to the theme of Eucharist as healing was made using three angles, namely, as a place that heals (that is, makes whole) the Pentecostal experience of Spirit baptism, a place for personal healing, and a place for the hope of cosmic healing. I argued that the process of SET taking place in the church is when the Eucharist opens up the Pentecostal community to be baptized by the Spirit, resulting in signs and wonders, while, at the same time, healing us from a showy understanding of Spirit baptism. Through a discussion on the doctrine of transubstantiation of Roman Catholicism, I argued that as the people receive the elements, they experience a life-giving touch of Christ that absorbs the broken bodies of the recipients into his own body. I maintained that the doctrine of transubstantiation provides an opportunity for Pentecostals to reshape and reconfigure their doctrine of healing in a more corporate way. Touched physically by the risen Jesus in the eucharistic elements, the community of believers is transformed into a healed community. The final discussion on the Eucharist as healing is that it is a place for the hope of cosmic healing. The Eucharist reminds us that the benefits of *Christus Victor* are not yet fully realized. Hence, it prevents an over-realized eschatology, maintaining the already-not-yet tension, but at the same time, it demands that we examine ourselves as a community in which our posture is in relation to the radical hospitality and healing that God extends throughout the cosmos.

The next discussion was about the Eucharist as mission, which is critical for Pentecostals because of the movement's missionary impulse. There are at least three ways the Eucharist is missional, namely, discernment in seeing the other; sending Christians to their mission (John 6); and finally, the sign of the great eschatological feast. Through a Pentecost event in the Eucharist, the Pentecostal church, people who have experienced divine embrace and hospitality, discern themselves as being invited to participate in God, embracing the world, offering and extending God's hospitality to others. In seeing the Eucharist as mission, the people are brought into the very act in which Jesus feeds his people with himself for the "spiritual nourishment" to go on their mission in the world. The Eucharist is also missional because it points to the great banquet that God will provide in the final kingdom. The meal's missionary significance comes in the fact that it is a foretaste of the universal triumph of his saving will and purpose. From this eschatological perspective, salvation is an experience of coming into the "training program" of a fellowship of missionaries; sanctification is experiencing a radical personal transformation from a life of the flesh to life in the Spirit.

Eschatology has become a very significant doctrinal issue for Pentecostals. In that section, I approached the subject of this discussion in two ways. First, I maintained that a greater appreciation of the Eucharist as eschatology offers Pentecostals a way to look into a more hopeful eschatology, having greater confidence in the gospel of Jesus Christ. Second, because of the greater confidence in the gospel, Pentecostals could work towards the hopeful eschatological unity of the body of Christ by celebrating an open and available meal. In this theme, I presented the Eucharist as a passage for the church to experience the Lord's eschatological nearness, not in the form of an over-realized eschatology, but in an experience of peace that transcends all understanding that precisely maintains the tension of "already" and "not yet." That brought my proposal for an open Eucharist. In celebrating an open Eucharist, Pentecostals can enact the foretaste of the eschatological righteousness, peace, and joy that will be made complete by the Holy Spirit. I also maintained that this openness could be done while upholding the standard of self-examination for anyone participating in the Eucharist, preventing it from becoming a free-for-all event that nullifies its meaning.

The final section in my constructive proposal was to discuss the Eucharist as a preview of *apokatastasis*, or the restoration of all things. I maintained that the somewhat controversial doctrine of *apokatastasis* is an authentic Christian doctrine. The *apokatastasis* doctrine holds that God's omniscience, omnipotence, and universal benevolence are incompatible with an understanding of the eternal damnation of those who do not receive Christ. The idea of a restoration of all things is not a surprise to Christians, as it is hinted at in many places, even in the Hebrew Scriptures. I pointed out that this doctrine shows us that for an image-bearer, judgment is the realization of how far one has drifted from the father's likeness. This image and likeness, which are genuinely found in Christ, are revealed to a person by the Holy Spirit and are impossible to reject ontologically. We are made in God's image and likeness, and one can turn away from that ontological reality only so far that, at one point, there is nowhere else to go but to return. There are at least two implications for seeing the Eucharist as a preview of *apokatastasis* within a SET paradigm. The transformation that is sought after and begins to take place at the altar in the church's encounter with her risen and living Lord is seen holistically. First, transformation *is* restoration. It is not just about transforming the people as a community but also about the whole cosmos created through and for and held together by Christ, who is before all things. Second, transformation cannot *but* be restoration because there is nothing transformative about annihilation and eternal damnation. In the Eucharist, we anamnetically remember that the Christian faith is built on the hope of a love that never ends nor fails.

IMPLICATIONS FOR THE LIFE OF THE PENTECOSTAL CHURCH

Here, my goal is to sketch the implications of this research for the life of the Pentecostal church. Pentecostalism today is regarded as one of the most exciting places to be as a constructive theologian. For the most part, however, this constructive conversation has not trickled down much into the average Pentecostal congregation. The Pentecostal church has some catching up to do—especially the Pentecostal church in the majority world, including Indonesia, where our worldview has always been one that is more enchanted than post-Enlightenment Western Pentecostals'.

To be a true Pentecostal church that is richly pneumatological, the task of understanding the relationship between the Spirit and the Eucharist is not just reserved for the theologian, but, more importantly, for the church to struggle with, reflect on, and live out on an ongoing basis. For this to happen, a departure from biblicism to a greater appreciation of sacramentalism is needed. The average Pentecostal church celebrates the Eucharist either only once a month or every once in a while. The typical reasons given are either too frequent observance would water down its meaning, or the Eucharist, like birthdays and wedding anniversaries, is a celebrations that happens only every so often. This is why we need a paradigm shift from looking at the Eucharist as a commemorative event to seeing it as Christ feeding himself to us so that we can become what we eat.

The way this takes place in the life of a Pentecostal church is to incorporate a weekly celebration of the Eucharist into our liturgy. I cannot emphasize this enough! I believe there are at least four reasons for this: first, liturgy is the language of faith; second, faith is learned by practice and participation; third, by having the sacrament of Eucharist central in the liturgy, the ministry of the word becomes complete, allowing the believer to be open to the work of the Spirit; and finally, by having the sacrament central in worship, Pentecostals will be even more ready to be sent into the world to fulfill their mission. I will explain each of these reasons briefly.

First, aside from its spiritual dimension, the church also has a sociological dimension. Its purpose is to make the spiritual dimension a reality precisely through a process of inscribing a paradigmatic pattern of the full Christian reality. In so doing, this shapes the church to become more like Christ and be the body of Christ. Becoming and being are two elements that go hand in hand because a person is a Christian only by becoming a member of the body. Being incorporated into the body is where we go through the inscription process and learn the language of faith.

Second, the intention of making these inscriptions is nothing less than to make it second nature to us, forming habits of good spiritual discipline so that we will want to seek, draw closer, and be more attuned to God. The liturgy in which we participate in the Eucharist is a snapshot of what is to come when the kingdom of God is finally fully realized. When the Pentecostal church participates in the Eucharist, we get a preview of what it is like living in God's reality, the reality of how things are intended by God.

Third, making the Eucharist central in the Pentecostal liturgy completes the ministry of the word of God, making the believer open and receptive to the work of the Spirit. The ministries of the word and sacrament are two foundational yet inseparable practices that make up the church. It is not by coincidence that Luke puts these two occasions in his gospel as a way to point out to us that they are not two separate acts but rather a unified event that Christ is instituting to the church as two things that form one single act of worship. The disciples recognized Jesus after the Great High Priest did two distinct but inseparable acts: preach and preside. As the church experiences the foretaste of the eschatological reality in its complete sense through reflection (word) and participation (sacrament), they are then open to the work of the Spirit.

The fourth and final reason, as we have seen earlier, is that mission is embedded in the DNA of the Pentecostal church. Mission, however, has been mostly understood as a cross-cultural mission, which is the mark of a Pentecostal church, and it is the canon by which we are measured. If the Pentecostal church seeks to be missional in a much fuller understanding, then we need to discover and fully understand the fact that there is a robust missional dimension of the Eucharist. Through the Eucharist, the church becomes a witness of Christ and the recipient of his Spirit, which is being made into a gift for the world. As we have seen earlier in the Orthodox liturgy, the Eucharist ends our journey of ascension, putting us back into a new beginning, competent and able to carry out our mission. The Eucharist is a place of radical hospitality. As the Pentecostal church celebrates the meal, they are turned into a community in which acceptance and mercy are found, making it a place of conversion and transformation of life.

In short, a greater appreciation of the Eucharist and its meanings that have been presented in this research could bring the Pentecostal church into greater confidence in the gospel of Jesus Christ, moving her from a biblicist outlook to a christologically pneumacentric and pneumatologically Christocentric outlook, making her into the Trinitarian image she is created to be.

IDEAS TO INVESTIGATE FURTHER

Having summarized this study's contribution and implication and realizing that the work of theological reflection is never finished, the following are ideas for future investigation. The first is in the area of practical theology. How would the meanings of the Eucharist, which are the main findings of this research, affect the life of the congregation if they are woven into the practice and the teaching of a local church? What sort of transformative outcome would the findings bring if they were embedded into the praxis of a local church? How would the transformative outcomes vary between a local Pentecostal church in the Western world and a local Pentecostal church in the majority world? How would those outcomes vary between a local Western Pentecostal church that is Anglocentric compared to a local Pentecostal ethnic church?

Second, in the area of biblical studies, it is worth investigating what a Pentecostal eucharistic reading of the Bible is—that is, to look into the text as having eucharistic provenance. In my opinion, such a reading would fit not only into a SET paradigm but also into a text-community-Spirit hermeneutical principle. The result of this kind of reading would bridge theology and spirituality.

Third, it would be worth investigating how the Eucharist as solidarity, justice, and hunger management, each or together, resonate within the marginalized communities, whether the marginalization is caused by sexual or gender identities, ethnicity, religion, socioeconomic status, including systemic racism, or any combination of these. Although I belong to a religious minority in Indonesia, I am a male with a privileged upbringing. My context would make it easy to miss many of the rich ways the Eucharist could address these themes in addressing the transformation for which we, as the body of Christ, long.

Fourth, in this study, I have proposed that the Roman Catholic doctrine of transubstantiation presents an opportunity for the community of believers to experience a life-giving touch of Christ. I maintain that the doctrine of transubstantiation provides an opportunity for Pentecostals to reshape and reconfigure their doctrine of healing more corporately. Since healing is central for Pentecostals, what would that look like if the community of believers were transformed by the physical touch of Christ in the eucharistic elements into a healed community? What does a healed Pentecostal community look like? Finally, in light of my proposal relating the Eucharist with eschatology and *apokatastasis*, what are some of the implications of the Pentecostal doctrine of soteriology? It is worth looking into, especially as the conversation in Pentecostal theology has predominantly been coming from the West. How would Pentecostal theologians from Asia, Africa, and, to some degree, South America, who belong to religious minority groups and are located within pluralistic societies, understand the Eucharist as a promise of the restoration of all things?

When we embrace our sacramental nature, we can take off "Saul's armor," which has been weighing us down. Therefore, let us eat and be nourished at Christ's table to have the ability to explore the undiscovered intellectual and spiritual treasures of our theology!

Bibliography

Albrecht, Daniel E. *Rites in the Spirit: A Ritual Approach to Pentecostal/ Charismatic Spirituality*. Journal of Pentecostal Theology Supplement Series 17. Sheffield: Sheffield Academic, 1999.

Alexander, Kimberly Ervan. "The Pentecostal Healing Community." In *Toward a Pentecostal Ecclesiology: The Church and the Fivefold Gospel*, edited by John Christopher Thomas, 183–206. Cleveland, TN: CPT, 2010.

Alfeyev, Hilarion. *Christ the Conqueror of Hell: The Descent into Hades from an Orthodox Perspective*. Crestwood, NY: St. Vladimir's Seminary Press, 2009.

Anderson, Allan. "Varieties, Taxonomies, and Definitions." In *Studying Global Pentecostalism: Theories and Methods*, edited by Allan Anderson et al., 13–29. Anthropology of Christianity 6. Berkeley: University of California Press, 2010.

Anderson, Allan Heaton. *An Introduction to Pentecostalism: Global Charismatic Christianity*. 2nd ed. Introduction to Religion. New York: Cambridge University Press, 2013.

Archer, Kenneth J. "Nourishment for Our Journey: The Pentecostal *Via Salutis* and Sacramental Ordinances." *Journal of Pentecostal Theology* 13 (2004) 79–96.

———. *A Pentecostal Hermeneutic for the Twenty-First Century: Spirit, Scripture and Community*. Journal of Pentecostal Theology Supplement Series 28. London: T. & T. Clark, 2004.

Aritonang, Jan, and Karel Steenbrink. *A History of Christianity in Indonesia*. Studies in Christian Mission 35. Leiden: Brill, 2008.

Arrington, French L. *Christian Doctrine: A Pentecostal Perspective*. Edited by Daniel L. Black. 3 vols. Cleveland, TN: Pathway, 1994.

Assemblies of God. "Affiliations." Assemblies of God, n.d. https://ag.org/ About/About-the-AG/Affiliations.

———. "Assemblies of God 16 Fundamental Truths." Assemblies of God, n.d. https://ag.org/Beliefs/Statement-of-Fundamental-Truths.

Augustine, Daniela C. *Pentecost, Hospitality, and Transfiguration: Toward a Spirit-Inspired Vision of Social Transformation*. Cleveland, TN: CPT, 2012.

Bailey, Kenneth E. *Jesus through Middle Eastern Eyes: Cultural Studies in the Gospels*. Downers Grove, IL: IVP Academic, 2008.

Banks, Patricia A. *Race, Ethnicity, and Consumption: A Sociological View*. New York: Routledge, 2020.

Barton, Stephen. "Dislocating and Relocating Holiness: A New Testament Study." In *Holiness: Past and Present*, edited by Stephen Barton, 193–213. New Century Theology. London: T. & T. Clark, 2002.

Basil the Great. *On the Holy Spirit*. Translated by Stephen M. Hildebrand. Yonkers, NY: St. Vladimir's Seminary Press, 2011.

Bauckham, Richard. *The Theology of the Book of Revelation*. New Testament Theology. Cambridge: Cambridge University Press, 1993.

Belcher, J. David. Review of *The Eucharistic Communion and the World*, by John D. Zizioulas. *AThR* 95 (2013) 207–9.

Biddy, Wesley Scott. "Re-Envisioning the Pentecostal Understanding of the Eucharist: An Ecumenical Proposal." *Pneuma* 28 (2006) 228–51.

Bloesch, Donald G. *The Last Things: Resurrection, Judgment, Glory*. Christian Foundations 7. Downers Grove, IL: IVP Academic, 2005.

Boersma, Hans. *Heavenly Participation: The Weaving of a Sacramental Tapestry*. Grand Rapids: Eerdmans, 2011.

Bouyer, Louis. *Eucharist: Theology and Spirituality of the Eucharistic Prayer*. Notre Dame: University of Notre Dame Press, 1989.

Breck, John. *Scripture in Tradition: The Bible and Its Interpretation in the Orthodox Church*. Crestwood, NY: St. Vladimir's Seminary Press, 2001.

Bricknell, Richard. "Ordinances: The Marginalised Aspects of Pentecostalism." In *Pentecostal Perspectives*, edited by Keith Warrington, 204–22. Carlisle, UK: Authentic, 1998.

Bromiley, G. W. "Introduction to Zwingli's 'On the Lord's Supper.'" In *Zwingli and Bullinger*, edited by G. W. Bromiley, 176–84. Louisville: Westminster John Knox, 1953.

Brown, Raymond E. *An Introduction to the New Testament*. New Haven: Yale University Press, 1997.

Bruner, Frederick Dale. *The Churchbook, Matthew 13–28*. Vol. 2 of *Matthew: A Commentary*. Rev ed. Grand Rapids: Eerdmans, 2007.

Bulgakov, Sergius. *The Bride of the Lamb*. Translated by Boris Jakim. Grand Rapids: Eerdmans, 2001.

Calvin, John. *Institutes of the Christian Religion*. Edited by John T. McNeill, translated by Ford Lewis Battles. Louisville: Westminster John Knox, 1960.

Cartledge, Mark J. *Encountering the Spirit: The Charismatic Tradition*. Maryknoll, NY: Orbis, 2007.

———. *The Mediation of the Spirit: Interventions in Practical Theology*. Grand Rapids: Eerdmans, 2015.

———. "Pneumatic Hermeneutic: A Reply to Respondents." In *Spirit and Scripture: Exploring a Pneumatic Hermeneutic*, edited by Kevin L. Spawn and Archie T. Wright, 186–88. Repr., London: Bloomsbury T. & T. Clark, 2013.

———. *Practical Theology: Charismatic and Empirical Perspectives*. Repr., Eugene, OR: Wipf and Stock, 2012.

———. *Testimony in the Spirit: Rescripting Ordinary Pentecostal Theology*. Oxford: Routledge, 2017.

———. "Text-Community-Spirit: The Challenges Posed by Pentecostal Theological Method to Evangelical Theology." In *Spirit and Scripture: Exploring a Pneumatic Hermeneutic*, edited by Kevin L. Spawn and Archie T. Wright, 130–42. Repr., London: Bloomsbury T. & T. Clark, 2013.

Castelo, Daniel. *Pentecostalism as a Christian Mystical Tradition*. Grand Rapids: Eerdmans, 2017.

Cavanaugh, William T. *Torture and Eucharist: Theology, Politics, and the Body of Christ*. Challenges in Contemporary Theology. Oxford: Blackwell, 1998.

Chan, Simon. *Grassroots Asian Theology: Thinking the Faith from the Ground Up*. Downers Grove, IL: IVP Academic, 2014.

———. *Liturgical Theology: The Church as Worshiping Community*. Downers Grove, IL: IVP Academic, 2006.

———. *Pentecostal Ecclesiology: An Essay on the Development of Doctrine*. Blandford Forum, UK: Deo, 2011.

———. *Pentecostal Theology and the Christian Spiritual Tradition*. Repr., Eugene, OR: Wipf & Stock, 2011.

Cocksworth, Christopher J. *Evangelical Eucharistic Thought in the Church of England*. Cambridge: Cambridge University Press, 2002.

Collins, Raymond. *First Corinthians*. SP. Collegeville, MN: Glazier, 2006.

Congar, Yves. *I Believe in the Holy Spirit: The Complete Three-Volume Work in One Volume*. Milestones in Catholic Theology. New York: Crossroad, 1997.

———. *The Meaning of Tradition*. San Francisco: Ignatius, 2004.

Cross, Terry L. "A Proposal to Break the Ice: What Can Pentecostal Theology Offer Evangelical Theology?" *Journal of Pentecostal Theology* 10 (2002) 44–73.

Dabney, D Lyle. "Saul's Armor: The Problem and the Promise of Pentecostal Theology Today." *Pneuma* 23 (2001) 115–46.

Duffield, Guy P., and Nathaniel M. Van Cleave. *Foundations of Pentecostal Theology*. Los Angeles: LIFE Bible College Press, 1983.

Duffield, Guy P., et al., eds. *Declaration of Faith: Foursquare Sunday School Lessons*. Los Angeles: Foursquare Sunday School, 1949.

Dulles, Avery. "The Eucharist and the Mystery of the Trinity." In *Rediscovering the Eucharist: Ecumenical Conversations*, edited by Roch Kereszty, 226–39. New York: Paulist, 2003.

Dusing, Michael L. "The New Testament Church." In *Systematic Theology: A Pentecostal Perspective*, edited by Stanley M. Horton, 525–66. Springfield, MO: Logion, 1994.

Episcopal Church USA. *The Book of Common Prayer*. Greenwich, CT: Church Hymnal, 1979.

Faith and Order Commission. "Baptism, Eucharist and Ministry." Faith and Order Paper 111, the "Lima Text." World Council of Churches, 1982. https://www.oikoumene.org/sites/default/files/Document/FO1982_111_en.pdf.

Farkasfalvy, Denis. "The Eucharistic Provenance of New Testament Texts." In *Rediscovering the Eucharist: Ecumenical Conversations*, edited by Roch Kereszty, 27–51. New York: Paulist, 2003.

Farrar, Laura. "Chinese Companies 'Rent' White Foreigners." CNN, June 29, 2010. http://www.cnn.com/2010/BUSINESS/06/29/china.rent.white.people/index.html.

Fee, Gordon D. *The First Epistle to the Corinthians*. Rev ed. NICNT. Grand Rapids: Eerdmans, 2014.

———. *Paul's Letter to the Philippians*. NICNT. Grand Rapids: Eerdmans, 1995.

Francis, Pope. "*Laudato Si'*: On Care for Our Common Home." Vatican, May 24, 2015. http://www.vatican.va/content/francesco/en/encyclicals/documents/papa-francesco_20150524_enciclica-laudato-si.html.

Gadamer, Hans-Georg. "In Response to Jacques Derrida." In *Dialogue and Deconstruction: The Gadamer-Derrida Encounter*, edited by Diane P. Michelfelder and Richard E. Palmer, 55–57. Albany: SUNY Press, 1989.

———. *Truth and Method*. Translated by Joel Weinsheimer and Donald G. Marshall. Repr., London: Bloomsbury Academic, 2013.

Gavrilyuk, Paul L. "The Eschatological Dimension of Sacramental Unity." In *Come, Let Us Eat Together: Sacraments and Christian Unity*, edited

by George Kalantzis and Marc Cortez, 170–83. Wheaton Theology Conference Series. Downers Grove, IL: IVP Academic, 2018.
Green, Chris E. W. *Sanctifying Interpretation: Vocation, Holiness, and Scripture*. Cleveland, TN: CPT, 2015.
———. "Saving Liturgy: (Re)Imagining Pentecostal Liturgical Theology and Practice." In *Scripting Pentecost: A Study of Pentecostals, Worship and Liturgy*, edited by Mark J. Cartledge and A. J. Swoboda, 108–18. London: Routledge, 2016.
———. "'Then Their Eyes Were Opened': Pentecostal Reflections on the Church's Scripture and the Lord's Supper." *Pneuma* 35 (2013) 220–34.
———. *Toward a Pentecostal Theology of the Lord's Supper: Foretasting the Kingdom*. Cleveland, TN: CPT, 2012.
Grumett, David. Review of *The Eucharistic Communion and the World*, by John D. Zizioulas. *Ecclesiology* 8 (2012) 245–47.
GSJA. "Pengakuan Iman GSJA" [Statement of faith of Assemblies of God of Indonesia]. GSJA, n.d. https://www.gsja.org/uncategorized/pengakuan-iman-gsja.html.
Gutiérrez, Gustavo. *A Theology of Liberation: History, Politics, and Salvation*. 15th anniv. ed. Maryknoll, NY: Orbis, 1988.
Harmer, J. R., ed. *The Apostolic Fathers*. Translated by J. B. Lightfoot. V. 12.3.7. Accordance Bible Software, 2000. Mac.
Hart, David Bentley. *The New Testament: A Translation*. Repr., New Haven: Yale University Press, 2019.
———. "'Thine Own of Thine Own': Eucharistic Sacrifice in Orthodox Tradition." In *Rediscovering the Eucharist: Ecumenical Conversations*, edited by Roch Kereszty, 142–69. New York: Paulist, 2003.
Hellwig, Monika K. *Eucharist and the Hunger of the World*. 2nd ed. Kansas City: Sheed & Ward, 1992.
Hollenweger, Walter J. *The Pentecostals*. Repr., Peabody, MA: Hendrickson, 1988.
Horton, Stanley M., ed. *Systematic Theology: A Pentecostal Perspective*. Springfield, MO: Logion, 1994.
Hunsinger, George. *The Eucharist and Ecumenism: Let Us Keep the Feast*. Current Issues in Theology. Cambridge: Cambridge University Press, 2008.
Interdicasterial Commission. *Catechism of the Catholic Church*. Translated by United States Conference of Catholic Bishops. 2nd ed. Washington, DC: United States Conference of Catholic Bishops, 2019.
Johns, Cheryl Bridges. *Pentecostal Formation: A Pedagogy among the Oppressed*. Journal of Pentecostal Theology Supplement Series 2. Eugene, OR: Wipf and Stock, 2010.

Johnson, Luke Timothy. "The Eucharist and the Identity of Jesus." *Priests & People* 15 (2001) 230–35.

———. *The Writings of the New Testament: An Interpretation.* Rev ed. Minneapolis: Fortress, 2002.

Kärkkäinen, Veli-Matti. "The Pentecostal View." In *The Lord's Supper: Five Views*, edited by Gordon T. Smith, 117–35. Downers Grove, IL: IVP Academic, 2008.

———. "The Spirit and the Lord's Supper." In *Toward a Pneumatological Theology: Pentecostal and Ecumenical Perspectives on Ecclesiology, Soteriology, and Theology of Mission*, edited by Amos Yong, 135–46. Lanham, MD: UPA, 2002.

Land, Steven Jack. *Pentecostal Spirituality: A Passion for the Kingdom.* Cleveland, TN: CPT, 2010.

Lash, Ephrem. "The Prayers of the Liturgy of St Basil." Anastasis, Apr. 12, 2016. https://web.archive.org/web/20160412130047/http://anastasis.org.uk/Basil%20noted%5B3%5D.pdf.

Lewis, Jeffrey R. "The Feeding of the Multitudes, Eucharist as Nourishment." *Catechumenate* 34 (2012) 8–14.

Lossky, Vladimir. *The Mystical Theology of the Eastern Church.* Crestwood, NY: St. Vladimir's Seminary Press, 1997.

Lubac, Henri de. *Corpus Mysticum: The Eucharist and the Church in the Middle Ages.* Translated by Gemma Simmonds. Notre Dame: University of Notre Dame Press, 2007.

———. *Scripture in the Tradition.* Milestones in Catholic Theology. New York: Crossroad, 2001.

———. *The Splendor of the Church.* Rev. ed. San Francisco: Ignatius, 1999.

Ludlow, Morwenna. Review of *The Christian Doctrine of Apokatastasis: A Critical Assessment from the New Testament to Eriugena*, by Ilaria L. E. Ramelli. *Journal of Ecclesiastical History* 66 (2015) 619.

———. *Universal Salvation: Eschatology in the Thought of Gregory of Nyssa and Karl Rahner.* Oxford: Oxford University Press, 2009.

Luther, Martin. "The Babylonian Captivity of the Church." In *Three Treatises*, translated by A. T. W. Steinhäuser, 113–260, 2nd ed. Minneapolis: Fortress, 1990.

———. "Sermons on the Catechism." In *Martin Luther: Selections from His Writings*, edited by John Dillenberger, 207–39. New York: Anchor, 1958.

Macchia, Frank D. "Babel and the Tongues of Pentecost: Reversal or Fulfillment? A Theological Perspective." In *Speaking in Tongues: Multi-Disciplinary Perspectives*, edited by Mark J. Cartledge, 34–51. Milton Keynes, UK: Paternoster, 2006.

———. *Baptized in the Spirit: A Global Pentecostal Theology.* Grand Rapids: Zondervan Academic, 2006.

———. *Jesus the Spirit Baptizer: Christology in Light of Pentecost*. Grand Rapids: Eerdmans, 2018.

Maximus the Confessor. *On the Ecclesiastical Mystagogy: A Theological Vision of the Liturgy*. Translated by Jonathan J. Armstrong. Popular Patristic Series. Yonkers, NY: St. Vladimir's Seminary Press, 2019.

McClymond, Michael J. "*Origenes Vindicatus vel Rufinus Redivivus?* A Review of Ilaria Ramelli's *The Christian Doctrine of Apokatastasis* (2013)." *TS* 76 (2015) 813–26.

McIntosh, Mark A. *Mystical Theology: The Integrity of Spirituality and Theology*. Challenges in Contemporary Theology. Malden, MA: Wiley-Blackwell, 1998.

Menzies, William W. *Bible Doctrines: A Pentecostal Perspective*. Rev ed. Springfield, MO: Gospel, 1993.

Milavec, Aaron. *The Didache: Text, Translation, Analysis, and Commentary*. Collegeville, MN: Glazier, 2003.

Moloney, Francis J. "John 6 and the Celebration of the Eucharist." *Downside Review* 93 (1975) 243–51.

Morse, Jonathan K. "The Presence of Christ in the Eucharist: From Scripture to the Fourth Century from a Byzantine Perspective." *GOTR* 57 (2012) 135–54.

Nelson, R. David. Review of *The Eucharistic Communion and the World*, by John D. Zizioulas. *International Journal of Systematic Theology* 17 (2015) 365–68.

O'Connor, James T. *The Hidden Manna: A Theology of the Eucharist*. 2nd ed. San Francisco: Ignatius, 2005.

O'Loughlin, Thomas. *The Eucharist: Origins and Contemporary Understandings*. Repr., London: Bloomsbury T. & T. Clark, 2015.

Pearlman, Myer. *Knowing the Doctrines of the Bible*. Springfield. MO: Gospel, 1937.

Peñamora, Aldrin M. "Ethics of Responsibility: Christ-Centered Personal and Social Ethics for Church and Society." *Journal of Asian Evangelical Theology* 19 (2015) 91–107.

———. "Eucharistic Justice: A Christ-Centered Response to the Bangsamoro Question in the Philippines." *Asian Journal of Pentecostal Studies* 19 (2016) 31–44.

PGI. "Sinode Gereja Anggota PGI" [Church synod members of the Indonesian Communion of Churches]. PGI, May 2, 2016. https://pgi.or.id/sinode-gereja-anggota-pgi/.

Phan, Peter C. *In Our Own Tongues: Perspectives from Asia on Mission and Inculturation*. Maryknoll, NY: Orbis, 2003.

Pruitt, Raymond M. *Fundamentals of the Faith*. Rev ed. Cleveland, TN: White Wing, 1981.

Ramelli, Ilaria. *The Christian Doctrine of Apokatastasis: A Critical Assessment from the New Testament to Eriugena*. VCSup 120. Leiden: Brill, 2013.

———. *God Is Near Us: The Eucharist, the Heart of Life*. Edited by Stephan Otto Horn and Vinzenz Pfnur. Translated by Henry Taylor. San Francisco: Ignatius, 2003.

———. "Reply to Professor Michael McClymond." *TS* 76 (2015) 828–35.

Ratzinger, Joseph. *Called to Communion: Understanding the Church Today*. Translated by Adrian Walker. 3rd ed. San Francisco: Ignatius, 1996.

Ricklefs, M. C. *A History of Modern Indonesia since c. 1200*. 3rd ed. Basingstoke, UK: Red Globe, 2008.

Robeck, Cecil M., Jr. "An Emerging Magisterium? The Case of the Assemblies of God." *Pneuma* 25 (2003) 164–215.

Rogers, Eugene F., Jr. *After the Spirit: A Constructive Pneumatology from Resources outside the Modern West*. Radical Traditions. Grand Rapids: Eerdmans, 2005.

Rybarczyk, Edmund J. *Beyond Salvation: Eastern Orthodoxy and Classical Pentecostalism on Becoming Like Christ*. Paternoster Theological Monographs. Repr., Eugene, OR: Wipf & Stock, 2006.

Salkeld, Brett. *Transubstantiation: Theology, History, and Christian Unity*. Grand Rapids: Baker Academic, 2019.

Schmemann, Alexander. *The Eucharist: Sacrament of the Kingdom*. Translated by Paul Kachur. Crestwood, NY: St. Vladimir's Seminary Press, 2003.

———. *For the Life of the World: Sacraments and Orthodoxy*. 2nd ed. Crestwood, NY: St. Vladimir's Seminary Press, 1973.

———. "The Missionary Imperative in the Orthodox Tradition." In *Eastern Orthodox Theology: A Contemporary Reader*, edited by Daniel B. Clendenin, 195–201. 2nd ed. Grand Rapids: Baker Academic, 2003.

Simatupang, Florian. "Christian Hospitality in the Celebration of 'Id al-Fitr: Participating in Halal Bi-Halal as a Way for Indonesian Christians to Learn Reconciliation from Their Muslim Neighbors." *Pneuma* 41 (2019) 218–35.

Smith, Gordon T. *A Holy Meal: The Lord's Supper in the Life of the Church*. Grand Rapids: Baker Academic, 2005.

Stephenson, Christopher A. *Types of Pentecostal Theology: Method, System, Spirit*. AARAS. Repr., Oxford: Oxford University Press, 2016.

Stott, John R. W. *The Message of Acts*. The Bible Speaks Today Series. Repr., Downers Grove, IL: IVP Academic, 1994.

Stylianopoulus, Theodore G. "Scripture and Tradition in the Church." In *The Cambridge Companion to Orthodox Christian Theology*, edited by Mary B. Cunningham and Elizabeth Theokritoff, 21–34. Cambridge Companions to Religion. Cambridge: Cambridge University Press, 2009.

———. *Scripture, Tradition, Hermeneutics*. Vol. 1 of *The New Testament: An Orthodox Perspective*. Brookline, MA: Holy Cross Orthodox Press, 2004.

Thomas, John Christopher. "Reading the Bible from within Our Traditions: A Pentecostal Hermeneutic as Test Case." In *Between Two Horizons: Spanning New Testament Studies and Systematic Theology*, edited by Joel B. Green and Max Turner, 108–22. Grand Rapids: Eerdmans, 1999.

———. "Women, Pentecostals and the Bible: An Experiment in Pentecostal Hermeneutics." *Journal of Pentecostal Theology* 2 (1994) 41–56.

Tomberlin, Daniel. *Pentecostal Sacraments: Encountering God at the Altar*. Rev ed. Scotts Valley, CA: CreateSpace, 2015.

Tupamahu, Ekaputra. "American Missionaries and Pentecostal Theological Education in Indonesia." In *Asia and Oceania*, edited by Amos Yong and Vinson Synan, 233–54. Vol. 1 of *Global Renewal Christianity: Spirit-Empowered Movements Past, Present, and Future*. Lake Mary, FL: Charisma, 2016.

Turcescu, Lucian. "'Person' versus 'Individual', and Other Modern Misreadings of Gregory of Nyssa." *Modern Theology* 18 (2002) 527–39.

University of Notre Dame. "Pope St. John XXIII." Faith ND, n.d. https://faith.nd.edu/s/1210/faith/interior.aspx?sid=1210&gid=609&pgid=16588.

Van Dyk, Leanne. "The Reformed View." In *The Lord's Supper: Five Views*, edited by Gordon T. Smith, 67–82. Downers Grove, IL: IVP Academic, 2008.

Vondey, Wolfgang. "Pentecostal Ecclesiology and Eucharistic Hospitality: Toward a Systematic and Ecumenical Account of the Church." *Pneuma* 32 (2010) 41–55.

———. "Pentecostal Sacramentality and the Theology of the Altar." In *Scripting Pentecost: A Study of Pentecostals, Worship and Liturgy*, edited by Mark J. Cartledge and A. J. Swoboda, 94–107. London: Routledge, 2016.

———. *Pentecostal Theology*. Systematic Pentecostal and Charismatic Theology. Repr., London: Bloomsbury T. & T. Clark, 2018.

———. *People of Bread: Rediscovering Ecclesiology*. New York: Paulist, 2008.

Vondey, Wolfgang, and Chris W. Green. "Between This and That: Reality and Sacramentality in the Pentecostal Worldview." *Journal of Pentecostal Theology* 19 (2010) 243–64.

Wainwright, Geoffrey. *Eucharist and Eschatology*. Akron: Order of Saint Luke, 2002.

Walter, Gregory. *Being Promised: Theology, Gift, and Practice*. Sacra Doctrina: Christian Theology for a Postmodern Age. Grand Rapids: Eerdmans, 2013.

Wandel, Lee Palmer. *The Eucharist in the Reformation: Incarnation and Liturgy*. Cambridge: Cambridge University Press, 2005.

Ware, Kallistos. *The Orthodox Way*. Rev. ed. Crestwood, NY: St. Vladimir's Seminary Press, 1995.

Warrington, Keith. *Pentecostal Theology: A Theology of Encounter*. London: Bloomsbury T. & T. Clark, 2008.

Westphal, Merold. "Spirit and Prejudice: The Dialectic of Interpretation." In *Constructive Pneumatological Hermeneutics in Pentecostal Christianity*, edited by Kenneth J. Archer and L. William Oliverio Jr., 17–32. Christianity and Renewal—Interdisciplinary Studies. London: Palgrave Macmillan, 2016.

Williams, Ernest S. *Systematic Theology*. 3 vols. Springfield, MO: Gospel, 1953.

Williams, J. Rodman. *Renewal Theology: The Church, the Kingdom, and Last Things*. 3 vols. Grand Rapids: Zondervan, 1992.

World AG Fellowship. "Statement of Faith." World AG Fellowship, n.d. /-/media/World-AG-Fellowship/Bylaws-Membership-Papers/WAGF-Statement-of-Faith.pdf.

Yan, Alice. "White People Wanted: A Peek into China's 'Rent a Foreigner' Industry." *South China Morning Post*, June 10, 2017. https://www.scmp.com/news/china/society/article/2096341/white-people-wanted-peek-chinas-booming-rent-foreigner-industry.

Yong, Amos. *The Hermeneutical Spirit: Theological Interpretation and Scriptural Imagination for the 21st Century*. Eugene, OR: Cascade, 2017.

———. *The Spirit Poured Out on All Flesh: Pentecostalism and the Possibility of Global Theology*. Grand Rapids: Baker Academic, 2005.

———. *Spirit, Word, Community: Theological Hermeneutics in Trinitarian Perspective*. Eugene, OR: Wipf & Stock, 2006.

Yong, Amos, et al. "Christ and Spirit: Dogma, Discernment, and Dialogical Theology in a Religiously Plural World." *Journal of Pentecostal Theology* 12 (2003) 15–83.

Young, Robert Darling. "The Eucharist as Sacrifice According to Clement of Alexandria." In *Rediscovering the Eucharist: Ecumenical Conversations*, edited by Roch Kereszty, 63–90. New York: Paulist, 2003.

Zizioulas, John D. *Being as Communion: Studies in Personhood and the Church*. Crestwood, NY: St. Vladimir's Seminary Press, 1997.

———. *The Eucharistic Communion and the World*. Edited by Luke Ben Tallon. London: Bloomsbury T. & T. Clark, 2011.

Zwingli, Ulrich. "On the Lord's Supper." In *Zwingli and Bullinger*, edited and translated by G. W. Bromiley, 185–238. Louisville: Westminster John Knox, 1953.

Name Index

Albrecht, Daniel E., 28, 28nn10–11
Alexander, Kimberly Ervin, 84, 93n144, 163
Alfeyev, Hilarion, 178n168
Anderson, Allan, 24n128, 140n3, 164n106
Archer, Kenneth J., 2n5, 10, 10nn45–46, 11, 11nn47–49, 41, 41nn63–65, 42, 42nn66–69, 43, 60, 98, 98n12, 99, 100, 100nn21–23, 101, 101nn24–28, 102nn29–31, 108n58, 111, 111n118, 173, 174nn146–47, 184, 186
Aritonang, Jan, 151n44
Arrington, French L., 7, 7nn23–25, 33, 33nn35–36, 34, 34nn37–42, 39
Augustine, Daniela C., 140n29, 141, 141n7, 147, 147n31, 148n32, 156, 156n69, 157n70, 158n73, 167, 167n117

Bailey, Kenneth E., 137n159
Banks, Patricia, 149, 149n36
Barton, Stephen, 146, 146nn21–23
Basil the Great, 93, 93n147, 121, 177, 187
Bauckham, Richard, 169n127
Belcher, J. David, 72n41
Biddy, Wesley Scott, 11, 12, 12nn56–58, 25, 25n3
Bloesch, Donald G., 169n126
Boersma, Hans, 22nn124–25, 155, 155nn64–65, 156n66

Bouyer, Louis, 64, 185
Breck, John, 105n43, 105nn45–46, 106, 106n48–51, 107n52, 107n54, 119nn114–15
Bricknell, Richard, 1n2, 68n23, 83n99
Bromiley, G. W., 86nn114–15, 87n117
Brown, Raymond E., 122, 122n123
Bruner, Frederick Dale, 131, 132, 132nn142–43
Bulgakov, Sergius, 179, 179n172

Calvin, John, 8, 19, 31–32, 37–38, 65, 85, 90, 90nn131–32, 91, 91nn136–37, 92, 92nn141–42, 185
Cartledge, Mark J., xvi, 1n1, 1nn3–4, 15, 15n81, 16, 16nn82–86, 21, 21nn116–17, 22n122, 23n127, 26, 26n4, 60n146, 63n2, 63n4, 64n5, 66n13, 74n51, 83n101, 84, 84n107, 85n110, 93n148, 94nn150–51, 95, 96n1, 97, 97nn6–7, 99, 99n13, 120, 120nn118–19, 137n161, 142, 158nn76–77, 159nn78–79, 162, 162nn92–93, 182
Castelo, Daniel, 160n86
Cavanaugh, William T., 143, 143n13, 156, 156n68, 167n119
Chan, Simon, 12, 12nn59–61, 13n62, 43, 43nn70–71, 44,

206 NAME INDEX

44nn73–77, 45, 45nn78–83, 46, 57n138, 84, 84n105, 139, 139n2, 159n83, 164n102, 164n104, 169n125, 170, 170nn130–31, 183n1, 184
Cocksworth, Christopher, 19–20, 179
Collins, Raymond, 124n126, 125, 125n127, 126nn129–30
Congar, Yves, 64, 64n6, 75, 75nn54–55, 76, 76nn56–58, 77, 77n60, 79, 79n77, 81, 81nn90–92, 82nn93–96, 108, 108n61, 109n62, 110, 110nn68–71, 119n117, 185, 185n2
Coulter, Dale M., xv
Cross, Terry L, 96n1, 98n8

Dabney, D. Lyle, 98n8
Duffield, Guy P., 8nn26–30, 35, 35nn43–48, 36, 36nn49–55, 37nn56–58
Dulles, Avery, 64, 75n55, 77, 77n61, 80, 80n86, 81, 81nn87–89, 186
Dusing, Michael L., 6, 6nn17–18, 27, 30, 31, 31nn23–27, 32, 32n28, 38, 40

Farkasfalvy, Denis, 121, 122, 122n121, 121n124, 126n132, 129nn136–39, 132, 132nn145–46, 160
Fee, Gordon D, 29n17
Francis, Pope, 164, 164n105
Farrar, Laura, 149n37

Gadamer, Hans-Georg, 20, 20n113, 21, 21n115, 22, 22n126, 94, 94n149, 94n152, 97, 97nn4–5, 111, 112, 112nn75–80, 113, 113nn81–87, 114, 114nn88–93, 115, 115nn94–98, 116, 116nn99–104, 117, 117nn105–8, 118, 118nn109–12, 119n113, 120, 122, 137, 137n160, 186

Gavrilyuk, Paul L., 171n135, 172, 172nn138–41, 173, 173nn142–44
Green, Chris E. W., xvi, 2n5, 14, 14nn70–72, 26, 26n7, 46, 46n84, 47, 47nn85–90, 48, 48nn91–99, 49, 49nn100–101, 50n102, 66n13, 75, 75n53, 84n104, 93, 93n145, 139, 139n1, 146n21, 148n34, 159n84, 160, 160n85, 161n90, 163n99, 165n107, 172n137, 180, 180n174, 184
Grumett, David, 66, 66n12, 70n29
Gutiérrez, Gustavo, 150, 15n41

Harmer, J. R., 158n74
Hart, David Bentley, 18, 18nn101–3, 177
Hellwig, Monika K., 146, 146nn24–25, 147, 147nn26–29, 148n33, 153, 153n54, 164n103, 175, 175n151
Hollenweger, Walter J., 8, 9, 9nn31–34, 13
Horton, Stanley, 6, 27, 30
Hunsinger, George, 77n64, 79, 79nn73–74, 89, 89nn127–30, 90n133, 171, 172n136

Johns, Cheryl Bridges, 60, 60n146
Johnson, Luke Timothy, 122n122, 126n131, 134n151, 135, 135nn152–54

Kärkkäinen, Veli-Matti, 9, 10, 10nn41–44, 66n11, 68n22, 83nn102–3

Land, Steven Jack, 82n98
Lash, Ephrem, 121n120
Lewis, Jeffrey R, 132n144
Lossky, Vladimir, 82n97
Lubac, Henri de, 16, 16nn87–88, 64, 80, 80n83, 108, 108n60, 109nn63–67, 119, 119n116, 142, 142n10, 144, 144nn16–18, 156, 156n67, 185

NAME INDEX

Ludlow, Morwenna, 175n150, 176, 176nn153–54, 176n156, 177, 177n164, 178n167
Luther, Martin, 31, 65, 85, 87, 88, 88n119, 88nn121–25, 89, 89n126, 90, 92, 185

Macchia, Frank D., xv, 71, 71n34, 102n30, 148n35, 159, 159n82, 161, 161nn88–89, 169, 169n124
Maximus the Confessor, 140m 140n6
McClymond, Michael J., 177, 177n164
McIntosh, Mark A., 141n8, 142n11, 143n12
Menzies, William, 1n2, 5, 6, 6n16, 27, 29, 30, 30nn19–22
Milavec, Aaron, 123n125
Moloney, Francis J., 126n133, 132, 133, 133nn147–50
Morse, Jonathan K., 129n140

Nelson, R. David, 67n14

O'Connor, James T., 64, 77n63, 78, 162, 162nn95–96, 78nn67–70, 79n72, 79nn75–76, 79n78, 80nn79–82, 80n84, 129, 130n141, 157, 157nn71–72, 163n98
O'Loughlin, Thomas, 17, 17nn93–95, 62n1

Pearlman, Myer, 4, 4n8, 5, 5nn9–11, 27, 28, 28nn8–9, 28nn12–13, 29, 29nn14–16
Peñamora, Aldrin M., 152, 152nn49–51
Phan, Peter C., 149, 150, 150n38, 165, 165n112, 166, 166n113, 166n115
Pruitt, Raymond M., 7, 7nn19–22, 32, 32nn30–33, 33, 33n34, 39

Rahner, Karl, xii

Ramelli, Ilaria, 175, 175n152, 176, 176nn154–55, 176nn157–61, 177, 177n164
Ratzinger, Joseph (Pope Benedict XVI), 16, 17nn89–92, 155nn62–63
Ricklefs, M. C., 151n43
Rogers, Eugene F., Jr., 145n19, 163, 163n97
Rybarczyk, Edmund J., 107n55

Salkeld, Brett, 77n62, 77n65, 78n66
Schillebeeckx, Edward, vii, 12
Schmemann, Alexander, 18, 18nn98–100, 68n16, 72n42, 73nn45–46, 143n14, 170, 171nn133–34, 179n169, 179n173
Smith, Gordon T., 19, 19nn104–6, 63, 63n3, 94
Soeharto, 151
Stephenson, Christopher A., 5n5, 14, 14nn73–74, 15nn75–76, 40, 40n61, 50, 50nn103–6, 51, 51nn107–12, 52, 52n113, 174n148, 184
Stott, John R. W., 135, 136, 136n155, 136n157, 137n158, 140n4
Stylianopoulos, Theodore G., 105n44, 106n47, 107n53, 128, 128nn134–35

Thomas, John Christopher, 21n119, 98n11, 99, 99nn14–17, 100, 100nn18–20, 108n59, 111, 111n74
Thurian, Max, 108
Tomberlin, Daniel, 15, 15nn77–80, 53, 53nn114–20, 54, 54nn121–26, 55, 55nn127–32, 56, 56nn133–35, 74, 74n52, 83, 83n100, 92, 92n143, 173, 173n145, 184
Tupamahu, Ekaputra, 165n108
Turcescu, Lucian, 66n9

Van Dyk, Leanne, 32n29, 86n11, 86n113, 91n135, 91nn138–40
Vondey, Wolfgang, 13, 13nn63–66, 25, 25nn1–2, 26n6, 57, 57nn136–40, 58, 58nn141–45, 59, 66n13, 144n15, 145n20, 159n84, 163, 163n100, 165n109, 165n111, 166, 167, 167n116, 168, 168nn122–23, 184

Wainwright, Geoffrey, 19, 19nn107–9, 98, 98n3, 125n128, 168, 168nn120–21, 172, 172n134, 180, 180nn170–71
Walter, Gregory, 151, 151n42, 152nn45–46, 174, 174n149
Wandel, Lee Palmer, 88n118, 88n120
Ware, Kallistos, 71, 71n33, 71n35, 177, 177n166, 180n176
Warrington, Keith, 3n7, 13, 13nn67–68, 14n69, 65n8, 74n51, 141n9, 170n129
Westphal, Merold, 21, 21n118, 98n10, 107n56

Williams, Ernest Swing, 5, 5nn12–14, 27
Williams, J. Rodman, 9, 9nn35–39, 59

Yan, Alice, 149n37
Yong, Amos, 3, 3n6, 11, 11nn50–55, 20n114, 37, 37n59, 95, 99, 102, 102nn32–33, 103, 103nn34–40, 104, 104nn41–42, 107n57, 111, 111n72, 158n75, 161, 162, 162n91, 162n94, 186

Zizioulas, John D., 17, 18, 18nn96–97, 21, 22nn120–21, 22n123, 64, 65, 66, 66n10, 67, 67n15, 68, 68nn17–21, 69, 69nn24–27, 70, 70n28, 70nn30–31, 71, 71n32, 71nn36–38, 72, 72nn39–40, 72n43, 73, 73n44, 73nn47–49, 74n50, 147n30, 159, 159n80, 165, 165n110, 173, 184
Zwingli, Ulrich, 28, 31, 65, 68, 85, 86, 86n112, 87, 87n116, 92, 185

Subject Index

Altar
    as a place of holistic worship, 54, 56
    a sacramental reality, 58–59
    in Roman Catholic understanding, 75, 80
    a constructive understanding, 160, 173, 180

Anamnēsis (Remembrance)
    as encounter, 138, 187
    a multidimensional event, 26, 64–66, 68, 165, 184
    Spirit-driven event, 10, 64–66, 68, 106, 144, 188
    relation to Epiclēsis, 10, 26, 68, 73, 147, 159, 164
    relation to interpretation of Scripture, 107–8, 119–20, 125
    roots in Jewish remembering, 126
    as exegesis, 108

Apokatastasis (Restoration of All Things)
    as an authentic Christian doctrine, 176
    variance in Christian understanding, 175
    see also Eucharist as a preview

Assemblies of God
    traditional view of the Lord's Supper, 4–6, 27–32, 38–39
    "initial evidence," 159
    "sixteen fundamental truths," 29, 38, 169

Hockley Pentecostal Church, 162
Indonesian Assemblies of God, 150
    variance in statement of faith, 169

Baptism
    as rite of initiation, 7, 9, 28, 174
    in relation to the fivefold gospel, 11
    as substitution for circumcision, 32
    as proclamation of faith, 87
    of the Holy Spirit see Spirit Baptism

Christ
    partaking in the life of, 5, 7, 18–19
    doctrinal understandings for eucharist, 12, 18
    incarnation as sacramental basis, 14–15, 83–84
    sacrifice in the eucharist, 16
    the church as the body, 17, 61
    Pentecostal understanding in the eucharist, 30–37
    as the gift of the Father, 58–59
    in relation to Transubstantiation, 77–78, 162
    redemptive power, 167, 176
    descent to hell, 178
    cosmic reality, 179–80

SUBJECT INDEX

Christology
  in relation to pneumatology,
    45–46, 67, 184
  as a dimension on the Lord's
    Supper, 51
  overemphasis in Eastern
    eucharistic theology, 67
  in Roman Catholic
    eucharistic theology, 75
    liturgy, 76
  Filipino, 152
  in Trinitarian encounter, 184
Church of God, Cleveland,
    Tennessee
  traditional view of the Lord's
    Supper, 7, 32–34, 39
Church of the Foursquare
  traditional view of the Lord's
    Supper, 8, 34–37, 39
Communion (Koinōnia)
  genuine implication, 48
  as the mark of pneumatic
    hermeneutic, 99, 137
  in the book of Acts, 136
  perichoretic *koinōnia* of the
    Trinity, 148
  as a process of SET, 161
Consubstantiation
  as an incarnational analogy, 89

Encounter
  as foundation of Pentecostal
    theology, 4, 74, 93, 111
  eucharist as place of, 10–11, 18,
    46, 47–49, 81, 86–91, 93,
    140–41
  role of Spirit, 52, 56, 61
  through Scripture, 47–49, 102–
    3, 109, 129
  in the book of Acts, 139
Epiclēsis (Invocation of the Spirit)
  in relation to Anamnēsis, 9–10,
    26, 66, 68, 165
  Pentecostal understanding,
    15–16, 158
  in relation to the Eucharist, 44,
    64, 73
  in Scripture, 70

post Vatican II, 75–77
  in Roman Catholic
    understanding, 80–82
Eschatology
  millennial vs. amillennial views,
    169–70
  as Pentecostal identity, 10–11,
    41, 43, 58
  as an important Pentecostal
    doctrine, 31, 169
Eucharist
  as a preview of *apokatastasis*,
    175–80
  implication for Pentecostal
    theology, 180, 194
  as eschatological meal, 169–74
    in Wainwright's view, 19
    difference with Wainwright,
      168, 173, 179
    in Zizioulas's understanding,
      66–73
    future hope anticipated,
      11, 55
    preventing an overrealized
      view, 45–46, 51–52, 164
  as healing
    physical/spiritual healing,
      42–44, 91, 166–68,
      183–85
  as hunger management, 154–58
    reversal of consumption, 156
    alleviating the world's
      hunger, 157
  as justice 148–54
    addressing injustice
      of racism, 149–50
      of white privilege, 151
      of religious intolerance,
        152–54
  as mission, 164–68
    Pentecostal's missionary
      impulse, 164–65
    missional meal, 166–67
    a place for discernment, 167
  as solidarity, 145–48
    political and prophetic, 11
    Christ with us and we with
      others, 144

as *kenosis*, 145
in relation to holiness, 146
as our *leitourgia*, 148
Eucharistic Theology
Eastern Orthodox perspective, 17–18, 65–75
Roman Catholic perspective, 16–17, 75–84
Protestant perspectives, 19–20, 67–68, 85–92
Ulrich Zwingli, 85–87
Martin Luther, 87–89
John Calvin, 90–92

Fusion of Horizons
explanation of Gadamer's thought, 111–18
at work, 118–20
the work of the Spirit, 21, 95
in relation to SET, 94
as an ecumenical awareness, 96, 119
Fivefold Gospel
in connection to the sacraments, 11

Healing
as the metaphor for salvation, 162
community, 163
see also Eucharist as
Hunger
human longing, 144, 172
for creative love, 146–53
the social problem Jesus addressed, 132
see also Eucharist as

Imago Christi
defined by solidarity, 145
the embodiment of *Imago Dei*, 163

Imitatio Christi
call to imitate Christ's self-giving, 83
In Persona Christi

priestly sacramental reality in Catholicism, 75
the place of pneumatology, 82

Justice
in relation to healing, 84, 163
in the book of Acts, 137
as a mark of a Spirit-filled church, 140
as the promise of God, 178
as mark of the kingdom, 180
see also Eucharist as

Lex Orandi, Lex Credendi, Lex Vivendi
in Pentecostal worship, 2–3, 23
in relation to *regula spiritualitis, regula doctrinae*, 14, 50–52
Liturgy
contemporary Pentecostal understanding, 46–48, 58
as a blueprint of life, 166
post Vatican II development, 81
torture as liturgy of the state, 143
in Eastern Orthodoxy, 72–75, 178–79
as a language of faith, 155, 158, 191
as an eschatological snapshot, 192

Mission
as Trinitarian identity, 57
primarily understood as *Missio Dei*, 59, 61
of Jesus, 107
connection to witness, 166, 168
empowering the church, 142, 165–68

Nourishment
Eucharist as spiritual sustenance, 42, 92
to be sent on mission, 167, 189

SUBJECT INDEX

Participation
  sharing in Christ's life, 7, 15, 22, 42, 51
  ecclesial/social dimensions, 11–12, 14, 57–59, 70, 89, 99, 137
Pentecostal Sacramentality
  historical views, 14, 29, 31, 38, 53
  renewed understanding, 41, 45–46, 57–58, 159
Pneumatological Imagination
  as methodology, 20–22
  reading Scripture in Spirit, 96–97, 102, 118, 120
  as a way to embrace other traditions, 93–94, 111
  in constructing Renewal Theology, 141

Racism
  relation to table fellowship and justice, 149–150
Regula Spiritualitis, Regula Doctrinae, 2, 14, 50–52
Renewal Theology (of Eucharist)
  constructive approach, 22–24, 94, 143–45
  seven meanings of the meal
    solidarity, 145–48
    justice, 148–54
    hunger management, 154–58
    healing, 158–64
    mission, 164–68
    eschatology, 169–74
    apokatastasis, 175–80

Search-Encounter-Transformation (SET)
  as a Pentecostal spirituality process, 1
  methodology defined, 20–22, 142
  mapping SET in the Eucharist,
    in older Pentecostal understanding, 27–41
    in contemporary Pentecostal theologian
      Kenneth Archer, 41–43
      Simon Chan, 43–46
      Chris E. W. Green, 46–50
      Christopher A. Stephenson, 50–52
      Daniel Tomberlin, 53–57
      Wolfgang Vondey, 57–59
    in Ecumenical Eucharistic Theology
      in Eastern Orthodoxy, 65–75
      in Roman Catholicism, 75–84
      in Zwingli, Luther, and Calvin, 85–93
  as fusion of horizons, 94, 120
  as a dialectic process in reading Scripture, 120–21, 128, 136
  as internal logic in the Eucharist, 140
Second Vatican Council
  influence on sacramental renewal, 16
  on epiclēsis, 75, 77, 81
  on pneumatology, 76
  on understanding tradition, 108
Spirit Baptism
  as a Pentecostal distinctive, 159, 168
  and spiritual fatigue, 159
  as a *shibboleth* test 160
  as *koinōnia* in the Trinity, 161

Text-Community-Spirit
  as a hermeneutical principle, 3, 21, 94–95, 96–98
  John Christopher Thomas's approach 99–100
  Kenneth Archer's strategy 100–102
  Amos Yong's Trinitarian hermeneutics, 102–4
Tradition
  its role in Easter Orthodox interpretation, 105–8

living tradition in Roman
    Catholicism, 108–9
  the role of the Holy Spirit,
    106, 110
  in connection to Fusion of
    Horizons, 118
Transformation
  as the outcome of *missio Dei*, 46
  through the Eucharist, 52, 140,
    143, 145, 147, 152, 154, 157,
    158, 168
  through encounter with the
    other, 142
  as the goal of ritual, 58
  bringing charismatic
    community, 71–72
  of the eucharistic elements, 73
  involving hermeneutics, 97, 109,
    136–37
Transubstantiation
  explanation of the Catholic view,
    77–79
  Pentecostal explanation, 12,
    22, 83
  pneumatological
    reconsideration, 162
  reshaping the Pentecostal
    doctrine of healing, 94, 163
Trinitarian
  opportunity for Pentecostals,
    45–46, 57–59
  framework for Eucharistic
    theology, 60–61, 69, 139

perichoretic participation, 81,
    99, 120
koinonia in the book of Acts,
    136
  in relation to Spirit Baptism, 161
  related to liturgy, 166

Via Salutis (Journey of Salvation)
  communal experience, 4–43
  as a pattern vs. *ordo salutis*,
    173–74
  Eucharist's role, 140, 181

Weekly Celebration
  arguments for, xiii, 191
Whiteness
  critical reflection white privilege,
    149, 151
  white-savior-complex, 151
  see also Racism
Worship
  common Pentecostal
    misconception, 3n7
  in relation to the Lord's Supper,
    9
  eucharistic liturgical worship,
    17, 44
  eucharist treated as addendum,
    25
  Pentecostal and Trinitarian, 45
  "liturgical exactness," 48
  Pentecostal distinctiveness, 53

www.ingramcontent.com/pod-product-compliance
Lightning Source LLC
Chambersburg PA
CBHW022015220426
43663CB00007B/1093